LOVE GAMES:

THE HIDDEN RULES OF RELATIONSHIP

Thomas M Jones

DISCLAIMER

This book details the author's personal experiences with and opinions about the dynamics of romantic love. The author is not a healthcare provider.

The author and publisher are providing this book and its contents on an "as is" basis and make no representations or warranties of any kind with respect to this book or its contents. The author and publisher disclaim all such representations and warranties, including for example warranties of merchantability and healthcare for a particular purpose. In addition, the author and publisher do not represent or warrant that the information accessible via this book is accurate, complete or current.

The statements made about products and services have not been evaluated by the U.S. Food and Drug Administration. They are not intended to diagnose, treat, cure, or prevent any condition or disease. Please consult with your own physician or healthcare specialist regarding the suggestions and recommendations made in this book.

Except as specifically stated in this book, neither the author or publisher, nor any authors, contributors, or other representatives will be liable for damages arising out of or in connection with the use of this book. This is a comprehensive limitation of liability that applies to all damages of any kind, including (without limitation) compensatory; direct, indirect or consequential damages; loss of data, income or profit; loss of or damage to property and claims of third parties.

Dedication

For Kathleen, Timothy and Michael, and all of my students and my teachers who have taught me with patience and love.

"Consider the following. We humans are social beings. We come into the world as the result of others' actions. We survive here in dependence on others. Whether we like it or not, there is hardly a moment of our lives when we do not benefit from others' activities. For this reason it is hardly surprising that most of our happiness arises in the context of our relationships with others."

—His Holiness the 14th Dalai Lama

CONTENTS

INTRODUCTION

In my years of counseling couples and individuals, I've learned a great deal about what relationships are and what they are not. I've noticed that we throw ourselves headlong into love without a thought as to where we will land or how things will work out. When we start a business, we create a business plan. We begin with a dream and a goal and we conceive pathways to achieve that goal. Why is this not the case with relationships? We dive into the river headfirst and worry about the rocks later.

Given the landscape of a relationship and the odds of succeeding (one of two marriages ends in divorce), it is amazing that we try at all. Hope springs eternal in this most unique area, defying logic and reason.

As a therapist, I have been a privileged witness over the years to the ways in which people choose to relate. I have had the opportunity to see which dynamics work and which don't, and I've outlined some of those principles and dynamics—the hidden rules of relationships—in this book. I believe that making relationships work is a learned skill. You can create a good relationship if you are willing to work hard.

Much of the work of this book will be undoing the fantasies, beliefs and expectations that we've grown up with and that are often toxic and unworkable. They are the obstacles to creating true love.

As I worked on this book, exploring the glue that holds love together, I discovered that there are pivotal moments in each relationship. Within these moments there are specific games that people are subject to; games that we must play.

Many of the actions we choose in love are pre-ordained. When we arrive at these junctures our beliefs, our programming and our expectations kick in. We are suddenly on automatic pilot, steered by the subconscious, arguably at the worst possible time. We blindly play out our parts and virtually no one is aware that he or she is following a script.

I am going to explore those games with you, along with the scripts and the programming that we fall prey to. I am going to help you navigate these difficult waters of love and I will teach you how to win.

I am going to share with you a method that I call "conscious relating." Conscious relating is the act of deliberately choosing and creating a love relationship; of being awake and aware of the choices you are making and the effect they will have. I assure you that you will not lose romance in the process. In a very real way conscious relating can prove to be a first opportunity for authentic romance. Your choices will no longer be guided by expectations and rules that make no sense in this century. It is my hope with *Love Games: The Hidden Rules of Relationships* that you will strengthen your power to love.

Lest you think I'm speaking in a vacuum, let me illuminate: I have rushed headlong into disastrous relationships time and again, and I have the scars to prove it. Though I consider myself fairly bright, relationships have made a fool of me and baffled me at every turn. Despite entering with dreamy hope and idealism, I have failed spectacularly and suffered.

With great energy and enthusiasm, I have tried to shape and control love. In my attempts to beat this rigged system, I've used every strategy: I have insisted on outcomes, and I have let it be. I have surrendered to fate. I've lavished affection and "taken space." I have given permission and spoken my truth. I have applied copious amounts of love and have even seasoned it with indifference. Through my ignorance of the rules and games of relationship, I have failed spectacularly.

The concept of conscious relating came to me like the slow dawning of the Pleistocene era. My understanding of the dynamics of relationships has grown with each failure, and conscious understanding replaced reaction.

Through my personal and professional experience, I have learned that our behavior in relationships is ruled by a series of predetermined moves and counter-moves. Like players in a chess game we tactically navigate our way around the chessboard in order to achieve gain.

As in chess, there is a finite series of moves for each aspect of the game of love. No matter whom the player or what the tactic, our overall strategy is the same: to be loved. Becoming consciously aware and knowing these plays, tactics and strategies will provide decisive power in the game of love. This knowledge can virtually ensure success.

We need a new language that gauges the success of a relationship by how much we've grown rather than how many people we've pleased or how long a relationship has lasted. The process called actualizing involves working through our neuroses to achieve authenticity within ourselves. That goes for a relationship too. We can actualize within a relationship and partner spectacularly in a way that we thrive individually and as a couple. The real value in a relationship lies not in how long it lasts, but in how much we learn and grow.

I tell people sitting across from me that relationship is temporary: love isn't supposed to last forever. Even if you live together all of your lives one or the other will die first. This pushes directly against the notion that love lasts forever, for good reason. When people believe that love is going to last, they go to sleep in their relationships. They tend to take each other for granted.

In order to succeed, we must be awake to create conscious relationship. We need to be as mindful as we would be if we were in business, operating in the world. A relationship is a living, changing entity. In order to be responsive to love we must be alert. Just as business can change and react to fluctuations in the market, so will our partnership change within its environment. We've got to be present to be powerful and effective in a relationship, not mired in our beliefs or expectations.

Love must be tended, like a living, changing life form. Most people give more attention to their family pet or their houseplants than they do to the love that they expect so much from.

There are powerful spiritual underpinnings in conscious relating, this new model of relationship that I present in this book. We're drawn to the lessons we've chosen to learn on this plane. We find the partners we've agreed to share these lessons with us. And we ask the essential questions in relationships: "What am I here to learn?" and "What am I here to teach?"

In this book I intend to make it simple and clear, and to give you a new model for love that works, and works elegantly.

Some of the answers concern the fantasies of relationships. By debunking these fantasies we get to the reality of what true relationship can be. We are able to create the love that we desire, but only after letting go of the fantasy.

We'll look at reality with real examples from the lives of the couples I've worked with. We will identify the dynamic that makes love work. We will shed light on common pathways that simply lead to the wrong place.

It is long past due to create a new model of relationship; the old model doesn't work. There is just too much unnecessary pain in the old "romantic" model, due to misunderstanding and confusion. The tragedy is that there is real love and willingness in most relationships, but individuals have lost their way and the road map is not there for them. Our patterns and expectations conspire to deplete that love and cooperation.

We can build again, intelligently. By arriving at an objective view of relationship and an understanding of our real needs, satisfaction and happiness can be found in partnership. It takes work, and a willingness to challenge the old ways and ideas, but with application and an open mind, a conscious, meaningful and enduring partnership can be created and sustained.

I promise you this: After reading this book you will have a whole new understanding of relationship. You will know what works and doesn't. You will know why. You will have a set of workable tools and skills to transform your relationship. You will have a roadmap to happiness in love.

My intention in writing this book is to create a dialogue. By entering into a conversation, we will ask and answer questions. To that end I have created a series of exercises to go along with many of the chapters. I suggest that you do the exercises after you have digested the text. Take it one chapter at a time, and work with that chapter until you have processed it thoroughly. Do the exercises when you have the time and space to go through them. They are designed to create an experience for you that will help you model the changes described in this book.

Thomas M Jones
New York City
July 2010

SECTION I

MANAGING RELATIONSHIPS

ONE

ROLES IN RELATIONSHIP

As I was contemplating writing this book my family and I took a trip through upstate New York. We have a little cabin in the woods in Washington Irving country, and I thought it would be a nice change of scenery to take in the fall foliage. As we visited the vegetable stand that we've gone to for years, I decided to ask the couple that runs the stand a few questions about their history together. Ana and Nico were more than happy to speak with me. The conversation went something like this:

THOMAS: How long have you two been married?

ANA: Forty-five years.

T: How did you and Nico meet?

A: He rape me.

T: What? (thinking I misunderstood)

A: He rape me.

NICO chimes in with: I rape her and her father say I must marry her! He chase me with gun!

T: How old were you, Ana?

A: I fourteen!

N: She lucky I marry her, ha ha!

My wife and I were shocked by this easy admission. Were they putting us on? When I looked from Ana's face to Nico's, I saw no anger, no guile. They might as well have been talking about the weather. They seemed to think that theirs was a natural circumstance; in fact, they have six grandchildren. Their narrative of love challenges conventional wisdom and breaks all of the rules of God and man, and yet, there they were, clearly at peace. How is this possible? I wondered. I realized that I had a lot to learn about relationships.

Admittedly Ana and Nico present a rather extreme example. But sometimes the most dramatic case makes the point most clearly. In my practice, as I talk to couple after couple about their partnerships I am amazed at the diversity of love. Each has an agreement and each agreement is unique. What is acceptable to one couple would be heresy for another, and yet within each relationship there is some basis for loving. These fundamentals of love are as unique and varied as the people themselves.

ROLES IN RELATIONSHIPS

Below is a list of some of the common roles people play in relationships. See how many you can recognize in yourself and in others.

THE CARETAKER: He or she promises to take care of you in every way that you need.

THE SEXPOT: This person relates strictly on a sexual level.

THE VICTIM: This person is always in crisis, not of his or her own making.

THE ROMANTIC: Sees the world through the lens of romance only.

10

THE DUTIFUL ONE: Always doing what is required, often righteously.

THE FREE SPIRIT: Carefree and irresponsible; charming.

THE CONTROLLER: Must be in charge and know everything.

MACHO MAN: Lives from his masculinity, demands respect.

THE NEGOTIATOR: Engages in endless discussion and constant arbitration.

THE HOLY ONE: Takes their righteousness from the sense of a higher power.

COMPENSATOR: Is always managing the experience of others.

WORRIER: Secretly controls their world through worry.

GOOD BOY/GIRL: Always does the right thing, but primarily for approval.

BAD BOY/BAD GIRL: Breaks all the rules.

THE INNOCENT: Holds childlike beliefs to get along in the world.

THE ALOOF: Doesn't get involved.

SOCIAL ONE: These people surround themselves with people rather than deal with life.

THE HERMIT: Malevolent view of the world.

SALESPERSON: Is always pitching something.

RESPONSIBLE ONE: Always does the right thing.

These are some of the roles we play in relationships and each role has an attendant game. Each has an approach and a recognizable set of qualities.

SOME BACKGROUND

Before we talk about roles and games, let's talk about the game board itself: the evolution of relationship. The rules that we are trying to follow are unworkable. In fact, they were designed to be unworkable. The model of relationship that we are working from is as antiquated as a Roman chariot. We base our rituals of love largely on the Roman poet Ovid's "The Art of Love," written around the year 25 BC. This was a rather cynical work that described in detail, how to make a woman fall in love through applied worship and adoration, the purpose being to seduce her sexually. This work was translated, largely without the humor and cynicism, by the medieval poets. Notably, Chrétien de Trois used Ovid as the inspiration for his "Lancelot" epic, which became a defining work and the basis of chivalry or courtly love. All the rage in the courts of France and later throughout Europe, chivalry promoted the correct behavior toward women when romancing them. The rest is history, as they say, and has become the groundwork for the rules we follow in love.

Try as we might, we cannot avoid disaster if we are following this model that we have been given. We truly are following a set of instructions that is unmanageable and a road map that leads to nowhere. Because of this history, we live by archaic notions of what love is and what it should be; we set out blind and dumb, to make love. Add to the mix that the secretive knowledge of sex is withheld from us as children and mystified; blend this with the confusing concepts of what a relationship should be and we have a recipe for confusion and pain at every turn. If it weren't so cruel it would be funny.

Even a rat in a maze has more chance of success. Does it have to be this way? The answer is a resounding No!

WHAT IS LOVE?

Accurately portraying love is not unlike the three blind men describing an elephant: The first man grabs the tail and says, "This creature is long and skinny!" The next holds the ear and proclaims "No, no! It is a smooth and velvety creature!" A third caresses the rear and says, "You're both wrong! It is a tough and bristly animal!" Each is accurately describing his own experience, but you would never know that they are talking about the same animal.

The aggregate that we call "love" is a series of games that must and will be played between the joint tenants in a relationship. As participants in these games we face critical passages that determine whether we will or we won't go forward together. Excitement and lust give us the strength to bully our way through the early twists of the maze, but inevitably, at some point we lose our way.

We don't imagine that we need equipment or knowledge for love; we throw in our lot, half-packed and ill-prepared. There is no other area in which we would dare to show up this unarmed. We would research and plan something as mundane as building a porch or losing weight, but we are cavalier about love: "Oh, let's just wing it!"

WHAT WE WANT FROM LOVE

There is the question: what do we want from a relationship? It is too simple to say that we expect to love and be loved. It can be said that we enter a relationship in order to find ourselves. We are attracted to what we need to learn. One part of the puzzle is the fact that we are trying to resolve childhood patterns and are searching for a partner who will assist us.

There is a reason that we can see the most attractive person in the world and have no interest—they don't match our patterns. When we find someone who does match our pattern, there is a gravitational pull that is compelling. We correctly or incorrectly identify this attraction as "falling in love." In a way, the search for love could be characterized as pattern matching, a process we go through until we achieve pattern lock. It is when we work through these patterns properly and learn what we need to learn, that we can achieve satisfying partnership.

Though singularly unromantic, this point of view is far more accurate in predicting our choices for love and the outcome of a relationship than just about any other factor.

It should be noted that these choices in pattern matching don't have to be gender specific. I can find my father in the woman I choose and be able to work through my pattern. Similarly, a woman can match her mother pattern with the man she engages.

There will be times when, having worked through the pattern, we move on from a particular relationship. We will see in this book that moving on can represent success, not failure. Too much value is placed on how the world perceives us in relationships. We are concerned that we have let down our world, our family and ourselves. On the contrary, to actualize—to become the potential that we hold as human beings, to learn what we have chosen to learn—should never be perceived as failure.

FIXING IT

Don't wonder why you end up in my office for therapy. What is it that you want when you get here? "Fix it! Stop the bleeding. Make it stop hurting." I don't blame you; I would want the same thing. And yet, putting on a Band-Aid won't transform your understanding or help you reinvent your relationship. Patching it together is like giving you an ice cream cone to soothe a broken leg. It may be distracting, but ultimately it is not that useful.

The work of a relationship counselor is to provide the vision that couples often lose in love or the vision that they never possessed in the first place. As therapists we attempt to leap the hurdles and reconnect the partners. We try to identify the roles in play, often while you fight us, tooth and nail. Unless we possess vision and awareness of the dynamics that are built in to the love landscape, unless we know the games that are being played, we spend most of our time kissing the "boo-boo" to make the pain go away.

Often, rather than providing an overview and an understanding that will create communication, we referee the game du jour, simply fixing the next broken bit. Our mission should be to empower couples to rise above their skirmishes and see that bigger picture; to sort through the dynamics and understand how these dynamics are interacting. To be effective we must put less emphasis on putting out the small fires and focus the couple's awareness on the mechanics that are breaking down the relationship.

So much of what is wrong has nothing to do with you, the couple.

The fault lies in the perception of relationships. As we identify the games and your roles we empower you. When you become objective observers and adopt a "no-fault" attitude toward relationships, then we can instill this vision. Together we can maneuver past the built-in expectations and pressures that are at the heart of most love problems.

EXERCISE 1

Identify the role(s) that you play in relationship and in life. Identify the role(s) your partners have played. Try to identify the origins of these roles. Try switching roles and see how this effects communication.

EXERCISE 2

Write a brief synopsis of your history of love including your current or latest relationship. Read it back and look for patterns and expectations.

TWO

LOVE GAMES

Our first order of business is to see the love games that we are subject to. Every stage of relationship has an attendant game. The Seduction game, our initial interface with each other is a fascinating set of deceptions and legerdemain. We set out to prove that we are much more than we really are. Like the Bird of Paradise performing the mating ritual we present what we consider the most compelling version of ourselves.

As we go deeper into relationship we confront the Power game. Here is a subtle and sometimes not-so-subtle grab for control in the relationship. Does your relationship have a COP (control-oriented partner) in it? Are you the cop? You may be in a situation where there are two cops. If so, you are the victim of your own orientation, not the villain in the match.

Dependence games, Status games, Identity games, Sex games, Dominance games, all show up within the context of relationship and each has a set of dynamics that will create conflict. The attendant roles are recognized universally: the good boy, the bad girl, the romantic and so on. Each is also, in medical parlance, a pre-existing condition that does not necessarily reflect problems in relationship. Knowledge is power, and when we identify these dynamics we go a long way toward eliminating the danger and creating understanding.

LOVE GAMES
SEDUCTION: We entice our partners with the promise of everything we have.

DEPENDENCE: We attempt to strike a balance in providing for each other's needs.

STATUS: One partner will lead and the other will follow, willingly or otherwise.

SEX: How we use our sexuality in relationship. Can be withholding or forthcoming.

POWER: The inevitable battle for control of the relationship.

COMPETITION: The built-in rivalry in every relationship.

NEGOTIATION: The ongoing courtroom of mediation.

BALANCE: The attempt to maintain order, usually in deference to our neurotic patterns.

We all participate in each of these games through the roles that were previously described. How we participate determines the quality of our relationships. Imagine the roles that you have identified in the first chapter being played within these games.

GAMES AND ROLES
Sooner or later we have to ask the question: What is the basis of a relationship? We approach love so casually that we seem to give more scrutiny to buying a used car than choosing a partner. Let us mix and match roles and see if the dynamics become recognizable. If I choose the "Innocent" as one partner in this relationship and the "Hermit" as the other, and

throw them into a game called "Competition," let's see how it plays out.

As you may recall the "Innocent" holds childlike beliefs in dealing with the world. The "Hermit" has a malevolent view of people and generally avoids them. The game of "Competition" can show up at every stage of relationship, but let's put the two of them in a social setting, like a party. "Competition" is the never-ending game of trying to gain advantage. The dialogue might go something like this:

INNOCENT: These people have really gone out of their way to make a spectacular party. I really like the decorations.

HERMIT: They've invited some work colleagues. That means this party is tax deductible.

I: Oh, I'm sure they're friends with those people, too.

H: Why do you think they invited us?

I: They enjoy our company, silly.

H: They want our business, you mean. Dave is an accountant and Sheila is a decorator. Don't be so naïve.

I: You're doing it again. You are making me feel bad. Why do you always have to be so negative?

H: Honey, I'm just saying that they might have another motive...

I: I just don't want to live in your world. You see the dark side of everything.

H: I'm just being realistic; and frankly, you could use a little more reality. You really have your head in the clouds.

And so it goes. Let's take the "Worrier" and the "Compensator" and throw them into the party, playing the game of "Seduction."

WORRIER: There are an awful lot of people here. I don't really trust crowds.

COMPENSATOR: Really? I only see one person that matters and she's pretty terrific. What can I do to make you more comfortable?

W: For starters you can stop talking so loud and drawing attention to us. I like it when we're quiet together.

C: I know. How about a dance? You like this song and it's a slow one.

W: I look silly when I dance. Let's go somewhere where it's just me and you.

C: It would be a shame to leave so soon; we just got here. How about staying for half an hour, and I will thoroughly entertain you and keep you busy, and then we can go off on our own.

W: Make it twenty minutes and you've got a deal.

Each role will eventually create tension and problems. Because these roles are neurotically driven they will create conflict. Sooner or later that conflict will polarize the couple and create difficult positions for both parties to negotiate.

THE META-GAME

There is a way of playing in relationship (or any game, for that matter) that will give us a huge advantage. First, there is the game, and then there is the meta-game. What is a meta-game? To play a meta-game we are armed with all of the information that each player knows. If I am immersed in a relationship game it means that I, as the character on the game board, am moving from one square to another. As a player of the Seduction game I am on the game board; I am aware of my surroundings: my opponent, the obstacles I face, the obvious gains and advantages, and the pitfalls. If I choose the meta-game, I am in a unique position: I am in position on the board and I am above the board, in a position of overview. I now have split vision and the benefit of both viewpoints. I become aware of the game being played, my chosen role in that game and my partner's role. Now I can play an informed game. I, as the player have more knowledge than the characters on the game board.

If you and I are playing chess, as the player, I see the board, I see your strategy and the moves that you make, and I have a strategy of my own. As the meta-player, I have information that I, as only a player, do not possess. I have knowledge that transcends the game. As a meta-player, maybe I have heard a rumor that you have a violent reaction to the color red. The meta-player in me will then be sure to wear a red shirt to the match. I, as the meta-player have more information than I, the player. When you become agitated and furious over my pawn to queen three, it is not the brilliance of my move that disturbs you, but the color I am wearing.

This is a position of huge advantage. In a game so evenly matched, even a five percent advantage can mean the difference. I am going to make you a meta-player in the game of love. The knowledge in this book is designed to give you that advantage and forever change your way of dealing in relationship.

BELIEFS AND URGES

The real origin of many of these games is the set of beliefs and perceptions of love that we have inherited. Who hasn't been inculcated with the fairy tale of love, the relentless stream of mush, like oatmeal being crammed into our ears? We are not broken or wrong. The problem isn't us, it is the information we've been given. Like the heirloom cuckoo clock that never really worked but has been kept for the sake of tradition, relationship is broken. These heartwarming fairy tales are major barriers to creating love. We've been given impossible expectations, and silent and unworkable rules. Are you looking for Prince Charming? Can you be Prince Charming? Of course not, and to try only creates heartache and disappointment.

We couple because we must, biologically speaking, but the vessel we're given to navigate is full of holes. There is no White Knight coming to the rescue, nor should there be. You wouldn't feel worthy of him if he did show up. The question isn't "Will this ship sink?" but "When will it sink?" A program of behaviors has been instilled in us by well-meaning people, all with shipwrecks of their own. The deck is stacked against us.

It seems a little arbitrary to risk everything and sacrifice all that we know for a set of sensations that we're not even sure we can reproduce. We gamble that this relative stranger, (aka "the love of my life"), can and will recreate the "chemical wash" inside of us that we identify as love. We all know those wonderful feelings we get when we think about him or her. Magic is in the air! Everything old is new again. Life is full of possibility! Yes, that "chemical wash." Reduced to its chemical components, these sensations are merely our neuroreceptors firing in a specific order. It seems extraordinary that we are so willing to give away our power for an ever-diminishing set of endorphins. As with any drug, it takes more and more stimulus to achieve the same effect. What happens when he or she can't stimulate our opiate receptors to quite the same height? Do we fall out of love? What about everything we've sacrificed; all the promises made and given, all of the changes we've put ourselves through?

In addition, in a very real sense, our unfulfilled childhood patterns are seeking a mate of their own. Until we have some self-knowledge we are doomed to the chemical and the psychological matches that we find.

EXPECTATIONS

In the midst of this fascinating confusion, decisions are still made and people still fall in love. We go eagerly forward with optimism, passion, but no clarity. It is a form of magical thinking to believe that by following our present dictates we will succeed in love. Navigating these treacherous shores would make for a daunting enough task, and yet our internal architecture makes it a thornier mission. Along with our historic inheritance, we have our programmed expectations of what love should be. Just eavesdrop on your inner conversation: "I expect to be adored." "I expect to be understood." "I need to be respected." "The one who loves me will anticipate my needs." The monologue is as different and varied as we are.

WHAT WE NEED

How do we answer the real questions: "What do I need from a relationship?" "How much should I give?" "How do I operate in the world while I'm in love?" "What is this supposed to look like and feel like?" "Am I in love?" "Will it last?" "How do I sustain it?"

Open up any *Glamour* magazine and you will find advice and guidelines for every problem of love: "How to please your woman!" or "Keep him wanting you, Ten sex secrets for captivating men!" If that doesn't kill the love, nothing will. Not long ago, there was a book about "The Rules" on how to capture and marry your man. It is an instruction manual with a series of calculated manipulations. The premise is this: if you put someone into enough pain, they'll cry "uncle" and marry you. Is that love? I'd like to be a fly on the wall when the guy who fell for this finds the book.

EXERCISE 1
Examine each love game and try to determine the role you play in that particular game. Determine your partner's role.

EXERCISE 2
Make a list of your beliefs and expectations of love. If you are currently in relationship, make a list of your partner's beliefs and expectations.

EXERCISE 3
Look through your relationship history and see if you can identify neurotic patterns in your partnerships. Look for what didn't work and the role being played.

THREE

A CASE STUDY

Despite my personal debacles in the arena of relationship, or maybe because of them, I have concluded that the only way to survive and ultimately thrive in love is to be conscious. As a child I believed that love would conquer all, and that everything could be solved if love was present. I was committed to this belief despite the great pain it caused me.

Unless we are awake we will be swept into the sea of beliefs and patterns that have grown around our rituals of love. Add to that the inner beliefs and programmed patterns that we have learned and we are navigating in a truly treacherous arena. "Conscious Loving" is the light that will light that mysterious room known as relationship. It will allow us to see through our beliefs and patterns, through our roles and the games we play.

Let's look at a couple in the throes of their relationship conflict and see what we can learn:

Marta and Lance are at a crossroads. They met when she was a dancer. At that time he was doing better financially than he is now. She no longer dances. Now, a deep divide separates the two. There is talk of separation, even the "d" word. We had a couples' counseling session and talked about their history and where they stand now.

THOMAS: So, what are you doing in this relationship?

LANCE: I don't know...

T: Hmm... Well, what made you get into it in the first place?

L: I met a strong beautiful woman. She inspired me. I felt like she understood me. I wanted to build a life with her. She was the most exciting woman I'd ever met.

T: And now?

L: I feel like I've been tricked. Someone kidnapped Marta and put this woman in her place!

MARTA: I agree. Aliens came down and replaced Lance with this control freak.

L: You always were funny...

T: Marta, how did it start for you?

M: Well, he was cute and dorky. He was very serious, and I didn't think of him as my type at all. I knew him for almost two years before we became romantic.

T: And how did that happen?

M: He was so determined. I like that. Finally, I thought, "maybe I should consider someone who's different. He's kind of cute and a very hard worker." He won me over.

T: So you both feel like victims of the old "bait and switch"?

L: Yes, it's so different from the way it started. I'm very discouraged.

What are Lance and Marta up to? What roles are they playing? Are they relating? What game are they in now? What can we see so far? Lance was inspired. Marta was charmed. Certainly the seduction game was a success. Lance fit well into the role of the "responsible one" while Marta played the "free spirit" to perfection.

Even Webster has difficulty making it clear: What is a relationship? Is it a mere attitude, a stance? The concept of being mutually interested makes some kind of sense. Essentially, a relationship is the act of cooperating for some mutual benefit. It is a contract, an agreement. But is this romantic relationship merely sex or is it destiny? They fit each other like hand in glove. Was this just a practical accommodation? Perhaps it is the fulfillment of each one's fantasies and expectations. Where do their rituals of love originate?

Despite the fact that being chivalrous was meant to caricature the church, in the late twelfth century chivalry ignited the imagination of all levels of society. This was not surprising in a time period where flogging and self-flagellation were all the rage. As if they'd read the latest article in "Seventeen" magazine, women were charmed and captivated by this new notion. "Oh, to have a man kneel at my feet!" It spoke to the men of this time, too. Something deep in the reptilian brain responded. It gave couples a roadmap, a model for behavior. The conceit became the reality. Chivalry was adopted wholesale and became the prototype of the behavior for love. They even competed to see who could fulfill this chivalry to its most extreme.

This is Lance and Marta's legacy. In a real sense it is the heart of the matter. The counterfeit goes on. Ovid's first century lampoon becomes a twenty-first century dilemma. That Roman has to be laughing up his sleeve. Not just our couple, but every man and woman today bases their behavior in love on this set of misguided precedents. What are Lance and Marta doing except comparing their love to how it should be. Never mind that our guidebook for love originated as a political statement, a parody and a protest.

Our behaviors are rooted deep in the past as the hoax continues. We need some serious course correction.

Back to our couple:

T: You realize that the beginning of the relationship was a fantasy, don't you? It's the courtship ritual. Everyone is on their best behavior and throws lots of sunshine.

M: Yes! For instance, he used to be very supportive of my dance, my career. Now he makes me feel like a whore forever doing it!

L: I never said that.

M: You've said it subtly from the time we were married. Suddenly I have all of these evil ways!

L: Well, I don't know who you are anymore. I used to trust you. I just don't know what you want. This isn't playtime. We have real responsibility now. I need a partner who can help me.

T: Did you ever know who she was? Maybe you fell in love with your concept of her. That is how love starts, you know.

M: You told me that you loved that I was an entertainer! It made you feel like you were a part of that world too.

L: And you used to love how "serious" I was. You said that I was your rock!

T: Marta, do you think you had an idealized version of him back then?

M: Obviously, because this version of him just judges me. He even tries to tell me what clothes to wear and how to wear my hair. It's too much control. I'm not a little girl that needs constant guidance.

L: You still want to act like you're single!

M: I want us to have fun. We're still young. We should be out dancing and making love, at least sometimes.

Marta and Lance are all over the map. There is a clear disconnect. Promises seem to have been made and broken. Each feels betrayed. Early on, each one has been charmed and seduced by the other. They made assumptions based on what each has seen. What was once special is now annoying and even upsetting. Have they changed so dramatically, or is there a stage missing in their growth?

Should we continue to do the "dance of the seven veils" for our partners or is there a pathway to becoming authentic with one another? We eagerly buy the "gift" called relationship and then proceed to make a thousand compromises to try to maintain the illusion.

To begin with, the couple is not communicating. Each assumed the other was in the same place, but effectively, they are strangers to each other. Through the kaleidoscope of beliefs and expectations, they see a distorted version of each other. Their first assumptions raised expectations that neither one can fulfill. The fault isn't in them; love is a no-fault process. Embrace that concept and digest it; no one is to blame. When the model fails, they each attack the other, but that only obscures the problem. If we can separate out the beliefs and expectations from the reality of their relationship, we can revitalize it.

It's amazing that they started a relationship at all, given that each has such varied expectations. Marta somehow convinced herself that Lance needed nothing; that the mere act of fulfilling her wishes was somehow enough for him. For his part, Lance expected Marta to be exotic and exciting only for him, twenty-four seven.

We make the assumption that we know what this relationship is and what it should be; that we know each other. We sledgehammer love into our lives and declare that it fits perfectly. What became apparent with this couple when the disappointments started is that they know nothing of each other's authentic self.

How can we hope to merge seamlessly our very diverse programs? Some of us want globetrotting adventure and consider that loving romance; others demand quiet and peace of mind and savor the image of doing the *New York Times* crossword puzzle together on a Sunday morning. Some see coupling as a team financially, and still others would never dream of combining their assets. Even our expectations of sex and intimacy are dramatically different. What someone considers sexy, another person may see as a turn-off. In almost every area there are bound to be vastly different expectations.

We demand to be known and understood without ever explaining ourselves. How many of us actually do the work in order to know ourselves? Can we expect to know each other? We need to look at what is at our core of our connection. Is it really a four-tissue match, wherein we connect mentally, physically, emotionally and spiritually, or are we engaging in the art of compromise for the sake of what we think we see?

Largely, Lance and Marta are driven by their unresolved childhood patterns in choosing this relationship. They yearn to complete the incompletion within themselves. These patterns determine what they think they want and need in love. Lance needs to be made to feel special because he grew up in an environment where he was never treated that way. He was ignored within an environment that provided him all of the creature comforts of life. Marta wants a partner to play with because she was never allowed to play. She grew up in somber house where most activities were forbidden or frowned upon. These are the gears that truly move their wheels and dials, and make this couple's choices in love. Their success in relationship will have a great deal to do with how much they know about these patterns and their willingness to break them.

For Marta and Lance the question remains: Can they hit the reset button and start again? Clearly, each watched in horror as the other slowly migrated from this perfect fantasy. Their loss has been a series of imperceptible shifts. The key to maintaining good business and good love is communication and awareness. They must let each other in. Step 1 can be painful, but it must include an honest assessment of what we have, what is working and what is not.

Back to our couple, looking for answers:

T: So, clearly, no one is getting what he or she expects in this situation. What's the solution?

M: Maybe we're just wrong for each other. Maybe this was a mistake.

L: Typical. Run away, Marta. That's what you always do...

T: That's an easy answer, and if it's true, we'll get there. But what if it's not true? What if you guys have all the love you need to make this work, and you're just not seeing each other clearly? Are you willing to risk giving it all up before you really explore that?

L: What's there to see? She doesn't want to be a grownup!

T: Way too simple. What message were you giving her when you first courted her? What was your through-line?

L: That I would take care of her. I was a good guy. Dependable. Not a flake.

T: Do you think that message has changed?

L: Yes, everyone changes, everything changes.

T: You mean like promising one thing and delivering another?

L: What am I supposed to do? Take care of her for the rest of her life while she goes and plays?

T: I'm not saying what you're supposed to do. I'm pointing out that your original promise has changed dramatically. She could feel cheated or tricked by this, right or wrong. Did you ever talk in the beginning about what you need or expect from each other?

L: I don't think we sat down and had a conversation about it. But we understood each other.

T: I don't think you did. I think the heart of the problem is misunderstanding. You both have unreal expectations. It's okay to change your agreement, but you have to communicate that change or you are effectively abandoning each other. You guys need a way of connecting again. I think you've lost all of your common ground.

You can see how this relationship evolved. They probably didn't even notice where they connected and where they didn't. It just "felt good." There was a compelling attraction.

When we meet someone, there is a physical, mental, spiritual or emotional hit or a combination of all of the above. That gets us into the game, but we don't stop there. Our minds are little fantasy factories that immediately go to work, creating a whole back story, a whole reality to go with this attraction. Lance opened up about his childhood and let her in. Marta was shocked and moved by his account. He was drawn to her affection and playfulness and saw it as the missing piece in his life. She, in turn saw his delight in her as all of the approval that she never received. His judgment came from the feeling that he was, once again, left out. Through many tears and discussions they opened their hearts to each other and the healing began. The healing can only begin through knowledge and vision.

It's no longer the Middle Ages, with feudal marriage. We have a better toolbox and more knowledge than ever before, but we still live with a legacy of archaic rules that leave us with unreachable expectations. Ask anyone what the rules of relationship might be, and each of us has a different answer. This means that the landscape is wide open to new input and new possibility. Yes, there is hope that we can escape history and our own expectations. It can all be changed. We are about to embark on a journey known as "conscious relationship." Let's untangle this Gordian knot.

EXERCISE 1

Identify the game that the couple in the example is engaged in. Identify the roles that each is playing. Identify the beliefs that each is holding. Identify the expectations that each partner has of the other. Identify the childhood patterns that each is driven by.

EXERCISE 2

Identify the relationship game that you are in.

Identify the role or roles that you are playing.

Identify the beliefs that you holding about your relationship.

Identify the expectations that you have in this relationship.

Identify the childhood patterns that are driving you in relationship.

FOUR

HOW WE RELATE

When we meet and relate, we connect and interact. The quality of our relationship depends on where and how we connect. The more varied and broad the connection, the more powerfully we are drawn. To borrow from medical terms we can say that a four-tissue match is a connection on all four levels at once. Here are four basic planes where we meet:

Physical
Emotional
Intellectual
Spiritual

Like opposite poles on a magnet, our physical attractors compel us toward each other. Biology is king and everything else takes a back seat. We feel a spark and it ignites between us, and we assign great meaning to this "chemistry." Oh, it's magical! If it ain't got that swing, it don't mean a thing. Without physical attraction we feel that the relationship can't go anywhere. In our earlier case study, Lance was very attracted to his dancer, Marta. It is easy to mistake this set of sensations for love, but it is not love; it is only the possibility of love.

We can use the model from the philosophical point of view that attraction indicates that we have met someone who has a lesson or message to teach us. We are drawn to our lessons, and the gravitational pull of physical attraction will compel us to learn these lessons. We will talk later about the importance of the physical; what it is and what it isn't. The physical is certainly the beginning of the equation for love.

Excitement, joy and nervousness, are all emotional reactions we have to a potential mate. The amount of emotion this meeting evokes, good or bad is a criterion for judging the potential of a relationship. When I was a teenager I worked at the A&P supermarket at the checkout counter. When that certain girl got on my check out line with her pretty blonde hair and her demure look, I became completely tongue-tied and red-faced. She evoked plenty of emotion in me. To this day I can still feel a blush coming on when I think of her standing in my line.

You've heard some variation of the phrases: "I'm miserable with her but I'd be more miserable without her!" "He gets under my skin!" All of these are examples of a response on the emotional level. We assign meaning to these responses and create a story to explain the emotions. In truth, this kind of emotional response can be the beginning of a connection. There are a thousand stories where this is the case.

In our example of the couple in counseling, Marta felt like Lance would protect her and this was very endearing. He, in turn, wanted to take care of her. He gained a sense of warmth and connection from this desire. Each evoked emotions in the other and they formed an emotional bond. They assigned great meaning to this bond. In fact, they married based on that bond and their interpretations of it. When the bond broke down the relationship needed repair.

What would an intellectual connection look like? Perhaps you are at a cocktail party and you overhear a handsome man with dark hair saying "Why isn't it obvious to the politicians of the world that we must inevitably go green? We are using up the resources of this planet! Aren't there any forward thinking world leaders?" You construct a story that gives this moment meaning and you fall a little in love.

We come together because we think alike. We see the world in similar ways and share each other's viewpoints. If you like the same candidate I do, it may grease the wheels for us to connect. We agree about global warming or the conflict in the Middle East. This mind-sync is compelling in its way. The mind can play tricks on us, though, and people do lie or change their minds. The magic of chemistry causes us to look for common ground and common ideas, whether or not they exist. This is not a case for or against intellectual connection; still, the Dalai Lama had a point: pick someone you can talk to, because, ultimately, that's all that you will have left at the end of the day.

Another valid way to connect is through the spiritual. We feel intimacy if we have similar spiritual beliefs. A shared philosophy can form a real bond between us humans, making us feel safe and cozy. We occupy the same universe together: same ethos, same Eros. Spiritual connection can include the belief that fate has brought us together. It can feel like karma. "I feel as though I've known her all of my life." Having lifetimes together can foster the sense of the eternal and the destined relationship. Creating meaningful connection can be difficult without this spiritual underpinning. It is very challenging if one partner believes and the other does not. Sooner or later there will have to be some renegotiation.

These are just some of the ways that we come together to relate, yet each is a path that can lead to relationship. Each path has its own evolution and ultimately intersects with the other planes of connection. They are by no means the only ways to connect, just some typical ways that we do hook up. It isn't accurate to have the same expectations for each way of relating, since each develops differently. You may be tempted to believe that your way is the only way, but as you can see, there are a many paths to falling in love.

Without these essential connections, these points at which we meet and agree, we feel disconnected. Wherever love starts, ultimately we have to fill in the missing dimensions. These are the lifelines that we have toward one another, and these lines need to be cultivated, fed and nurtured. When we broaden our relationship we give it strength and sustainability.

Look at your past relationships and even your present one. Where did you initially connect? Think back to the time you first met. Maybe it was all about the talking. Perhaps you would spend the night on the phone, talking 'til the wee hours. What did you talk about? Or, were you so physically rapped up into each other that you didn't come up for air? Sooner or later the relationship will have to migrate to other planes or it won't survive, but each connection gives us strength and opportunity to broaden our base of relating.

RECONNECT

Reconnecting on the physical plane doesn't mean that you try to jump back into the sack without foreplay. That would be comic and probably end in disaster. Connection takes a gradual rebuilding. If you've gotten away from the physical, go slow. Try some mutual massage or a deliberate attempt to hug. Touch your partner. Affection is a simple way back to physical connection, but use plenty of patience and ease.

Strike up a conversation about something you know he's interested in if you want to meet on the intellectual plane. Stay away from topics you don't know and have no interest in, as this will doom your effort. He has an interest in vitamins and how they affect healing. Do some reading about it and share what you've read. This little investment will yield interest and results. Do not get discouraged; this is about developing your communication skills, not necessarily about pleasing your partner. If you keep trying you will get a response. A conversation about the meaning of life will put you squarely in the spiritual, but it isn't always the easiest to approach. Any dialogue that includes what we are building together or what we represent in the world is rooted in the spiritual plane. Discussions about life lessons and what we are learning now, speaking about our purpose in life, our mutual destinies, all of these are fodder for the bigger picture conversations that meet on the spiritual plane.

What moves your partner or your potential partner emotionally? What does she care about passionately? Think back to a time when you heard he or she excited or agitated about something. When you can answer this question, "What is my partner passionate about?" you have a key into their emotions. When you talk about this topic, find ways to share what you feel about it as well. The emotional connection is the most accessible to reestablish, and maybe the most meaningful. A good "feeling" conversation can make you feel instantly connected.

Building a relationship means laying these planks as the foundation for how we relate. Rebuilding is much the same. Take an honest assessment: see what is good in our communication and what needs repair. Whether building connection or reconnecting, we can weave thread upon thread until we have created a strong fabric that will sustain us.

EXERCISE 1

Take any relationship that you are in that you would like to deepen or improve. It can be a love relationship or friendship, or even a potential love relationship. You could even focus on a sibling, a parent or your child. From the four planes of relationship, (emotional, physical, spiritual, intellectual) pick one and start a discussion. Make it your business to deepen that aspect of your relationship and notice how it changes.

Here are some examples.

Emotional: Share your passion about a movie or a world event.

Physical: Challenge a friend to a racquetball game; hug your mother-in-law.

Spiritual: Discuss a life lesson with your partner. Discuss meaning and purpose in your life and theirs.

Intellectual: Share a book you love with someone important. Start a discussion about it.

Get into the spirit of it and you will come up with your own examples.

EXERCISE 2
Have a "feeling discussion" with the following rules: Each participant fills in the statement "I feel..." with what they are feeling in the moment or about a chosen topic. In this exercise, there is no judgment, no right or wrong and no attempt to fix anything. Simply observe. When one partner has finished sharing the listener must then "empathize" and reflect with the sharer, by using the following phrases: "Do you mean...?" Or "I heard you say..." Find comparisons and similar situations that you have been in, and recap what your partner has said. When the first person is done, switch partners. Let this lead to a discussion.

FIVE

STAGES OF RELATIONSHIP

FREEZE-FRAME!
If only we could freeze time in the beginning of a relationship. Love starts out like a house on fire! Everyone's having a fabulous time and we can't believe our luck. Somewhere in the festivities there comes a moment that is the turning point. Joan Baez talks about this moment in time when "your perfect lover looks like a perfect fool." We suddenly see him or her in a way we hadn't before, and instead of making us feel grander, it diminishes us. The music stops, the lights go up and the scales fall from our eyes. The magic is gone. In a flash, our entire program of beliefs kicks in and we start to circle the drain in an inexorable spiral of expectation/ disappointment. We are still in love with our concept, but we are no longer in love with the person we've chosen. In fact, that person starts to become annoying and to get in the way.

WHAT'S LOVE GOT TO DO WITH IT?
Imagine a rocket headed for outer space. As we see the plumes of smoke and fire, we observe parts of it falling away. In order to achieve escape velocity and reach deep space, the rocket fires in stages. One after another, the boosters fall away as the projectile sweeps through space. Though each is discarded in turn, all are indispensable in reaching the charted destination. Love is a gradual unfolding of necessary stages. Here they are in a nutshell:

41

Identification

Attraction gives us liftoff. To say that this is the only stage is like focusing on the candy wrapper instead of the candy inside. Oh sure, it's pretty and eye-catching, but it's not the goods. This is the stage where we marvel at our sameness. "We're so alike!" Everything about each other is great and we sacrifice parts of ourselves that don't seem to fit in the relationship. We collapse into identification with "us." This stage can last from 2 weeks to 6 months. No one seeks counseling in this stage.

Differentiation

Now we see our differences, often in stark contrast. One of the difficulties of this stage (and all of them) is that couples are rarely on the same schedule. I can still be in the romance of the first stage while you've moved on to seeing our differences. This can lead to feelings of betrayal and loss. This stage is about power and autonomy, defining who I am in this partnership and how to go forward. "I need my space" replaces "I need you." A time of necessary disillusionment, this stage is often read as the beginning of the end.

Assimilation

Assuming survival of stage two, we move on. Almost a state of truce, this third stage is marked by a deceptive quiet. Whereas stage two is usually indicated by fighting and conflict, stage three almost feels like resignation. What's really going on is that our focus is no longer on the relationship itself, but on whom I am in the world and how this partnership fits in to that world. Though it can look like the "magic is gone," the real bones of a sustaining partnership are being created here. Real communication begins, and how you build will define the quality of this partnership. It is a stage that is constantly misread, but absolutely necessary in the formation of a healthy partnership.

Integration
In this stage we can consider a future together. We have explored enough of who we are in the world and lived with the reality of each other for long enough to know that we can build together. A willingness to commit shows up in this stage and a return to the relationship starts to occur. Intimacy is again sought after and even a renewed blush of romance can show up as we consider new ventures and possibilities together. Big external moves might occur at this time, such as moving in together or getting engaged.

Creation
In this stage we have put together a durable enough partnership so that we are willing to take on an outside enterprise together. Whether this implies having kids or co-partnering in business, the relationship feels strong enough to sustain a joint participation in the world. The danger in this stage is that we can lose each other in the mix, but clearly we feel strength in the relationship that supports creation of some kind.

CONFLICTING STAGES
The breakdown is obvious for the couple in the next excerpt. They've clearly migrated from that "isn't it great that we both love foreign movies" stage to the very real question "Who are you?" Small wonder; none of us can compare to the idealized version of him or her. Because of the expectations of our next couple, each is deeply disappointed in this relationship. Both feel betrayed by a partner who hasn't lived up to their fantasy. The "never agreed upon" agreement has

broken down. They were going to build an empire together. Now they feel like they've grown apart. If the lines of communication had been open along the way, these changes would have been handled differently. As it stands now we see the crumbling of romantic love.

Let's listen in on Karen and Martin:

KAREN: Wait a second, here. I'm being made to look like this indulgent little brat that lost her toys and is having a temper tantrum. I just want what we had.

MARTIN: I don't know who you are anymore! I can't trust you. You're ridiculous.

T: Without characterizing it like that, aren't you both angry? What do you think you promised him? What were you bringing to the mix?

K: (laughs) I promised to be beautiful and sexy; and to make him look good in the world.

T: You think you're kidding, right?

K: Yes, I don't know what my message was. We were crazy about each other. We literally couldn't take our hands off of each other. You know, we were both in other relationships when we first met. Maybe I was supposed to provide romance. To give him something he didn't have in his life.

T: Yes, maybe all of that and more. You did provide warmth and comfort, even a touch of the exotic. And he provided stability and dependability?

M: We were an unbeatable team. When I met Karen my life came together. My work made more sense; I think my whole life made more sense. Now she's always angry with me.

K: Wow, did we screw up! Is this an unfixable mess?

T: Given your model for love, this had to break down. Maybe it's supposed to break down to create something new. Somewhere along the line you have to become aware of what you give and what you need. I don't think you know who you are to each other. In a way it doesn't matter how this relationship started, your needs change with every stage of relationship. You have to recognize that and find a way to communicate. Stop blaming! This is a no-fault situation. You haven't failed each other. You two are stuck in different stages of this relationship. Now, it's our job to be smart enough to see where each of you is stuck and try to connect with each other. You both had to outgrow the old model. Now you need to create a new agreement that actually addresses your needs and can work.

K: Yes!

These two have a couple of wild cards to deal with. To start with, they built a relationship while still being in their original partnerships. This implies guilt and mistrust from the beginning. Putting history aside, let's look at the dynamics in play.

What stage is this couple in the example in? In fact, they are in two different stages and therein lay the problem. Karen seems stuck between stage one and stage two, Identification and Differentiation. She wants it to feel the way it used to and yet she is finding out who she is in the world. Martin is somewhere in stage three, Assimilation. He wants stability and commitment and a real foundation for building, but he isn't paying attention to what Karen needs right now. How do we reconcile this? First, we identify the problem in simple terms, and then we fix it. Communication and agreement will hit the reset button and put them in the same stage.

Now, back to our couple in their respective stages:

T: What do you think about all of this? Martin, what do you need?

M: She knows! (Laughs)

T: that's the whole point! She doesn't know what you need. She can't know until you tell her.

M: I need to know that she believes in us. That she wants to build a life together. I need to know that I'm more important than her friends, more important than "hanging out."

T: Can you give him that? Do you want to build this, Karen?

K: of course I do, but I need validation.

T: What does that look like?

K: Acceptance. Respect. Respect is huge! I feel like I can build anything with him if I get that. I need him to stop trivializing me and my life. I can see myself going forward with him if he gives me that.

T: That's a start. What about you Martin? Can you give her what she's asking for?

M: I can give her that. I just felt like she was leaving me behind. That hurts. As long as I know she wants a future with me, I'll give her the world.

This became the basis of a new relationship. Through communication and connection they jump-started the process and found their way to the same stage together(Stage three). They will now continue the conversation that they should have had years ago. Finally, there is a chance to give each other what they need. By being in the same place and time, Martin can feel the safety and trust of partnership and Karen can receive the validation that she needs. It is a dramatically different world for them when their needs are being met.

We ask so much from relationships and we know so little about them. No one has taught us how to negotiate the stages of relationship. The passion and fireworks are merely the first stage of love, but they are the part we see most in the movies and we identify as love. When this projection falls apart, as it must, then only do we have the opportunity for the succeeding stages, the booster rockets of love.

You see the dilemma: we have an unreal "formula" for love and vague notions of how it should unfold, yet we are attached to the very stage that cannot last. *Real love can only show up after disillusionment.* We must first get through and dispel the fantasy before we can begin to love. After the disappointment that is inevitable we can start to question, "What do we have here and how can it work?"

What most people call love in the beginning of a relationship is a form of self-infatuation. We're thrilled with how we feel; we marvel that we can feel this way again. We are blissfully unaware of whom our partner might actually be. Underneath it all, our patterns, our psychology our lessons have bonded deeply. If not for this fluffy fantasy, people might never couple at all. Only after the first stage is worked through and breaks down can we begin to create a workable relationship.

WHAT STAGE ARE WE IN?

According to this framework we may ultimately find ourselves in five separate relationships. Each stage is so dramatically different that each creates a unique experience of the relationship. When answering the question, "What is relationship?" we have to start with what it is at any given time. Initially, it is the most stimulating fantasy ever and then, when it breaks down, it is not that fantasy. It is the opportunity to feel emotionally connected and yet it evolves to a place where we cannot get all of our emotional needs filled. It is the experience of being seen and understood, a most fulfilling experience. Having accepted that reality, it migrates to a stage where we are connecting with the world instead. It does not remain a guarantee of sex and intimacy, or of eternal passion, though it starts with that promise. Neither is it a static, never-ending situation. We don't grow simultaneously and in lockstep with one another, but we are always growing together or growing apart. The fact is that relationship, like everything else in nature, is in a constant state of change. If we don't acknowledge this truth, we will feel tricked and betrayed.

As we start to separate what we've been taught to expect from the objective reality of relationship, we see real differences. According to the old model, our partner should be psychic. She must know the "real" me (whatever that happens to be at the time), and deeply value that, whether I reveal that or not. He must know my special "code" for love: exactly how I need to be loved and when. The old model demands secret hidden knowledge. We'd have more luck guessing the combination of someone's gym locker than knowing their formula for love.

In the new model, conscious relating, there is a gradual unfolding of great potential through the use of observation and communication. There is purpose and meaning to every conflict. We see the arc of growth in our partnership and we expect change. Disappointment and sadness may show up, but these are only the signals of work that needs to be done. Every stage has an order and logic to it, and each can be exciting and naturally build to the next, as we construct a durable model that sustains us.

In the Identification stage, we yearn to surrender who we are. We gladly collapse into an "us" and fall under the spell of this dream-like state. Oddly, even within this fantasy there is a certain reality. What we see in this first heady stage is the potential of that person and this partnership. Life first takes us to the top of the mountain to show us the view and then brings us down to the valley with a message. The message is "earn it." Stage one gives us a vision and a mandate.

Real and workable dynamics need to be mastered, and when we master them, we can navigate these waters called relationship. Only within the disillusionment of the second stage can we start to see these dynamics. There is the adventure of discovering whom we are with, and what they are all about, but we must not abandon ourselves. Differentiation provides the opportunity to see who I am in the context of relationship and in my life.

Forget the magical thinking. Let go of the promise of stage one to magically transform, and take the opportunity to find out who you are and who your partner is. Stage one is sameness, Stage two is difference. Without hostility or blame we can discover where "I" end and "you" begin. Without this vital information we cannot proceed. It is essential not to lose our sense of self or give it up for an illusion. There can be great conflict in this stage, because we are angry and conflicted. The magic is gone, the pain of self has returned and the promise of the situation seems to be broken. Only after the flower dies, can the plant begin to bear fruit. We must be willing to give up the semblance of happiness for the real possibility of connection. If we had been taught to expect this stage, there would be less conflict. We can and should embrace this necessary disillusionment. Stage two gives us independence.

A sobering stage, Assimilation brings an uneasy truce, and with it the possibility of building a real foundation. The first two stages could take two years, or six months. This period is also not determined by length but by content. We discover that this love will not take away pain, it will not manufacture happiness, or bliss. This is a time to honestly assess the assets of the union. Perhaps she is great at seeing the bigger picture, while he is a master of detail. He is wonderful at generating money where she has a great sense of balance and style in the world. By now we have done our time on the outside and once again look inward towards the partnership. Communication shows up in this stage because we genuinely want to know if we can go the distance with each other. Enough of an investment has been made and now we need to know what we have. We gain objectivity in this stage.

Commitment comes with the fourth stage, Integration. The timeline of this stage begin from one year onward. At this point we have explored the previous stages and are ready to build a future. The wariness is gone and with it that sense of separateness and suspicion. There is a sense of real acceptance in this stage and even a growing feeling of contentment. We sense a union that is not based on dependency but on choice. This can be an exciting time; we embrace that which we have held at arm's length for so long. The relief and release of this time brings a lot of joy, and the good will to move forward. This can take the form of long-term commitment, moving in or getting engaged. We are ready to formalize our union and declare it to the world. More than ever, communication and awareness are necessary tools for this stage. When the love and good will overflows, when we have enough emotional equity in this partnership, we want to expand. Perhaps a year or two into the relationship we reach the stage of Creation. We feel so secure within this partnership that the good will literally spills over into other areas. We are ready to add more moving parts. We have successfully forged a new concept of "us" that wants to take on the world. It is a heady state that allows us to trust what we've created; we believe that the partnership can support creating a family or building a real enterprise in the world.

This synthesis of concept and reality makes us stronger, like alloyed metal. We build businesses, buy houses and have babies with faith that we have the strength and agreement to do so. Creation adds a dimension to relationship that gives us participation and validity in the world. We affirm ourselves through what we create. It is an exciting stage that can be sustained for the life of the relationship.

START AN INQUIRY

Partnership is creative and challenging; it requires passion and commitment. We have to abandon the idea that relationship runs itself, and roll up our sleeves to do the work. Awareness is the beginning of a process to create conscious relating.

For something we want so much from, we give love very little attention. Truthfully, if the relationship were a houseplant it would not survive with the little nurturing and attention that it is given. We don't even investigate what agreements we've already made or what patterns we are behaving from. To start an exploration we need to ask questions: What do each of us want from this situation? Is this partnership we have created addressing our mutual interests? How does the world experience us as a couple? Does the world like what it sees in our interactions? Do they (the world) know more than we do about our own dynamics? How are we changing and how have we changed?

If we start with the assumption that we don't know what this relationship is, then we are at the beginning of an exciting inquiry. Only by living in the question of "who are we" do we have a chance to examine and change the inner workings of our lives.

The couple in the example made a huge discovery: they learned that they don't know who each other is, or what each wants. They did not know that relationship unfolds in stages, or what each stage means. Knowledge is power: they are now able to start addressing these issues. It is their first real opportunity to love consciously.

EXERCISE 1

1. Write down the stage of relationship you think you and your partner are in.

2. Determine what stage your partner is in and why you see it that way.

3. Determine what stage you think your relationship should be in and how to get there.

4. Start a dialogue about the stage you are each in, without judgment. Have a "feeling" discussion about it.

EXERCISE 2

Start an inquiry: discuss your mutual patterns and origins, not in order to assign blame, but in order to shed light on your relationship. Try your best to stay objective, and if the discussion gets heated, put it aside for another time.

EXERCISE 3
Identify the role that Karen is playing; identify the role that Martin is playing. Change those roles and see how the conflict would show up differently.

SIX

YOUR WORK OF ART

A NEW MODEL

It isn't easy for people to make the adjustment from the appearance of romance we've come to know to the very different reality of partnership. We can survive the transitions of every stage, and make sense of the work and the play of it. The question is: will there be enough love and good will at the end of the day to sustain us?

In my experience, the reality of relationship is better than the fantasy. This point of view takes into account all the work that must be done and still allows for romance and joy. With fantasy comes uncertainty and insecurity. If love is too good to be true, then we don't feel worthy of it; if partnership is based on truth and hard work, we can earn our happiness.

A NEW VISION

Conscious relating is based on the merging of equals coming together for the purpose of spiritual growth. Love is defined as spiritual cooperation to mutually learn what we have chosen to learn. Attraction is based, not on the physical, but on our being drawn to our lessons. We are destined to come together to learn and to grow. There are no accidents in the spiritual model. We have chosen each other, in our wisdom and clarity, to work in perfect spiritual cooperation for our highest good and personal happiness.

In psychological terms we say that our patterns attract each other. The unresolved issues of childhood are being unconsciously acted out. We seek resolution through a partner whose patterns dovetail with our own. This model can live side by side with the spiritual model without conflict.

You and your chosen partner are in perfect spiritual agreement with every issue and every lesson. The issues that arise in relationship are perfectly designed to reveal patterns and to give each of us the opportunity to resolve them. We have conspired to create the events that move each of us forward on our journey. Everything that happens in this relationship is for our highest good. We serve each other best when we understand that we are the catalysts for each other's growth.

CONFLICT

Conflict is a necessary part of partnership. We look at love, and even disagreement, as a part of spiritual synchronicity. In this context there is no such thing as pointless argument. All events have a purpose for growth and learning; when we empower this model we are never lost. This framework assigns meaning to every exchange and allows us to keep our power in the relationship. From this point of view there are no accidents. Nothing has "happened" to us; we have chosen everything.

We are together because we are destined to be together. There is no unnecessary pain, just unfinished business between us. Rather than having the experience of "having the same old argument," recast it as ongoing work on issues that we have agreed to resolve. Every matter is a piece of spiritual business: from the bedroom to the public arena we are always in the process of our learning and growth. This powerful model gives meaning to our interactions and purpose to going forward together.

A PRACTICAL PHILOSOPHY

As we migrate through the different stages of relationship this philosophy of conscious relating is a beacon that will light the way for change. Everything evolves and so should our model for love. This new model is more serviceable than the conventional viewpoint, and it works to solve problems. Don't waste time debating whether or not it is true; rather, use it as a template to see what this model reveals and explains.

YOUR WORK OF ART

If you and I are painting a mural together we confer, discuss and agree. There will be conferences and brainstorming, even disagreements. Passions will run high. Each of us will have a point of view that reveals our inner world and our choices. Through our common goal and purpose we get to know each other. We create a connection, an intimacy. We relate. Communication is essential. We build on the skills that each of us brings, on the mastery that we both possess.

Every great artist first mastered structure and form before creating their masterpiece. How do we create our own "work of art," our masterpiece of love? There is structure that we must master. There are dynamics that need to be understood, strategies to be explored, and real understandings that need to be in place to build a partnership. In addition, there are the tools of relationship: vision, communication, empathy and a working knowledge of dynamics.

We need to become clear about what we are fighting for: what is the truth and what is not. We need to know what is possible. We also need to know where we stand right now. Are we as a couple in the same place? Is our communication functional?

The easiest way to find answers is to go on an inquiry and a fact-finding mission. There is a show on the home network called "This Old House." In this show the host systematically goes through the house and looks at the plumbing, the electricity and the basic structure of the home. He makes an honest assessment of what is working and what needs improvement. Only by doing so can he determine the value of the house. He will not even begin to market the house until he has an objective view of it. This doesn't mean that he isn't looking at the homes' potential; within this very real scrutiny the "art" is to see what this structure can be at its absolute best. It is at once a thorough scrutiny and a projection of the best possibility of what the house can be. This is our artistry in relationship.

THE STATE OF THE UNION
This attention to detail and focus on the relationship allows us to see it much more objectively. If we are going to improve anything, we can and must take an honest look at the state of the union. We also need a path or structure to compare what we have. In the house we have plumbing and electric; an entire checklist of features to assess. In relationship we have our own value points. We can assess the health of the partnership through the following: How are we relating intellectually, physically, emotionally and spiritually? How are we doing socially, sexually, financially? This is a fair checklist through which we can take the temperature of the relationship.

CHECKLIST
Intellectual: Do we have a healthy dialogue with a range of topics?

Physical: Are we physically active, together and separately?

Emotional: How in touch are we with our feelings and our partners?

Spiritual: Do we have a compatible spiritual viewpoint?

Social: Do we interact well with our world, together and separately?

Sexual: Do we still feel vital and connected sexually?

Financial: Do we have an agreement on how to build financially?

A quick perusal of this list will give insight into the state of your union, and give some indication of where work is needed. We have to find ways to maintain our enthusiasm and vision while doing this work. In any creative project, vision is the ability to see where this partnership needs work now, while holding a picture of its highest potential.

Conscious relationship is a way and a path. Instead of placing blame and being frustrated, we choose to concentrate on where we need to improve our skills. We become a team with a purpose. Love becomes a work of art to be proud of and excited about, as well as a very real framework that demands attention and care. This model gives purpose to every moment in relationship and causes us to assess more powerfully and with a workman's eye. There is a pride and delight that shows up when we care about our work and real progress when we make substantial improvements. When we can recognize the place that each of us is in within this partnership, we have something powerful to communicate to each other.

WORK TO LOVE

Abandon the fantasy. It got us to the dance but it won't keep us there. Be in the stage that you and your partner are truly in. There is joy in every stage and there is appropriate work for each stage that you are in. In the spiritual model of conscious relating, we choose to deal with the dynamics of partnership and see those dynamics as a set of agreements. We take full responsibility for how we show up and the issues that we find.

We wouldn't expect to get behind the wheel of a car and automatically know how to drive. Let's be realistic and honest with ourselves; rather than expect love to work magically, let's have an understanding that, like any partnership or project, love means work.

What we create together will be as unique as we are. We come together spiritually, emotionally, intellectually and physically to create a synthesis that only our partnership can produce. Be fascinated by what will be forged when we combine our skills and interests. Take inspiration from whatever the highest evolution this union can attain. Your love of theater and my delight in the outdoors can live together and inform each other in ways that we haven't yet imagined. Be present with the question of "What do we create?" We can't be afraid to look under the hood and see the engine.

We need communication and an accurate assessment of where each of us is within the relationship. If you are still in the identification stage and I am in the differentiation stage, only communication can bridge the gap of potential disconnect and disaster. Without seeing this we are blind and will cause each other unnecessary pain.

Instead of being reactive, let's find out who the stranger is across the room. Remember the initial excitement about your partner; that was real. Don't abandon the potential of who you can be together. Determine to continue to use every tool available in order to understand and recapture the power and the magic. We are the raw material for our own creation.

EXERCISE

Make an assessment of the state of your union, using the checklist in this chapter as a guideline.

SEVEN

THAT MAGIC FEELING

WHAT RELATIONSHIP IS NOT

We've now explored some history and background about relationship, and how the concept of love has evolved. Let's look at what we have learned so far. Clearly, we've learned much of what relationship is not. Relationship is not Chivalry. It isn't just sex. It is not the fantasy we've projected on to it. It isn't a vehicle for our expectations, nor is it a promise of getting our emotional needs filled. It is not our attachments; nor is it the chemical wash that surrounds us when we first meet.

We now are equipped with a great deal of information about roles and games and how these roles interact with each other. We are not those roles, nor are we the games we play. We know that we are in one (or several) stages of relationship, often exclusive to where our partner is. We also know that we are operating on several different planes and that we may or may not be connecting with our mates on these planes. We are driven by the unseen rudders of childhood patterns that live within us, and these patterns also interact with each other and have volition all their own.

All of this information begs the question, "Who is relating to whom?" We can't honestly claim to know ourselves very much, apart from this information. It can be difficult to determine why and how we are connected. A key aspect of this information is this: within every inauthentic connection there lies the potential for an authentic one. For every "bad" reason we are involved, there is the potential for real connection. The underlying spiritual and emotional potential exists, even within our neurotic patterns.

With respect to our self-knowledge and motivation, we know even less about our mates. How many of us can name our partner's likes and dislikes? Not many of these preferences get communicated. We have an experience of each other which quickly collapses into a concept, and we relate and react to that concept, rather than the person in front of us.

AGENDAS

To further obscure the truth, each of us has an agenda, a hidden agenda and a secret hidden agenda. My agenda might be to buy you flowers; my hidden agenda may be to be seen as the romantic. As my secret hidden agenda, I could be seeking love and approval in order to feel safe in the world. It is far easier to see these agendas from the outside. We are often unaware of our own agendas, yet we somehow expect our partners to know this information and to respond to our needs. We will touch on agendas again later.

SOCIAL LANDSCAPE

Putting aside the internal dynamics for a moment, within the social context, love is an ever-evolving concept in our society. What looked right yesterday is not acceptable today. Partnership is so wide open now that we can define it any way we choose. Watch vintage movies from the 30's and 40's and you will see a very different version of love than the one that we know. To start with, there's that cigarette dangling from Bogey's mouth. In their time that was the new "sexy." Bacall teaching Bogey how to whistle was so risqué. That wouldn't pass muster these days.

The changing social landscape offers the challenge of how we want to appear to the world. We don't know what love should look like or whether we are doing it right. There is pressure to make our partnership conform to the acceptable form of the day. We will discuss the impression that we create as a couple and how to create a mindful and user-friendly image in the world in later chapters.

MAGIC

Can that "magical feeling" really be the signal for true love? Maybe... Every love relationship I've been in began with that crazy, out of control feeling and a sense of the magical. It can be the beginning of a real and important relationship in your life. If we keep in mind that every inauthentic aspect of relationship has its authentic counterpart, we needn't be alarmed by the knowledge that some of how we interact is fantasy.

If you are already in a relationship, you know that you are involved and connected in some very particular ways. We need to explore the dynamics and see what this animal called relationship actually consists of in its simplest form.

SIMPLE RELATING

Let us take a simple relationship with few moving parts. Let's visit your local Key Food and look in on your relationship with the grocery store clerk. There is an exercise in enlightened self-interest resulting in mutual benefit. You have an agreement with the grocer. He provides bananas and cheese; you bring the money. You make your choices and pay for your delicious items. An exchange occurs and you are in a functioning relationship, clean and simple.

So what goes wrong when we add "romance" to the mix? What bitches' brew causes the migration from an easy exchange to one of obligation, pain, and betrayal? Our pesky expectations lead to the confusion. The moment we add love to the equation we unleash our emotion-backed demands.

Try putting these expectations on your store clerk and see what happens. What if you demanded of him: "You should anticipate my needs and know who I am! How dare you not have Gouda?" Try asking him "Why don't you respect me? If you loved me you wouldn't give me fruit from Costa Rica!" "You should know what I want and have my bananas waiting!" You are likely to get some strange looks from the clerk (or start something you didn't bargain for)!

We all remember grammar school: the sights and sounds of the erasers, the surreal noise of the classroom. Oddly, Mrs. Belford was teaching us about relationships then, and not just between teacher and student. Relationship was at the heart of every subject that was taught. Each topic was really about dynamics and interactions. English was about the relationship of subject to verb and object. In mathematics, how two numbers interact describes their relationship to each other. There is elegance in how the numbers relate, multiplying, dividing, adding or subtracting. It is so simple. We human beings have a set of dynamics that can be understood with the same simplicity.

NECESSARY MAGIC

When I fell for my first girlfriend, it started as attraction. "She's so hot!" morphed quickly into "She's so kind, so sweet, so understanding!" I barely saw it happen. I saw through the filters of my attraction. She had her own "chemical wash" or set of endorphins that triggered and she immediately began interpreting through that filter. We become the willing partners in this charade. Our patterns locked and we assigned feelings and projected on to each other, based on our internal experience. This experience cued up each of our expectations of love. I "knew" I loved her and this signal triggered my internal programming. Her schemata of expectations were mobilized as well. It didn't matter that we didn't really know each other; we were quickly becoming intertwined.

Perhaps it is true that without the fantasy we would never choose relationship. I could argue that if I knew how that first love affair was going to end I wouldn't have participated. If I hadn't gotten involved, though, I never would have learned those early lessons that I needed in order to build healthy relationship today.

THE IDEAL MATE

Lance and Marta from Chapter Three barely had any experience of each other before they were off to the races with their fantasies. Maybe if they compared notes and communicated early on and broadened their base of communication, this couple could have avoided the pain of misunderstanding. We all face that same dilemma.

The decks were stacked against them as it is with all of us. Our expectations are encoded in every aspect of our culture: movies, music, TV. We see what we want to see. As human beings we are storytellers. We create a "story" about our love interest and we tell that story to everyone, including ourselves. We begin living in the concept of love, rather than the experience. Suddenly she or he is the best, the brightest, the sweetest, and, why not? The deception is completely self-serving: if he or she is "all that," then I am terrific for attracting her. We subtly weave a fantasy in which we are the hero and we are delighted with who we are and what we have accomplished. We then have a huge stake in making sure that he or she stays the best and the brightest, for the sake of our story. We are more attached to the "story" than to reality, and reality can become an intrusion onto that story.

FANTASY PEOPLE

A fantasy woman is always kind. She is endlessly patient and giving. Incredibly supportive, she always understands. She is the soul of tenderness: beautiful, yet nurturing. Infinitely creative in bed (and always interested!) she is a great sport and a real pal. An insightful partner in business and personal matters, she has a great sense of humor and a down-to-earth quality.

The fantasy man is always charmed. His love is a source of endless delight for him. He is generous to a fault, and endlessly attentive. He cares about her every thought, her every experience. He beats a path for her and makes the world a safe and inviting place. He shows her off to family and friends as the jewel that she is to him. Every need and want is anticipated by him. He shares her same hopes and dreams for the future.

Charming though this story is, this is a formula for disaster; a time bomb waiting to explode. Sooner or later, one or the other partner will become disillusioned. He or she will vary from the path. There is great pain when a partner deviates from this fantasy. It feels like a loss and we don't respond well; we feel cheated, tricked and even punished.

AUTHENTICITY

In truth, we're lucky if we experience our mate authentically more than a few times, before we are immersed in the fantasy. We very early are experiencing our own creation, rather than reality of our partner. We observe this in others, this inability to see the partner they are with. "How can he be with her?" we ask; or "Doesn't she see what a bad guy he is?" The answer is no. She sees only the fantasy she has woven. When the fantasy does break down, it tends to break down all at once. Like scales falling from our eyes, we see everything that we've ignored for so long. Our house of cards falls apart.

When we ask the question: "What is relationship?" it is not a simple answer. The more we see of ourselves the more we see that different parts of us are in relationship with each other. As we become more conscious we begin to make new choices and we are able to bring relationship into the realm of the authentic. We will not sustain the relationship that it started out to be, that isn't possible, but we can build with conscious determination and practical magic.

Let's use our discovery to answer the more compelling question "What can relationship be?"

EXERCISE 1

State a list of your partner's interests and preferences. Ask your partner to do the same. Compare notes.

EXERCISE 2

Target a relationship and identify your agenda, hidden agenda and secret hidden agenda.

Identify your partner's agendas.

EIGHT

INTENTION

Chapter Seven spoke of the magic of relationship, perhaps the glue that holds it together. We have discussed the model of conscious loving and awareness. Now let's talk about the power of intention within love. Intention has the ability to transform us from being victims to being the creators of our reality. It allows us to set our own course and choose our destiny. We choose the reality that we find ourselves in. When we create an intention we set a course for a hundred different conscious and subconscious choices that align with that intention. Intention becomes the roadmap that we follow to create the reality that we want.

What follows is an excerpt from a session. Henry has been given his walking papers after six years of marriage.

HENRY: She says it's over. I blew it. I know there've been problems, but she says she's had it. She doesn't feel the same way any more. She says she loves me, but she's just not in love with me any more...

THOMAS: And you believe her?

H: She's really mad!

T: So what are you going to do, lie down and die? Have you ever heard of the concept of fighting for your relationship?

H: I think she's really done. She says this has been going on for years and she can't take it any more. She says I never come through for her. That I don't listen to her and I don't care.

T: Maybe she wants to see if you'll fight for her, fight for the relationship. Isn't she worth it?

H: Oh God, yeah...

T: Than how come you're not fired up? Why isn't this opportunity to show her how much she means to you? Take a chance and make a heroic effort. Listen to what she is actually saying. She's saying that you don't care. Are you trying to prove that she's right? Make a fool of yourself for this; pull out all the stops! Storm the barricades! If she's worth crying over, she's worth fighting for. Are you a victim or do you want to create what you want? What exactly is your intention here?

H: What if it doesn't work?

T: Well, how well is the crying and suffering working?

The man in this excerpt has already given up. He is weaving the "sad story of me" and doesn't want to stop. The only trouble is that he is burying the body before it's quite dead. Of course she doesn't love him the way she used to. Unless we are frozen in a bubble of time, love changes. If he understood the stages of relationship he would see that. Of course the relationship has changed; this is great opportunity, if only he has eyes to see. Instead, Henry is giving his power away to the apparent circumstances. He wants to whine and complain instead of making it his intention to recapture the love. His choice of giving up is boring and powerless.

The first thing he doesn't know is that when we have relationship we will have conflict. That is inevitable when we merge two worlds, two different points-of-view. We would expect to disagree in business, so why should love be exempt from the concept?

PERFECT DESIGN

Here's an unromantic notion that is true: any relationship we choose is going to have dramatic shortfalls and those flaws are built in to the design. The distance between our needs and what we receive is the space where our lessons show up. It is important and sometimes even necessary that love not give us what we think we need. We seek contentment so that we can fall asleep in our cozy nest. We will only evolve when we are out of our comfort zone. If our intention is to make our relationship work, this discomfort will be the signal to learn and to grow. It may also signal the beginning of challenging times and a new stage of the partnership, but that is a positive, not a negative.

Let's examine the concepts of the spiritual model of relationships, the precepts of conscious relating. We are here to teach each other. It is no accident that we push each other's buttons, and hook in to each other's patterns. Don't assign diabolical intentions to your partner; there really is an elegant plan.

Our issues fit together like a hand in a glove and that is no mistake. This is why we picked one another. Nothing is as attractive to us as our lessons, all wrapped up in an exciting new person to play with. Without the motivation of attraction we would never choose to learn our lessons and change our patterns. When we can choose to see love as a design instead of proof of some mistake, we can get meaning out of conflict. Then we can take control and exploit the situation for what there is to learn. Conflict doesn't mean that the relationship is bad or that it is a failure. Conflict is a signal that this union is functioning the way that it should: there are lessons here to learn.

INTENTION

In order to manifest any reality we need only three things: personal power, burning desire and intention. By taking our power back from everything that we've given it to, we gain the fuel for creating reality. Burning desire is cultivated through visualizing the reality that we want to create. None of this can work, however, unless we intend. We must complete the sentence "I am going to create _____" Whether it is writing a book or creating a relationship, intention is the arrow of direction that life follows in order to form our reality.

FAILURE AND SUCCESS

The cheetah is the most successful hunter in the animal kingdom. It's true, she is the most successful; she's number one. She's the leader and yet she only makes a kill one time in ten. This means that she fails nine times out of ten. I wonder if we could consider ourselves "most successful" with those numbers. Alex Rodriquez may be one of the greatest hitters of all time (I didn't say the most popular). He fails at bat on the average of seven times out of ten. If you rounded off the numbers in these two examples to the nearest ten, they would fail all the time. Sound like good odds? Do you think they see themselves as failures? I doubt it.

When I was a child my parents always had the magazine *Reader's Digest* in the bathroom, and to this day I always associate that magazine with that location. I can't see that logo without it calling up the sense memories of blue tile and pink wallpaper. There was an article in one particular copy of RD about how a CEO of a large corporation is chosen. Surprisingly, one of the qualities sought after in a corporate head of the company is a history of failure. Their reasoning is that unless someone knows how to fail and how to negotiate their way through that failure, they will fear failure and they probably won't take the company to the height of success. The point of the article was this: your success is based on how you interpret failure.

Is Henry from the previous session excerpt correct? He believes that he has failed and lost the love of his life. Henry believes that he should give up. Whenever relationship is discussed, there is no tolerance or even value for failure. Henry isn't succeeding yet, but he shouldn't just bag it. He has invested an awful lot into that relationship. To leave now would be like building half a house and walking away.

We are missing something that the greatest successes know: failure doesn't mean stop. It is not a signal to quit. When our intention is clear, failure is merely a step toward getting exactly what we want. Henry Ford said it best when he said "Failure is the opportunity to begin again, intelligently." Conservatively, a child falls on the average of five hundred times before he succeeds in walking and falls many times thereafter as he masters the skill.

As adults we would interpret this seeming failure as a reason to give up. We would still be sitting and never get up. With our experience of failure we might never get off the ground. We have all failed. We will all fail again. We don't have to take failure personally or interpret it as a stop sign. Failure is an opportunity, a gift. We can use failure for the value that it holds and choose to learn what is being taught. Failure will never again be an obstacle once we change our interpretation of it.

FUTURE REGRET

Henry is so busy focusing on his pain and personal loss that he isn't listening. Sometimes fighting and even leaving is just a strategy we use in order to be heard. If Henry doesn't do everything possible to save the relationship now it will be incredibly painful for him later. Regret is the greatest cause of pain at the end of a relationship. We go over what we could have and should have done a thousand times in our minds. The regrets never stop. For his sake, for the sake of the "witness within" he needs to make all of the heroic efforts now to save his relationship. That part of himself, or "witness" that is watching his choices and behaviors will hold him accountable for everything he does and doesn't do, all actions taken and not taken. The "witness within" is always watching; we are always accountable.

RELATIONSHIP IS FOR LESSONS

Learning our lessons in relationship means that we become the person that we are meant to become. Henry needs to step up to becoming the man that he can be. Only by growing can he hope to transform this relationship. This is the synchronicity that exists in relationship. Both parties come together to learn what each must learn for their own highest good. Everything is perfect exactly the way it is, for everyone's growth.

FOREVER AND EVER

We don't have any guarantee that our relationship is going to last forever. It isn't supposed to. Even if we manage to live together all of our lives, chances are someone is going to die first. We certainly have no surety of an afterlife where we can hang out together. The concept that love will go on forever is insidious in its way. It gives us permission to put off the work that needs be done in the partnership. We are not supposed to have the complacency that "lasting forever" would give us. We are designed to feel the urgency of the moment and the uncertainty of the future to motivate us to do the work. Uncertainty is our ally. Only with uncertainty will we be vigilant about protecting and improving our relationship. Only with uncertainty will we stay awake.

We can count on the lessons in relationship as sure as the sun rises. They are supposed to show up. Let's welcome them like the opportunities that they are instead of reacting as though something has gone terribly wrong. In business we expect obstacles; in relationship we should expect the same. It is no less an enterprise.

OUR DESIGN

When we start to own that we have designed this partnership on some higher level we are no longer taken by surprise when issues surface. We've all seen the individual who picks the same type of person to have relationship with over and over again. This is not a self-defeating act: they make this choice because they are picking the same lesson over and over, until it is learned. How different relationship would be if we understood this. We'd stop blaming our partners for his or her perceived faults and start looking at ourselves and the lessons that we've chosen. We might even welcome these challenges as the opportunity to work on what we've chosen to master. Our patterns show up in order to be healed. We have picked the perfect partner to assist us in that evolution. When we understand this model and determine to change, we don't waste time and effort casting blame.

CHANGE THE RIGHT PERSON

Let's see how, in this model, we go about effecting change. We start with the fundamentals. We are the projector and life is the screen. Instead of trying to change the results that we see, we can change our internal projector. We look at our patterns and history for clues to our behavior. We examine our feelings and emotions with a ruthless honesty. We take full responsibility for the conflict or upset and start unraveling the truth from there. Ask the dangerous questions: "Why did I create this? What am I up to?" Only by looking within can we gain any real power over the situation and create real progress. We have been given the power to change everything, but they say that God hid the knowledge to change where man would be least likely to look: within.

We can change the old patterns and create healthy new ones only when we seek these patterns and recognize them. The measure of a person's power is their ability to handle truth about themselves. The path to gaining real power is seeking truth. We have seen all of our issues before in our other relationships. If we are honest, there is very little new in this "new" situation. When we go to the source of the problem within, we can actually gain power over the issue and ultimately resolve it forever.

It is such a foreign idea that we have come here to learn. We have been groomed with expectations to the contrary. According to our legacy and our history, love is supposed to look perfect; instead it is perfect, but in unexpected ways. We are in the midst of an elegant design that allows us to learn and grow together in perfect synchronicity. Every event is designed and agreed upon as an opportunity to learn. We simply have to understand and properly use the system we find ourselves in. Within this model there is very little use for victim status.

People who try to change each other in relationship are doomed to frustration and pain. I can't change you, I can only change me. We have control over one person, ourselves, and that is enough. Let's stick with controlling our own identity and see how much it can change.

When we talk about control, let's be clear: all that we control is our experience in life. We do not control our circumstances. We don't control our partner any more than we control the weather. This is the tactical error that most people make: we try desperately to change our partner in order to gain happiness. It is never our circumstances that make us unhappy, nor is it ever someone else; it is our experience of those circumstances that makes us miserable. Unless we go to the source of the problem, to the areas where we actually have control, we cannot "fix" the problem.

We all tend to master the victim game and the blame game. This is the surest way of giving away our power. If I say that you can make me happy or unhappy, I have given you the power over my experience. It isn't true and it isn't effective to give our power away to any person or circumstance. We can roll up our sleeves and take on the job of self-transformation and then we are at the work site of our own happiness.

BE A STUDENT

Being a student of life means that we choose to learn. There are three or four things we can do right now to make the relationship better. I can forgive, I can be kinder, I can stop criticizing, and I can stop acting so disappointed. I can do all of this without the cooperation or even knowledge of my partner. I can stop taking it personally and honestly look at what isn't working in me. I can take responsibility without guilt. I can be a master of my own fate and decide to change my experience. I can take an honest inventory. If we don't learn from history, we are doomed to repeat it.

HENRY: I've tried everything!

THOMAS: I doubt that. You mean you've taken your shot and you can't think of anything else. You've got to give up the idea that this is some Greek tragedy. Obviously she's still talking to you. It's an opportunity.

H: You think this is an opportunity?

T: What if this is the moment in time that when you look back changed everything? What if this is the chance to get back on track and revitalize your relationship?

H: It doesn't look like that, at all.

T: Did you ever see a diamond in its natural state? It's dull and irregular and looks like an ordinary rock. You might pass it by. Yet, if you can recognize it, you've made a fortune. Don't wait for it to look right. Make it your intention for this to be the beginning of your new relationship! Take it on. Make it great.

APPEARANCES

We are fascinated by what a successful relationship looks like. Brad Pitt and Angelina Jolie are the subjects of endless articles. We may try to emulate a Hollywood couple but we will seek form without function. I have a friend who is an accomplished artist and whose work I admire. She invited me to see her studio one day. I was excited to check out the workplace where such art was created. "Don't mind the mess, I'm at the beginning of a new project." she said, as she led me into the studio. I looked around and took in the half-squeezed tubes of paint, the unfinished sketches lying all around. "Out of chaos comes order!" she giggled, as she took in my facial expression. I realized that this is what greatness looks like.

Let's continue to define our new model. Just because there is disagreement does not mean there isn't the potential for a good relationship. We should expect to fail at communication and connection from time to time, if only to perfect these skills. Human beings learn by failing, not by succeeding. We will be thoughtless from time to time and even arrogant and rude. This is still within the bounds of a great love affair. "I love you" has room and heart enough in it to also contain "I'm bored of you!" It's a big room that also holds "I don't like you right now!" Love is big enough and strong enough to take our greatest conflicts and from them forge a lasting relationship. It is not always a pretty picture, but it contains powerful potential. We are destined to screw up dramatically with infinite creativity and still we are working toward perfecting love. We can't give up on love just because there is not always harmony or agreement. Let's make it our intention to fight for love with the understanding that it does not always match the picture we've been given.

A good relationship doesn't show up with a lot of fanfare. When we have worked through our conflicts, love is a nurturing cooperation between two independent people, with common goals and common interests. There is little drama, but a sweet, easy agreement, a quiet trust that lends strength and power to us in the world. "We are together, through choice, not need. We are building safe haven for ourselves (and maybe our children) in this world." It's a partnership that makes one stronger, but without pressure. It isn't protection from life, but a clear space to refuel and renew us: a good relationship is a mutually beneficial background structure that gives our life definition and purpose.

CONFLICT AND INTENTION

The spiritual model makes conflict inevitable and valuable. It is an opportunity to grow. Conflict is not an unwelcome guest, but it can be a difficult one. To know that we have chosen each other to teach turns a clash from a battlefield to an inquiry. "What am I here to learn?" "How do I teach through this encounter?" "What does it look like if I take full responsibility for this conflict?" We get to change our relationship with disagreement; we begin to understand that isn't hostile or filled with shame. If this, too, is perfect, then nothing is wrong. We haven't failed, and far from being the wrong person for each other, we are the exact right ones to bring forth the issues necessary for change. Is relationship an idyllic respite from life, free from all conflict? Let's be realistic. Any partnership is going to face conflict because we are human beings, with different points of view. It isn't the fact that we have conflict that means anything; that is to be expected. It's how we resolve those conflicts and the meaning we place on them that will define the quality of our relationships.

The only "failure" in relationship is the refusal to learn, to grow, to challenge oneself to make it the best situation it can be. Everything else is just a work in progress. To fail would mean to give up when there is more for you to learn and more solutions to try. And, yes, there are some relationships that are too far gone to save, but we can't know that with any certainty until we give it a real effort. In fact, we can't reasonably leave a relationship until we've brought it to the best place it can be. Only then can we judge whether it is workable.

We're happy in relationship because of who we are in that relationship. It is ourselves that we have to live up to. When we are proud of our efforts, our learning and our results, we will be content. I have a client who was very excited to start a new relationship. She claimed that he is everything her former boyfriend is not. "This time I'm going to make it!" She declared. Of course, the same old issues came up again, and she was tremendously discouraged. I told her to stop looking for someone "different" and to be "different" herself. Unless she changes how she approaches relationship and what she expects from it, she will always get the same result. The definition of insanity is doing the same thing over and over and expecting different results. That is the good news and the bad news. The bad news is that it is her job to change. The good news is that it is within her power to change.

When we take a road trip we set an intention to get to a specific destination. We don't hope to generally arrive in a location. We have a plan, a roadmap and directions that include our journey's end, including a specific address.

Whatever stage you are in, even if you are at the end of a relationship, it still matters how you behave. You can still end it with dignity and kindness and there are still lessons to be learned. You are the one watching you and judging you. There are still issues to resolve, even at this point, and you can still succeed in ending it with your power intact.

The only "failure" in relationship is giving up—giving up who you are and who you want to be, and even how you want it all to come out. See relationship as an opportunity to learn and grow. Take it on as a situation that you are in to see how good you can make it. Success is an inner experience. Don't try to succeed for the sake of your friends or your family. Try because the issues that come up here will come up again and again. They are your issues and you get to solve them in this situation or in the next.

EXERCISE 1

List all of your intentions in your relationship. Use the prompt: "I intend _____"

List all of your intentions for yourself in your life; again use that same prompt.

List everything that you have achieved in your relationship, and those intentions you still want to fulfill.

EXERCISE 2

List all of the lessons that you think that you need to learn in relationship.

List all of the lessons your partner needs to learn.

Compare the two. Acknowledge what you each have learned and the lessons yet to be learned.

SECTION II

COMMUNICATION

NINE

DIALOGUE

When I visited China, I found that it was easy to understand the gist of most conversations, even though I knew nothing of the language. Because of the nature of my business, I respond to a hundred different cues that have nothing to do with being verbal and everything to do with making our desires known. I literally "read" people visually as I went along and was never really lost in the dialogue. We are always communicating what we want, whether we know it or not.

A relationship cannot exist without intention. It is essential to be able to communicate that intention, or nothing will develop in the relationship. Communication occurs on many different levels: Conscious, subconscious, verbal, non-verbal. We communicate through thought, word and action. We signal our intentions through body language and dozens of facial expressions. We are always making ourselves known. Language is the last clue in a puzzle that we are already interpreting before we even speak.

Jon and Colette have come in to discuss their communication issue. Each has their point of view.

JON: I don't even know what I'm doing here. I didn't ask for any of this. (He's looking down.)

COLETTE: See, I knew you'd do this. You said you would come and now you're denying it!

J: I said I was willing to fix this relationship, not come here. (He looks at the ceiling.)

C: But that's what we're here for!

J: I never agreed to this! I don't know him (pointing to me).

C: You are lying!(she looks at me, pleading.)

J: No, you are manipulating!

T: Can I...

C: Wait! This is exactly what happens all the time!

It didn't take much to get to the disconnect in this situation. It was easy to pick up the non-verbal communication. Each was in a separate well-rehearsed conversation in his or her head and just waiting for the cues from each other. Jon felt trapped and Colette felt tricked. They were off to the races. I didn't get a word in until ten minutes into the conversation, when they each had to catch their breath. And he was mightily pissed off...

T: Why are you so angry, Jon?

J: I am sick of being made to look this way. I'm the bad guy? I just can't take this constant attack. I'm always wrong... it's always me that didn't see something, or said the wrong thing. It just isn't fair.

T: I agree.

J: What?

T: I agree. It isn't fair for you to constantly be cast as the bad guy, and it isn't true. The fact that you're here shows me that you are at least willing to try. That's more than ninety-nine percent of the men out there. I think that's terrific.

J: Why don't you tell her that?

T: You really think she's not listening? I just said that you're right. I think it's safe to say we have her attention. I'm going to end this battle for a couple of reasons: one, it's boring! Two, neither of you actually means it; you are just in the habit of communicating this way, and neither of you knows how to put their weapon down. I hesitate to say "Hey, there's a lotta love in this room!" but I will say that you wouldn't be fighting if you didn't care. Now let's start saying what you guys really want to say instead of giving me your "stories."

What is the single largest obstacle to communication in a relationship? "He doesn't understand." "She's not willing to listen." The block is in how we communicate. We arm ourselves for war! Deborah Tannen points out in *The Argument Culture* that the basis of our communication is battle. We immediately embrace a conflict mentality, even in our personal lives. It truly is "the battle of the sexes" instead of the meeting of the minds. We engage in a war of words rather than seeking agreement. Watch television and see if you can find a civil discussion on any channel. Fox News's political coverage has mastered the baiting and bashing that passes for dialogue in our public conversation.

Because I counsel couples I am uniquely positioned to see this breakdown in communication. You might think that folks put on their Sunday-best manners for a therapist, but the reality is that they quickly forget that I'm in the room. In the heat of battle, the conversation between couples looks more like prosecutors sparring than lovers talking to each other.

This couple caught my interest because there is an underlying affection beneath the battle. I could see the love peek through from time to time, even if they couldn't feel it in the moment. Yes, they were angry, but there was a tenderness and familiarity beneath the pain. Many of their physical gestures were conciliatory rather than hostile. Both had found themselves in a place that they did not want to be. They looked sick and uncomfortable, but underneath it all, they were begging for the conflict to end. We've all been in the position of defending something we don't necessarily believe. Logic and sanity are abandoned when we draw the battle lines. We're caught up in an insatiable need to win, and it makes us stupid and stubborn.

We've all been there. Fighting for the sake of fighting causes us to lose sight of the love, the humor, the sensitivity. We're busy chasing our tails. The "discussion" degenerates into a contest about who can hurt each other more effectively. Like a dog chasing meat we are rabidly attached to being clever and causing pain. Still, we are at cross-purposes with ourselves. We want an end to the conflict.

This couple was stone deaf to each other. They were only listening for their next opening to insert a nasty barb. I came into the conversation and decided to agree with someone, in order to disarm them. I needed to break the pattern and shut them up. Since each was armed for disagreement, agreement was the only tactic they weren't prepared for. They were so taken aback by this new twist that it stunned them long enough to hear something different. I could see a glimmer of hope in them.

THOMAS: What do you really want, Jon?

JON: I want her to appreciate how hard I work! I want more sex! I want more love. I don't want to be nagged.

COLETTE: What??

T: Uh, uh, uh! Don't stop him or cut him off. He's trying to tell you something.

C: Yeah, he's trying to tell me to shut up and put out!

T: Okay... what's wrong with that?

C: Are you kidding me? You're just as bad as him! What am I a robot? I should just do what he wants and smile like a Stepford Wife?

T: I don't know. Maybe. What do you really want?

C: I'll tell you what I don't want. I don't want this ignorant idiot that replaced the guy who used to open the door for me, and listen to me and actually care about me. Jon, you used to be so different!

I had the hazardous job of taking the weapons out of their hot little hands. The bomb was ticking and about to explode into shrapnel of recrimination and hatred.

J: What have you ever done for me? I'm sick of you!!

C: My mother was right!!

Tick, tick, tick...

T: I can't decide who's more stubborn. I think I have to go with you, Colette; you win.

Like boxers in the ring, they circled around one another. Each was ready to pounce, yet they both continued to show more vulnerability. Once I broke their pattern I could give them a road map. They needed a way to get to the love and caring that they had for each other, before the next escalation.

T: You know, there's a conversation going on between you two beneath this one. There are requests being made; a subtext. Do you want to know what you're really asking, Collette?

C: "I want you dead so I can collect the insurance?" (she smiles; so does he.)

T: No, good try, though. You're saying "I want the man that I love to show up again. I want the guy that knows how to treat me well. I miss the man who was head and shoulders above the rest when it came to caring for me. He was gentle and tender, and I knew that he really cared. I could see it in his eyes. I loved how that man loved me, and I would do anything for him."

C: Okay, that's true. (she looks scared.)

J: Really? That's not what I'm hearing...

T: And what do you think you're saying, John?

J: "I miss you?"

T: Not a Hallmark card, but close. You're saying "Where are you? I miss the girl who loved being loved by me. I knew we had something special, something better than what is out there, and you know it too. We had a deal. I feel left out, cheated. I want that feeling again. Nobody did it better than us, nobody! I want to know that that's still there. I want in."

J: Yeah! That's it. That's what I'm trying to say.

T: Do you two hear what's really being said now? It's a lot different than these stories you're telling. (finally, they are looking directly at each other.)

I was the translator for each of them. I stripped away their stories and showed them what they actually meant. I showed them their common ground: he wouldn't be there if he didn't want this love. She wouldn't put herself through this frustration if she didn't believe that it is better than this moment. They were starving for the affection that each one had for the other. By miscommunication, they'd fought their way to the edge of the cliff without having a clue as to how to get down. It was my job to help them down. Oddly, language was their biggest obstacle.

I had them role-play and switch positions. I put Jon in her position in order to see where all of Colette's judgments were coming from. Quickly he realized that even he would be exasperated by his own behaviors. He saw some of his patterns and even where they came from. He understood that he needed to explain some of these behaviors, without assuming that she knew his intentions. He became willing to participate once he saw that he is loved.

She in turn, recognized her pattern: if anyone comes at her with a medley of complaints, she turns off immediately. It was an old childhood mechanism. She'd done it with her mother. It was her way of defending herself. She laughed in relief. She realized that he could no longer hear her when she shut down like this.

They came to some new understandings and really saw the underlying wounds beneath their fights. We had stopped the battle; now we had to end the war. We had to establish some new ways to communicate or they would quickly degenerate to "he said, she said" once again. Changes had to be made. I taught them to communicate through agreement rather than conflict. It wasn't easy.

T: The "yes, and... " exercise is a simple one: one person starts by taking a subject and making a statement. Your partner answers with agreement no matter what the other one say. She then adds what she wants to say at the end of the statement. For example: in answer to "You need to come home on time.": "Yes, and I will when I can do that, but sometimes we need the overtime to pay the bills." Etc. Okay? Who wants to start?

C: I will.

C: You get so frustrated with your career that I can't even talk to you. You just grunt and grumble. You act like you hate life and you hate me.

J: Hmm. I have to say "yes, and" to that?

T: Yes. That's the exercise.

J: Great, Okay. Yes, I do hate life when I see a dead-end at work. I'm going nowhere and I can't just walk away. All these guys have seniority. It's going to be fifteen years before I can advance.

T: and?

J: Oh yeah, and. And, I wanted you to be proud of me, and see me as a success. If I'm not going anywhere how can you be proud of me?

C: Can I respond to that?

T: That's the point.

C: I've always been proud of you! Always. I'm proud that you want more, even though you're not where you want to be. Jon, I've never stopped being proud of you, or believing in you.

J: Seriously?

C: Don't start up again. Yes, seriously. I brag about you to my friends... (she starts to cry.)

T: How does that feel hearing that? Does that change anything?

J: Yeah, Absolutely. I didn't know. If I don't feel like I'm letting her down it makes it a lot easier to think about my career.

T: How do you feel about Collette?

J: I feel much better. (Jon tears up.) I'm surprised. She's on my side.

T: Now, how about treating your ally a little better? Remember that part of what made you feel good about this relationship was how well you treated her. You've gotten a lot of pride from being the kind of guy you are. You give that up when you lose your way. Because you feel like you're letting her down, you take it out on her. You think it's her fault that you feel like a failure?

J: What do you mean?

T: You aren't letting her down at work, you're letting her down at home. She just wants back the guy who treated her so wonderfully. You were a master at it, but you gave it up. That makes that treatment seem like it was a trick, instead of the real deal. When you give up who you are in this relationship, you give away your power; you stop being yourself. Then you feel bad in two ways, instead of just one. Do you get this, Collette?

C: Yes, I just didn't know that any of this was going on...

T: Communicate! Assume the love and then start asking questions. Look beneath the surface of these fights. There's so much more going on than we know. I feel a lot of love in the room... (everyone smiles, finally!) Never mind! Just hug each other.

They could have gone on with miscommunication, right up to the moment of serving each other papers. It was only by looking beneath the surface and finding common ground that they managed to save the situation. Simple agreement changed the conversation and let them see what they couldn't otherwise see. Their special relationship gave them the resources to deal with anything they faced. They knew they were better than the rest of the world in this way. This "shared secret" made them a very powerful couple. Somewhere they lost sight of that and it all came undone. Allies had become enemies because of shame and miscommunication. How many of these conversations do we find ourselves in, because we won't look beyond the surface? We must see everything that is being communicated, not just those negatives that happen to fit into our patterns.

Whether you are at the beginning of a relationship or in an established one, or trying to create relationship in your life, communication revitalizes connection.

EXERCISE ONE: "YES, AND... "

One partner starts a discussion with an opening statement.

Partner Two responds positively with "yes, and..." And adds to the discussion.

Continue the discussion with the rule that you must remain positive and must continue to add to the conversation.

TEN

NEW FORM OF COMMUNICATION: CHANGING STATUS

At Camp Kiwago I graduated from senior camper to junior counselor. I was staffed at the trading post, a grand name for a convenience store for the campers. I was in charge of chocolate bars and sleeping bags. Big doings for a 12 year old, but I reached for it like a champ. One of the honors of being a staff member was that you got to sit at the head of the table during meals. Oh my God! Having my own table! I would rule with a velvet glove, benevolent yet firm. The problem was that I was short for my age. I was always mistaken for one of the campers, to my constant chagrin. Every meal was a campaign of strategy to find and secure the chair of honor. I plotted to get there early and jump into the throne. I suffered through the scrutiny as more senior counselors gave me the hairy-eyeball, challenging and questioning. Each meal was a battle and a victory! (Except when they unceremoniously threw me out of the chair.)

Oh, status! It makes fools and martyrs of us all.

Status is defined as position or rank in relation to others. What does status look like in a relationship? Sometimes it looks like the upper hand; at other times you appear to be at a disadvantage. It is rarely what it seems. The victim can rule and the bully can be a slave. You can conquer from below or be toppled from on high. If you learn to be a status chameleon you will master every negotiation you find yourself in, whether personal or professional.

Every relationship has a leader and a follower, no matter how slight the advantage may appear. Joannie makes all the decisions, and Rob goes along willingly. You'd be tempted to say that she "wears the pants" in the relationship, but as we are discovering, everything is not as it appears.

We swap leads in a relationship, depending on circumstance and our perception of advantage. I'm in charge of the bills, you handle the social schedule. You and I are more comfortable in one status or another and we gravitate toward that status, high or low. If we were to arbitrarily switch, neither of us would be comfortable. In every kind of relationship you are in, you are one status or another, right now.

Want to figure out where you're at? Ask yourself "Who's in charge here?" When the answer is 'not me,' you're low status. Let's try not to feel bad about our status, let us just identify it. Status isn't good or bad. It is only the position we are in relative to others. Remember that: status describes the position you are in, relative to others.

Jim grew up with a domineering mother, and because of this history would feel like a fish out of water in high status. Depending on our patterns and conditioning and each of our particular psychologies, we are trained to gravitate to one status or another. Negative or positive, status will out. I can be a bully, or an inspired leader, but I will take high status. You can be the victim or the arbitrator, but low status is your comfort zone.

Despite our predilection, we can change status at will depending on the situation. If I'm at the garage with my mechanic, I will take low status: "Gee, I dunno what happened. The red light went on and it just stopped running." I'm going to let him lead, since he knows a lot more than I do. To take high status in that situation would be foolish, and might even cost me money. If the situation takes a turn where I think low status is going to cost me the advantage, I can turn on a dime: "No, I don't think I need a whole new transmission. Last time this happened it was the alternator." Status is flexible.

Some situations dictate our status and we take it from there. If you are the supervisor at work, you have built-in high status. What you do with that status is up to you, but you are given the high ground to start with. People that are aligned with high status tend to manage it better than those who are not. Some of us will fumble, others will be sure-footed.

How can status inform communication? Can it become a tool for change? By understanding and recognizing status, we have an opportunity to influence the outcome of any situation. In conversation, we have a choice: take high status or low status. We often ignore the choice or default to our natural tendency, but we do have a choice. The first unspoken issue is a fight for status. You could, instead of fighting for the high ground, deliberately take low status instead. Can you control the outcome of any situation by choosing your status? Always. Look at the person across from you and determine what status they are in. What status do they need? What do they crave? Where are they comfortable? Watch a skilled salesman and see how they play the status game masterfully. All of the following are low status phrases:

Salesman:

"May I help you?"

"The customer is always right!"

"If you're happy, I'm happy."

"Say, you really know your stuff!"

"I wouldn't presume to tell you your business... "

"You're the boss!"

"You're the best!"

It is a good idea to do the unexpected. There is enormous power in this choice. For myself, if I take the correct status I am guaranteed the outcome I want. We can fight for high or for low status. Watch as two people fight for low status and see how nothing gets done:

"Oh, no I insist, after you!"

"Oh, no, no, you first, please."

Ad infinitum.

What would it look like to master status in relationship conversation? We listen with different ears. Instead of ignoring the truth and waiting for our turn to talk, we actually look for agreement. We get to shape the outcome and even the tone of the dialogue. We can choose low status phrases like:

"You're right!"

"I see what you mean."

"I'm sorry, my fault."

"You tell me what you want."

"You know best."

"You see it better than I do."

Instead of assuming that I know, I might ask for clarification. By putting myself in the other person's shoes, I automatically see a different viewpoint. We can disarm through empathy and understanding instead of playing into the same old roles.

Instead of getting sucked in to the boring old patterns, ask early in the conversation, "What is it that I am trying to achieve? How do I want to go about that? What should it look like? How do I want it to feel?" These are powerful questions that will turn the conversation in a different direction. Low status doesn't mean concession or agreement. It simply means low status. By being the empathetic one, the caregiver, we show understanding and sympathy. We set the tone.

High status will set us up to be assertive and aggressive; it almost always guarantees a conflict. Choosing low status allows us to receive and comply. Let's not commit to being right, but commit instead to connecting. If you haven't tried changing status you are in for a real treat. It is no longer the same old conversation. We create new possibility and new outcomes. We greatly increase our chance of getting what we want when we can change status at will. Is it a better manipulation? Possibly, but it is also the way to real communication.

Early on in courtships, we willingly give up status. We realize what a useful tool it is. "You're wonderful! You are the best" "You are the smartest man I've ever met" "You are the most beautiful woman I've known!" These are all examples of taking low status in order to control the outcome. We instinctively go there, knowing that it works. As we get invested in relationship, we become more reluctant to give up status.

Giving up or changing status costs us nothing and can get us everything. Play with it and watch how it changes dynamics. Try changing status at work. We unlock power and put ourselves in the present when we consciously change status. We should never become so rigid that we can't give up the positions we find ourselves in, and when we do find rigidity, we should challenge those positions. The purpose of any position is to get what we want, after all. We have the right to expect different results when we make different choices. The following is an example of changing status:

You: (high status) I've been working here for eight years and I deserve a raise. I'm loyal, hard-working and always on time. People who have started after me are already making more than me!

Boss: (high status) Sorry to hear that, but raises are given out here based on seniority and performance! No one gets preferential treatment.

You: (low status) I know you are doing the best you can, and I appreciate you being in my corner. I'm just frustrated because I don't understand how to make this work.

Boss: (high status) Tell you what. I will look into it and see what I can make happen for you. I know you're a good worker. (Switches to low status) To tell you the truth, I don't understand half of what comes from the front office these days.

As you change status, you will create change in whomever you are communicating with.

MAKE A PLAN

We can develop a strategy to talk to our partners. In leading up to a job interview, we would certainly prepare. In fact, in almost every situation we find ourselves in, we give it thought and preparation. Let us sit down and arrive at a strategy to talk with a mate. Give it some time and some effort. Why make our personal life less important than other areas? Anticipate the problems: if you know you have a short fuse, plan for ways to de-escalate. Build in breaks and learn how to key down. Have an exit strategy. The topic is not nearly as important as the communication itself. Let go of being right and looking good. Let your pride come from how well you can communicate. Let us put away two perceived needs immediately: being right and looking good. By taking these off the table we greatly increase our odds of success in communication.

I have done a lot of work with couples to prepare for a discussion. There is great value in creating a roadmap to communication. "This is where we are, and this is where we want to get to." We talk about the meeting that is about to happen. How does it start when you sit down for a discussion? Where do you get plugged in? Where does he react? What do you want from the conversation? What does he want? How do you go about getting what you need? You both have a strategy and a set of tactics that you operate from. Concede that you have an issue with communication and that it is an area that needs work. You aren't supposed to be an expert at communicating, only a willing participant.

One way to understand the situation is to view it from the biggest picture that we can. See it as a story, maybe even one that we can be objective about. For a change, if we tell it like a fairy tale, we see what kind of insight this brings. Start with "once upon a time... " and go from there. Make it romantic and dramatic. Give permission to exaggerate, give it color and light. We will see it very differently as we continue to reframe the story.

CHANGE UP

If you know that your tendency is to take high status, or to be the leader in the conversation, try something different. Take low status and listen. We've all had the experience of someone going "high status" on us. It is as it sounds: to take high status means to be aggressive, to insist on being right, being "in the know." If you are high status, you are going to teach, or inform. If you take "low status" you are likely to be in the receiving position, to supplicate or be the peacemaker. It is a great exercise to switch status and see how you communicate from that new position. When two people take high status, no one gives ground and nothing gets done. When two people take low status, no one takes the initiative and again, nothing gets resolved. If you have the habit of being the aggressor, try being receptive or low status. If you've never take the lead, try that on. Determine where your partner is, and take the opposite status and watch how much more smoothly the conversation goes. Experiment with status and you will discover new and more powerful ways to make your point.

Limit your exposure when you first start a discussion. See how it goes for five minutes. If you can manage to communicate in that time, then you can expand the conversation. Continue to limit the time until you feel like you are connecting.

DON'T MAKE YOURSELF "DISMISSABLE"

Whenever we try to communicate through an upset, we make ourselves dismissible. Our anger is seen instead of our point, and anything we say is not heard or is invalidated. If I show up hurt, my partner is likely to get guilty and frustrated. We want our upsets to show in order to make the point that we are that we are hurt, but this defeats the communication. The upset becomes the focal point instead of the issue. If a point is worth making, it's worth being heard, and we need to find out how to be heard. We would be better off postponing a discussion until there is some good will to work off of, rather than diving in while the issue is hot.

Using an emotional upset is the least efficient way to get anything resolved. Backing away from the situation and trying to get objective about the issue is far more effective. Of course, we all want our partners to know just how upset we are, but why? Isn't it because we want things to change? Ultimately we want to avoid this upset in the future. We show our upset in order to say, "Stop hurting me" or "Change this behavior!" The impulse to change the situation is right, but the strategy is wrong. It is our intention to make the situation better. We have to take the actions that can make that happen, instead of satisfying the impulse of an emotion. We can't place the blame on others until we've done everything in our power to create meaningful communication. Clear thinking creates clear action and clear action creates clear results.

BE THE MOST EFFECTIVE VERSION OF YOU

When we deal with the world we understand that we get what we want through agreement, not conflict. In any given situation in the world we automatically put on a certain persona way of presenting ourselves, in order to achieve what we want. We decide to be civil, or kind, or friendly, or whatever it is that our personality does to get what it wants. I take out a version of me that will get results I am looking for. When we visit relatives we have another version, and when we are with friends, yet another "me" shows up. Is this being phony and manipulative? No, we are making choices based on the circumstances. So why is it that we give so little care to how we show up with someone we claim to love? We want strangers to think well of us, but loved ones? Who cares, right? Yet these are the people largely responsible for our experience and personal happiness. It makes no sense to be less prepared for them than for the counter-clerk at Wal-Mart's.

What if we put our best self forward toward our loved ones? Can I put on my best persona for my significant other? Which is my most effective persona? Is it through humor, or kindness? Is it when I go the extra mile to be that understanding? How would we decide to show up if we knew that the whole world was going to be seeing us in action? Wouldn't we be intelligent, understanding, and easy-going? You bet we would.

Let's take a moment to see ourselves at our absolute best; looking great, feeling great. Isn't that the "me" that the world responds best to? When I fill myself with all of my best qualities: generosity, ease, and playfulness, I am compelling in the world. Picture the world's response. We know the world loves us this way and is willing to cooperate with us. The world holds a special place for this version of me. It shows kindness and generosity. Is there any reason to believe that our partners won't respond the same way? After all, that is who they fell in love with. Isn't it likelier to get what we want by being this person?

Take this version of you into your life. It is always available and it works better than any other version. Let the world experience this persona. Let your partner experience this persona. Let yourself experience you this way!

Remember, we are attached to looking good, and with the whole world watching, we want to show up like a million bucks. We automatically behave better when we know we are being seen, when we are accountable. So why not take that on? In your next discussion with your partner, put on this great persona of love and ease and act as though the whole world is watching, and see how much more effective you are. When you put this version of you on, you get smarter, kinder and wiser. You also get results.

KNOW WHAT THEY WANT

How much are we really going to communicate unless we know what the people across the room from us want? How much do we really know of their hopes and dreams? If it were a business client we would be clear about what they want. We might even take special pride in being aware of their interests and special needs. We would not resent it, either. It would be a matter of doing the job at hand. In many ways this is the person responsible for our happiness. Doesn't it make sense to know where they are coming from and what will satisfy them? We make assumptions that we know what our partner wants or needs, and more often than not, we're not even close. We are operating on assumptions made from the first time we met. We'd never assume that the store clerk knows why we are here and what we intend to purchase. That would be silly. Yet, we readily expect our mates to be mind readers, and we are disappointed and hurt when they can't perform. Let's get real. Communication needs all the help it can get: tell them! Ask them! By making ourselves crystal clear in what we need, we greatly increase the chances of getting what we need. By making a study of our partners and what they desire, we are doing the work we are meant to do in this partnership.

How much do you know about what your partner wants in life? Not what they want from you, but what they want from life? What are his interests and hobbies? What is her secret dream? What are all of the details, from the profound to the mundane? "She likes English Toffee" or "He has a secret dream to own a motorcycle." These are the details that make a life. This is the knowledge that can lead to happiness and satisfaction in relationship.

It will be a revelation to see how much (or little) you know about your partner. Are you really paying attention, or are you just "phoning it in" at this point? How much do you know about what your partner wants from you? "He wants me to appreciate how hard he works" or "She wants me to listen more." Maybe this and so much more. In our heart of hearts, we need to be paying attention to the details. When we look at what they want from life and from us, we begin to understand the person we are dealing with. Honestly, if I go to an art gallery and spend five minutes staring at "Starry, Starry Night" I begin to see details that I hadn't seen. I get wiser about the painting. Similarly, if we spend five minutes thinking about our partners, we will become so much more aware of them and their needs and wants. Think about his sense of humor, or the expression on her face when she is figuring something out.

Think about some of the ways we spend our time. How long have we stared at the "boob tube" in deep concentration as though it would give us some answers? And yet, here is someone who has great influence over our happiness and well-being. If we honestly concentrate on them for just two minutes a day, our relationships will vastly improve. It will arm you with information and fill you with good will. And don't forget, knowledge is power. When we don't know who we are dealing with, we haven't got a chance of making them happy. When we do know, we have knowledge and opportunity. When you know what is wanted from you, you have a chance to give that. Without that knowledge, you have no chance.

Every person is like a puzzle, like a mystery to be solved. It was the reason you were so intrigued in the first place: the excitement of the unknown and the delicious journey of discovery. To give up now is like a child who half-unwraps a present and then loses interest. There is so much more to see and learn. If you are having conflict, it means you have not discovered everything you can discover. There is still the unknown to explore and solve, and it can be just as exciting and challenging as it was in the beginning. Remember, the discovery is for us and our experience, not our partners. We can't allow ourselves to get cynical and bitter, or we have nothing.

ASSUME THE LOVE

Here's a concept called "assume the love." Think about what you want from your partner. Not a list of your complaints; everybody knows them already. Besides, complaints are a result, not a cause. Think truthfully about what you really want, mentally, spiritually, physically, and emotionally. Do you want to be held, listened to, left alone, or talked to? Is it about more physical nurturing, more sex, or more shared interest? Get clear about what it is that you are yearning for in this partnership. Now let's examine this. Notice the feelings those desires bring up. Is there resentment or jealousy? Does it bring up past pain? Of course it does. These are your obstacles to your communication, the very resentments that you cannot see past or move past. Now, for the sake of the experiment, assume that you are receiving everything that you are longing for. Imagine having it all: She is your biggest advocate. He really comes through for you. Let yourself experience getting all that you want, effortlessly. Notice that when you let this thought in you experience a sense of well-being, whether it is the truth or not. Your mind doesn't make a distinction between what is real and what you imagine. It automatically responds with the appropriate emotions of gratitude and peace.

This is the reason we can respond to fantasy. On the darker side, it's why we can believe our suspicions, even in the face of hard evidence. Nevertheless, your mind will respond as though this premise is absolute truth; that you are being nurtured and appreciated. Isn't it amazing that we can create the very feelings that we assign to our partners? We give our power away for something that is always a thought away.

What is the value of this? It will change your behavior toward your partner. The feelings will go from resentment to joy. You are much more able to be loving when you perceive that you are getting what you want. We can create an atmosphere of good will within yourself and the relationship. We will attract whatever we hold in our minds. We are literally magnets for whatever thoughts we have. Through our own choices we can create a better experience than living in want and pain. We are much more in control in of our experience. Being at someone's mercy tends to create resentment and rage. Oddly, your partner is more likely to give you those very things you want because you are now in the receiving mode for them. We'll talk more about control versus real power later on.

WHAT'S YOUR CASE?

Let's talk about "cases." Did you know you have a "case" against your partner, and that you work on that case all the time? That you look for "proof" for your case, in everything they do? We weave a negative story about the person we are with. We assign motives, and we see punishment and loss.

In the beginning of a relationship we are in the presence of the person we are with, and it's great! There are no patterns, no tendencies, just newness and fun. As the relationship gets a little more serious, we have little complaints, but we overlook them. We have enough good will to handle the little disappointments. As the stakes get higher, we start to worry a little. "He's not as attentive as he used to be." "She really does think of herself a lot!" We start to use what we know about them in our case. "You're just like your mother!" "You're like this because your father was cold!" And it's off to the races with our "case." It's really quite a construct and soon everything fits in to this story.

There's a whole conversation in our heads about this person, and any little slip or flaw goes right into the case! We build defenses and reactions to this case, including reasons why we must behave badly to protect ourselves. Of course, the thing about a case is that, like a fantasy, it's not necessarily true. In fact, it's more often not true, but it doesn't take much to keep a case going once you've got it established. It needs only a little truth to enforce the big lie and we become very invested in our story.

The problem with holding a "case" against someone is that they haven't got a hope of changing the story. That look on their face could be passing gas, but we interpret it according to "the case" and it becomes yet more disapproval or anger. We have made the transition from being in the experience of that person to being in a concept, a story; and it's a lousy one at that!

Guess what? They have a "case" against you, too! Oh yes, you haven't been left out. All of your tics and foibles, all of your worst qualities have been knitted together to fashion a hair shirt just for you. You have been tried and convicted and sentenced for crimes unknown, and are living out the punishment, even now. That punishment you sometimes suspect is often real, though the cause rarely is. At some point, the "cases" fight each other, and you two are merely prisoners of war!

What a mess! One can see where this might be an obstacle to communication. We're no longer in the experience of that person and we are no longer present. The story is very compelling; in your "case" you are the hero. You get to be right and look good in that story, struggling mightily against long odds. It is tremendously addictive. It is not a story we willingly walk away from, unless we see it, and determine to change it.

You know your case against your partner. You know the story you tell yourself about how they are so bad and you are so good. How, if it wasn't for them you'd have x, y and z and be so much further along in your life? You will find that it is rich and full with beliefs and feelings, "facts" and interpretations. There is danger and threat, hurt and consequences. You are the hero and the victim all at once; and, of course, you are right and they are wrong. It is a story that we never get tired of retelling. All of our friends and family know much, if not most of our "case." Is this the story you want to be living in? Don't you already know the ending? Can there be a good outcome?

CHANGE THE STORY

How are our stories the opportunity for communication? Much of the power of the story dissipates when the story is shared. Tell each other your "case" and take the power out of it. Refuse to be held captive to this fantasy.

Having done this, construct a best version of the story together. Based on what each of you know, build a positive "case." No one owes any allegiance to that sad story. Remember, a relationship is a constant opportunity to reinvent yourself. You have enough facts and materials to come up with a great story that is uplifting and romantic, with hope and possibility. Isn't this where you want to be? Burn the old story and keep the new one. Let it become a road map for the two of you.

We are not going to effectively communicate unless we know what we want and have a plan for how to get it. Communication at its best is cooperation. We already have a strategy, we just don't know it. It is a strategy of despair and petulance instead of power and clarity. However, we can't sulk our way to happiness, or rage our way to contentment. We need knowledge and a willingness to see. Share with each other and take the power away from these ridiculous stories that we tell. If we are honest, we've heard this story before, long before we met our current partner.

We need to find the strength to try something different. We cannot always believe our feelings and emotions! They don't call your conscious mind the "liar mind" for nothing. Throw history out the window and dare to be different, even if it's uncomfortable. Change is always uncomfortable. Don't do it for your partner's sake. Change because you want a better experience for you. Human beings have enormous power to make our situation different, but we must seize that power.

As we share our stories, it begins to fill in the blanks and we start to understand how we are perceived. We immediately gain insight and power. Work with the idea that you and your partner have common goals and interests, instead of delegating blame. Treat your partner at least as well as you would a stranger. Commit to hearing what is being said without prejudice. It is a critical time when partners trust enough to share their stories, so you must honor this time. The pain at the end of a relationship has a lot to do with regret for not having tried or tried hard enough. Share, listen, respond, without judgment. Work together to build a new, positive story.

EXERCISE 1

This is the "persona" exercise. Close your eyes and picture yourself at your absolute best. Looking great, feeling great: see yourself smiling, with the most loving attitude you've ever had. Fill yourself with all of your best qualities: generosity, ease, and playfulness.

Now picture the world's response to you. Really let yourself feel the world loving and approving of you. As you open your eyes, take this version of you into the world. Live through it for the day, especially with your partner.

EXERCISE 2

Get a pen and paper and make a list of what your partner wants in life; not what they want from you, what they want from life. Add all of the detail that you can, from the profound to the mundane. "She likes English Toffee" or "He has a secret dream to own a motorcycle."

When you're done, read it. It will be revealing to you to see how much (or little) you know about your partner.

Write out a list of what your partner wants from you. "He wants me to appreciate how hard he works" or "She wants me to listen more." Really work on this, and find at least five things they want from you.

Now look at these two lists and start to understand the person you are dealing with. Armed with information, now share these lists with your partner and compare notes.

EXERCISE 3: THE "CASE" EXERCISE

Sit down and write out your "case" against your partner. To do this honestly, you must give yourself permission to rant and rave.

Don't believe what you're writing, just write it out. When you are done, read it.

Now write out the best version of your "story" together. Based on what you know, build a positive "case."

When you are done, read both cases to each other. Burn the old stories and keep the new one. Merge it into one story and let it become a road map for your partnership.

EXERCISE 4: ASSUME THE LOVE

Make a list of what you want from your partner. Write as truthfully as you can about what you really want, mentally, spiritually, physically, emotionally.

Now look at this list. Notice the feelings it brings up. Is there resentment or jealousy? These are your obstacles to communication.

Now assume that you are receiving everything on that list. How does that feel? Mentally allow yourself to receive all of those things that you want.

Maintain this ongoing assumption and watch how it changes your experience in your relationship.

ELEVEN

CONFLICT

RULES OF CONFLICT

Give up being right and looking good

Give up your positions

Attack the issue, not each other

Empathize: take each other's point of view

Fight for a win/win scenario

Teach with love, not pain

Look for and learn your lesson

Take a time-out

Write it down and present it at a time of good will

Allow it be okay

If you've ever been on the debate team you know that you can be arbitrarily assigned to one side of the argument or the other, and you will be expected to make a case for either side. What you would also know, is that debating is not about believing what you say. The goal in debate is to create a strong argument for your point of view using the material at hand. In fact, there is one debate exercise where you switch points of view and argue the opposing side. This is revealing because it shows you that you can argue any point whether you believe or not, and you will be committed to your case, whether or not you think it's true or right. How many times have we caught ourselves in relationship doing exactly that? We argue for the sake of arguing, regardless of the point or the truth. We forget what we are fighting for, and become committed to being right and to being heard and ultimately to winning. Soon we are not exactly sure what there is to win.

GIVE UP BEING RIGHT

As we previously referenced, when we give up two attachments in a relationship, we will eliminate 90% of conflict: give up being right and abandon looking good. We are so committed to making our point that we go deaf and blind. Imagine the freedom and pleasure of being in an argument and not having to be right. There is equal freedom in not trying to look clever or smart. When we take a position, we are trapped in it, and forced to defend it, much like the debaters on the team. Imagine the flexibility of being positionless, even in a situation where there appears to be something to lose.

Somehow we have to determine what we are fighting for: we are fighting for truth, or are we are fighting to win. If we are fighting to win, we hope to gain the satisfaction of being right and looking good, regardless of where that satisfaction can bring us or what we will have gained. There are reasons to fight but looking and good and being right shouldn't be among them.

Something inside of us creates a primal need to be right. At one point, being right was essential to our survival, to preserve our very existence. Looking good was key to being loved and lovable. These are survival tools. Though this was appropriate once, this is no longer the case, yet, we fight with vehemence as though we are still in a life or death struggle.

In this contentious society we watch as politicians do anything to be right and anything necessary to win. It is the model for our society, illustrated by the "talking heads" who are more interested in how they look than in any real substantive or constructive argument. The modus operandi of our society is that we fight for the sake of fighting. Most of the time we have no idea why we are fighting, but that still doesn't stop us. We are on automatic pilot and in defense mode.

We accept a new model when we embrace conscious relationship; a model that gives us new purpose for conflict resolution. In our model, the meaning of conflict is to learn what we have chosen to learn. We can fight for understanding and recognition, if that is our chosen lesson. We may be doing battle in order to be heard. Conflict becomes opportunity; then there is purpose and order in it.

WHY FIGHT?

There are some simple rules that will make fighting useful rather than a painful exercise. Let us start with the simple idea that when two people care, they will disagree. If everything that happens is meant to be and for everyone's highest good, then take away the guilt about fighting. See conflict for the value that it conflicts. More often than not, guilt is the fuel that keeps us fighting. Feeling that we're wrong makes us fight to be right, so give up right and wrong and we eliminate a great need. In our model there is no right or wrong: conflict is a no-fault proposition.

I had a colleague who used to ask, "Would you rather be right, or happy?" It's an annoying question because it points out that we can choose the way our experience shows up. We have enormous power over our happiness. As we learn to master the art of fighting instead of being sloppy and abusive, we gain mastery over ourselves. We will fight cleanly with skill and care when we are fighting to learn and grow.

The trigger for a fight can be a feeling of being wronged and misunderstood. Often there is a buildup of many events and the feelings that those events create that crystallizes in one moment.

When I say, "I'm sick of this!" or "I'm not taking it any more!" I can be sure that the fight isn't about what happened five minutes ago. An upset is always a compilation of feelings and events that come to a head in one moment in time. We explode because we haven't built in safety valves to gradually let off the steam in a relationship. We haven't created acceptable ways to download a little at a time, so we overflow, literally filled beyond capacity.

Sometimes the purpose of a fight is to make a connection. We are really saying "Are you there? Can you hear me?" Each of us has an emotional body as well as a physical one. To our emotional body, any emotional exchange is better than none, so we reach out, however inefficiently. Some of us have been raised in an environment where fighting is a natural way to communicate. To you the conflict may seem like a horrible fight, to someone else it is the norm.

Whatever the initial motivation, the purpose of fighting is to resolve an underlying conflict. Be a scientist; be more interested in what that conflict is, rather than in gaining the upper hand. Conflict, by definition means there is something unknown and unresolved: something not understood. Change your purpose from being right and looking good, to understanding and making real connection.

ATTACK THE ISSUE

The Geneva Conventions consist of Treaties and protocols that set standards for the treatment of combatants.

Since we're going to fight, let us also agree on some ground rules. Attack the issue, not the person. Too often we aim at the personality flaws of our partner, instead of getting to the heart of the matter. We have all left scars and done permanent damage by attacking the person. "You're fat and lazy!" or "You're terrible in bed!" These statements will sustain long after the issue is forgotten, and they will be huge obstacles to overcome. We have a perverse pride in our ability to cut to the bone. Let's ask ourselves "What am I trying to accomplish?" Out of our pain we may want to lash out, but that won't further our cause. Those scars will become the very obstacles that we will have to overcome in order to communicate.

If your lover were a business client, you wouldn't take anything personally; you would be more interested in getting what you want. Even if there was a conflict you would handle it diplomatically. All of your communication skills would come to the fore and you would handle it masterfully, trying for a result that works for all parties.

In relationship we try to prove how hurt we are, how wronged we've been. When we see conflict as a business transaction we start to handle the person we care about with some mastery and care.

When we attack the issue instead of the person, we can afford to see the other's point of view. We utilize different negotiating skills that might never come into play if we were personalizing. We can afford to make concessions. We become "positionless" and we have nothing to defend. Remember the debating team: we can just as easily argue the other side.

EMPATHIZE

Tai Chi Chuan is the physical expression of the principles and philosophy of Taoism. Within it there is an interesting and disarming technique. By empathizing with our opponent, we send a signal that immediately lowers his guard. As we stand in front of our opponent we look for reasons to identify with them. We deliberately try to find common ground and open our hearts to our "enemy." We think positive thoughts about them and project warm feelings toward them. The act of identifying with our adversary brings an energetic result of harmony, and gives us the strategic advantage. They lower their guard which allows us in. We position the person in ways that they will hear us, and are inclined to cooperate with us.

Of course we want to be heard. Naturally we want to be understood and respected, but we set the energetic tone: If we give respect we have a better chance of receiving it. If we are open to listening, we will probably be heard. Does it matter who is heard first, or is it more important to get the outcome we want? When we fight for a win/win scenario, our motives are unassailable. We automatically have the moral high ground and ensure successful communication.

We quickly lose site of what is wanted in conflict. Find out what it is that your partner wants in this conflict: what his/her real objective is. When we know this, we have the ability to end the conflict. When we think we know this answer, but don't, we are fighting blind. The reason most fights have a familiarity to them, is that we are usually fighting for the same thing that we have been fighting for. What is it that we aren't getting? That they aren't getting? What is it that we could give that would change everything? The answer to that holds real power. People generally fight for love, acceptance or approval, gain or vindication. What do you fight for? Are you compensating for something you don't have or didn't get? People often think, "Why don't I feel the way I used to feel in this relationship?" A more powerful question is: "Am I giving what I used to give?"

LONELINESS OR SOLITUDE?

Life is a solitary journey. We are born alone, we live alone in our experience and we will die alone. Somehow relationship has become the perceived answer to this aloneness. It is not the cure or the answer, but when we first find love, it feels like it takes that pain of being alone away. It doesn't take the pain away because it cannot. The mere hope that love can take pain away creates relief. The possibility that relationship represents lifts us up above the pain, momentarily. When we discover that we are still alone, we can feel great anger, even betrayal at this disappointment. We can no more bridge the gap of loneliness through love than we can change the nature of our atomic structure. Perhaps we are not meant to bridge that gap, but rather, to negotiate it together.

So much of what shows up in conflict in relationship is really our own work. Even the loneliness and anger are our feelings. No one can make us feel anything, and no one can take those feelings away. Partnership is not a remedy or a cure. The danger in relationship is that we can always find something to complain about, and even to be right about, but often it's not the problem. It's just the place we hang your hat, because we can't or won't get to the real issue. Before we continue a conflict let's ask ourselves if what we are fighting about is really the issue. More often than not, we will discover that the problem is inside, not out. If we could take two minutes to do a little self-examination we could save hours of heartache. Loneliness can turn to solitude and even partnership when two partners agree to face it together.

TEACH WITH LOVE

The spiritual point of view of relationship is that we are in this partnership to learn some elements and to teach others. We have agreed in perfect spiritual cooperation to illuminate lessons through conflict. The core of every conflict is about learning. Ask yourself "What am I supposed to be learning from this?" What am I supposed to be teaching?" We are attracted to the lessons that someone has to teach us. Look for those lessons. When we ask these questions we are at the work site.

Ever notice that your partner has qualities that you don't? That there are qualities that you admire and would even like to possess? These may be some of the lessons that they are meant to teach you. If you take an honest inventory, you admire some of their traits too. That may be part of what they are teaching you. Of course, you can teach with pain, or you can teach with love. Teaching with pain means finding fault; it means having a short fuse and taking the luxury to react without patience. It is using the whip hand to educate. An animal that has been taught with pain will always flinch; will always have a certain amount of distrust. Teaching with love is the kind of teaching we would do with a little child: gentle, patient, caring. A moment's reflection will let you know what kind of teacher you are.

The good news is that we can choose to teach in a different way; even if we were taught with pain, we can still decide that we want to teach with love. Take a minute and think of how specifically you can change your method of teaching with your partner now.

TIME IS ON YOUR SIDE

There is a quick and easy way to disrupt the negative patterns we find ourselves in while in the midst of conflict. Take a time-out. Even boxers take a break between rounds. If something is worth fighting for, it's worth taking some time to think about. Take a break from the action and go to your respective corners.

Remember, these are the heightened times when permanent damage can be done. We must handle relationship with the delicacy of a fine jewel. Some things said can never be unsaid. Take five minutes to think about what you are really trying to accomplish. Are you communicating? Do you want to hurt, or to get through to your partner? We can all experience feeling powerless in a personal conflict, but inflicting pain is no remedy to that powerlessness. Breathe, think, refocus and relax.

Are you going to be more upset or less upset when you disengage? When we take a minute to reorganize, even in the hot zone of a discussion, we are giving the moment its due. If the issue is as important as it seems, it probably deserves a little time to mull over. By taking that time, we will more readily see what's important or not. We should often rethink our strategy and our tactics, making sure that they are serving everyone's highest good.

If you find it difficult to walk away, practice. Learn to excuse yourself. Take a bathroom break. Declare a truce. If you can't walk, then run away. Go to another room, or leave the house. Have "fire drills" taking time outs so that you are practiced and you know how to do it. It only takes a moment to do damage that a lifetime of effort may never undo.

WHAT IS THE GOAL?

Sun Tzu in *The Art of War* declares, "The true object of war is peace." He goes on to say that victory should be secured ideally without shedding one drop of blood. If the greatest general of all time has the goal of peace in mind without pain or bloodshed, perhaps it's a worthy strategy for us to adopt.

Webster defines "strategy" as a plan for accomplishing goals from beginning to end. A "tactic" is an action chosen to fulfill a strategy. We need both. We need an overall strategy that describes the goals we want to achieve in our relationships, and we need the tactics necessary in order to achieve those goals.

A good general never loses sight of why he is fighting. Put aside the ego reasons and take a self-inventory: ask yourself what are trying to achieve. Your deeper purpose is not that "I'm trying to inflict as much pain as humanly possible." What will that achieve? Let's assume you have put him into agony; now what? That is just a short-term goal, a tactic. Is this a tactic that will achieve your overall strategy? What is the result you are trying to achieve and will achieve through these tactics? Follow the logic: he's in pain and this cause will have an effect. Is this an attempt at communication wherein I am trying to get him to see how much pain he caused me, so that he will never repeat his behavior? Am I trying to get him to treat me better? Get clear about what you are trying to achieve. Choose the tactics that will achieve your goal.

Too often we pick tactics that will relieve our momentary pain. This short-sightedness can only lead to a continuation of hostility. Start with the basic assumption that our goal is peace, not war. We need to become aware that we are taking action and that our action will have reaction. Whether we know it or not, we do have a strategy and we are employing tactics to achieve that strategy. A good general knows what he is doing and never causes devastation for no reason.

PREPARE

Write it down. If the point is so important to you that you want to make sure that you communicate it, put it on paper. Write it clearly and accurately without emotional charge, and then present your point at a time when there is good will. The best point in the world will not matter if no one can hear it. We must be smart enough to prepare a mood and an atmosphere so that our points can be heard.

When we argue using anger or pain, all that will be seen is that upset. We will not be heard; in fact, we will be dismissed. We make ourselves dismissible when we are in the grips of our emotions, because all that can be seen is that emotion. We are not inclined to listen when we are being shouted at. We must present our case at a time when we can be heard.

Find a time when the two of you are getting along, and then make your points. Now the two of you have some emotional equity to work with. When you've had a time of good connection or have just had some fun, try presenting what you need to say. Do so with compassion and humor, but without blame. A good salesman picks the right time and opportunity to sell.

Having created timely opportunity, make clear and understandable points. Stay simple and clear. Make one point at a time. Don't try to get everything done and said at once. Be prepared to say what it is that you are trying to communicate in several different ways. Be patient and respectful. This would be an appropriate time for the golden rule: do unto others as you would have them do unto you. Be aware that it may take you more than one session to get your point across.

GOOD WILL

There must be willingness to come to agreement. Often people are so hurt that they don't want to resolve conflict. They feel so hard-done-by that they want something back for their trouble. The same way that a child can get stuck in his emotions, so we can get lost in our upsets. Often, we want to let go but we are not able to find our way out. Upsets are sticky, like flypaper.

You are presented with an opportunity: let the conflict resolve. Letting it be okay is a real act of love at a time of conflict. We all intuitively know how to do this. We can simply let it be okay; we can surrender. We have the power to drop our anger, our demands, even our positions. We can allow peace and sanity to be restored. We all know how to be the bigger person; this is the opportunity to teach, to show the way for our partner.

By taking the opportunity to let conflict resolve, you can create a real turning point, an unforgettable moment in the relationship. You would be amazed at how much power and good will you add to your relationship when you take this action. You also become a living model for how to be, at times like this, and your partner will never forget it.

COMMON ISSUES

Money, sex, work, children, future and division of labor are all hot buttons for couples, often in that order of importance. Each one of these topics has the potential to send us to our corners and square off in the ring. These are the central themes that we wrap our emotions around and about which we create positions. They may not be the actual issues of our upsets but they are the site that our conflicts show up in.

Money is such a personal issue that there is bound to be disagreement among couples. We have all been raised with different values and attitudes toward money. Of all issues that couples find themselves in conflict about, this one is the least discussed and agreed upon before we seriously commit in relationship. There will be conflict in this area and the only solution is communication.

If you have managed to have a dialogue early on that defines who each of you is financially and where you each stand, you are well ahead of the game. This rarely happens. In the development of a relationship there is so much to do and attend to that this area is often overlooked or taken for granted. Rather than create agreement, folks polarize in their positions and dig in.

Very often, this issue, though the subject of conflict, is not the issue, but merely an excuse to express our anger or discontentment. It would be much easier to have a dialogue about money early on, while you're still in that "we talked all through the night" stage. Having a baseline communication and understanding of where each other stands, financially, emotionally, and sexually, could avoid so much unnecessary pain, but this happens infrequently. No one wants to bring up the heavy issues when there is so much fun to be had.

Sex is another core issue that is avoided early on and later rears its head as a source of conflict. Because we go through different stages in relationship and our sexual temperature changes with each stage, sex is a veritable minefield of issues. As with money, our identities are bound up in our sexual beliefs and programming. Without communication we are guaranteeing conflict in this area. Every issue from the desired frequency of sex to our choices and preferences in the bedroom will become a venue for dissension.

Work ethics, views about children, even whether you are a late or early riser, all become fodder for discussion and ultimately conflict. Without a reasonable expectation that we will have discordance and disagreement, we are hopelessly unprepared for the reality of relationship. To be realistic we must have a plan, a strategy. We must have tactics that are effective and that we can live with in order to navigate the inevitable conflicts. There is just too much that is too different in all of us to expect anything else.

The good news is that it isn't too late to implement tactics and strategies. We can still have that discussion in our relationships and it's still essential. We can start from where we are now on each issue and build a strategy for communication. We can come together with good will and create an intention to build a platform on which we can understand each other.

Initially, attraction was the bond that brought us together. Now, we need a construct that promotes telling each other what we want and need, a vehicle that empowers us to express our needs and wants to each other with little conflict.

This way of communicating must reflect our intentions, our desires and our needs to be heard and understood. Through the journey that relationship is, this forum has to give us shelter. It must be a safe and inviting space where we can tell our truth and bare our souls. When there is a certainty that conflict will arise, there is a clear need to manage it powerfully and efficiently. There is no shame in not having created this system before, but once we acknowledge the need for some form of communication, we would be wise to provide for that need.

LIVING IN THE QUESTION

We don't have to know what communication should look like. We don't even need to know how it should function. There is a way of exploring the issues that starts, not with the answers, but with the questions. Living in the question of an issue means that we start with the assumption that we don't have all the answers, but we do have some information. We start with the information we have and ask questions from there. For instance, "What should our conflict look like if we are caring about each other?" "What does effective communication look like?"

Willa and James came to me because they couldn't find a way to talk to each other. Too much had been said in too many harsh ways and they were out of words:

WILLA: I'm tired of arguing. I felt like if we could talk to someone together, maybe we could agree on something.

JAMES: Interesting how you're blaming me for this communication breakdown.

W: Did I say anything about whose fault it was?

J: You think I don't see what you're doing?

W: OK, now what am I doing?

J: You've set this whole thing up so that we would fail and then you'd blame it on me. You think I don't know you?

T: Can we take a time out here?

These two had fought so much that they leapt to the end of fights without even bothering with the beginning. It was amazing to experience being dropped in to round six of a heavyweight battle with no preliminary.

T: James, can you hold the possibility that she genuinely wants to communicate with you, despite what may have happened in the past?

J: It's hard to trust her when I've seen this before.

W: Why should I go to all this trouble just to prove that you're the problem?

J: Well, if I hold that possibility, what are you going to make her do? She's got to give something up too.

T: I'm going to ask her, (you, Willa) to hold the assumption that you're madly in love with her, right now, despite however it might look. (they both laugh)

T: Let's start with the premise that you both really want to come to a new place of connection. Hold that about your partner and then look at him. See someone empathetic, but lost; willing but a little wounded. Now how would you talk to her?

J: I'd tell her that it's okay. Everything is going to be fine. We just got a little lost for a minute.

T: Tell her.

J: I mean it, Willa. This is what I always want to say, it just doesn't come out the way I mean it.

W: I swear I feel the same way. I just get in my head...

T: Now, live in the question that this is what is always going on underneath your conflict. No one wants that other way.

They were remarkably tame after this, and started making a new contract with new rules. They were on their way.

FIGHT FAIR
Despite our best efforts there will be times when we find ourselves in conflict. There are some dos and don'ts to fighting. Don't take the opportunity to bring up the time she embarrassed you in front of your family. This isn't the time to dig in and be adamant and decide that you have some power. Don't refuse to resolve issues. Let the issue be the issue, and if you need to, do start a discussion at another time about your underlying resentment. You probably already have a loose set

of rules that you fight by, but it isn't a bad idea to articulate them. Include some simple tools for fighting fair: deference, compromise and agreement to disagree.

Deference means that we take the high road, right or wrong, and concede to our partner's point of view. It is a powerful and persuasive tool, but it can be, at times, unmanageable. Try deference and see if you can manage that position. If not, keep it in your back pocket; there are other tools to try.

Compromise allows that we come to a middle road where each get something of what we want and each give something up. A very powerful tool, compromise is the key to the art of negotiation. This is the essence of what we are up to. We are either negotiating badly or well, but have no question that we are trying to get what we want. The only question is whether we will master getting what we want in a win-win scenario or just go about breaking the lamps and furniture and peace be damned.

There are times when we will still be living in the question without the ability to come to a conclusion. Instead of rushing to some agreement that nobody wants, we need to provide space in our relationships for this very real occurrence. Agree to disagree. It is okay not to finish every discussion in one sit-down. When we think of what is at risk, we can agree that we deserve all the time necessary to come to workable answers.

Conflict is the opportunity to learn. It is the basis of all change and growth throughout history. It is also the opportunity to show up differently and to create something new. Few situations offer more opportunity to grow and redefine ourselves, so choose to see conflict as opportunity. It will make us stronger and smarter, and give us the chance to like ourselves and our partners better.

EXERCISE 1

Have a "mock fight" for fifteen minutes, practicing all of the rules of conflict. At the end of 15 minutes, discuss it, notice what came up and how it felt, and then switch positions, taking your partner's point of view. At the end, stop, discuss and see what you've learned. (Warning: stay within the 15 minutes, even if you have to use a timer. This is a "mock fight" not a real one.)

EXERCISE 2

Re-scripting conflict: answer the following questions individually.

What is your goal in this conflict? What do you hope to achieve?

What does your partner hope to achieve?

What would you like your partner to do to remedy the situation?

What are you willing to do to remedy the situation?

What experience do you expect to have if you achieve your goal?

What is the experience your partner is having now?

What does he/she think of your tactics?

What do you think of his/her tactics?

Are they effective?

Do these tactics make you more or less inclined to give what your partner wants?

How would you change your partner's tactics?

If you added respect to your approach, how would it change your tactics?

If you added understanding to your approach, how would that change your tactics?

If you reversed goals, how would you fight for your partner's outcome?

Why do you think he/she wants what they want?

Is there room for compromise in this conflict?

What would the compromise be?

Would you describe this as a win/lose scenario?

Is it a lose/lose scenario?

Can it be changed to a win/win scenario?

What is your conflict style? Combative or cooperative?

Do you feel diminished if you concede?

Do you feel augmented if you win?

Are there implied or stated threats in this conflict?

Does your style of conflict reflect your values? Your beliefs? Your spirituality?

Can you change your conflict style to more accurately reflect these aspects of your belief system?

What is the basis of your resistance to resolving this conflict?

Can you accurately paraphrase your partner's position and requests?

If this conflict didn't exist, what would these feelings and emotions be about?

What is your hidden agenda in this conflict?

What is your partner's hidden agenda in this conflict?

If this conflict escalated to a conclusion, what would it be?

If this conflict de-escalated to a conclusion, what would it be?

If you and your partner had to brainstorm your way out of this, what would that look like, and what would the outcome be?

What are the facts of this situation?

What are your respective opinions of this situation?

What would you advise a friend in this situation?

How is the conflict different when it is public, and when it is private?

What do you agree about in your partner's stand?

What do you think they agree about in yours?

Are you willing to admit being wrong?

Is your partner willing to admit to being wrong?

Are you trying to dominate or avoid domination?

Is your partner trying to dominate or avoid domination?

What can change here? Can the facts change? The feelings? The interpretations? The intentions?

Imagine this resolved. What does it look like?

How will you feel when this is resolved?

Can you feel that way now?

Can your partner feel that way now?

Make it your intention that this will be solved to everyone's satisfaction.

Start a discussion based on some of these points.

TWELVE

THE MAGIC IS GONE

In the previous chapter we discussed conflict and how to handle it. One of the casualties of doing battle is our sexual passion for one another. It can be extremely difficult to get "turned on" when we are in the midst of unresolved issues. Men have a tendency to still want sex, even during conflict, while women are traditionally wired a different way. How do we negotiate this illusive yet essential element of romantic relationship while getting the real business of love and resolution handled? That is the question that we will live in, in this chapter. Let's examine the evolution of our desire.

When I was a teenager, I never would've imagined that marriage could be boring, because, in marriage you are allowed to have sex all of the time. You could perform the magic deed whenever you wanted. That's like a child being told that he can have all the candy in the world. It is a testimony to human changeability that we can go from the excitement of "whenever" to "whatever."

Without our ability to fantasize we might never get together at all, yet a fantasy cannot sustain itself forever in the face of reality. Ultimately, familiarity leads to boredom and resentment. Of course, if we don't expect the honeymoon to end, we will feel cheated or betrayed when it does, and who are we going to blame? We blame the stranger sitting across from us.

LOVE GAMES

Christina and Arturo have come in with a common complaint. Their passion has waned and they can't find their way back...

CHRISTINA: We never make love anymore. It isn't natural to go this long.

THOMAS: When was the last time you made love?

C: Probably a month ago.

ARTURO: That's not fair. I try to get things started.

C: You mean you try to get me to service you!

A: It has to start somewhere.

T: So what happens between you? Do you try?

C: We just both let it slide and neither one of us bring it up. I think we're afraid that if we mention it, we'll have to do it.

T: Why, don't you want to?

C: I just feel nothing. I don't feel remotely turned on... I feel like we're miles away from that.

T: Sounds like you're angry.

C: I am angry. I'm frustrated, I'm disappointed. I don't know where to go with this... I don't know what I want.

THE GOOD OLD DAYS
We can all long for those first romantic days of a relationship, when everything was possible, and there was no pain. Remember when you first met, and you couldn't wait to see each other again? Nothing was as interesting as thinking

136

about your true love. There was no need for work or friends or anything else. It was idyllic; it was great. This state of mind, however, has nothing to do with reality: real love can only show up once the honeymoon is over.

The fantasy blocks our ability to see accurately; when the smoke clears and the dust settles, then we can begin to build. In fact, the initial excitement may have had more to do with what was missing in our lives before our partner showed up than what we've actually gained. When someone looks like the antidote, it's wise to identify the disease. Oh, but the pain of losing that wonderful feeling: it is like being thrown out of the Garden of Eden all over again. Some people never get over this loss, and live in mourning. In fact, the whole country music business is based on that pain. "I'll never smile again, etc."

IS THERE POSSIBILITY?

This doesn't mean that we have to stoically do without romance in our relationships once the passion wanes; it only means that we have to work to recapture the romance. Life has a habit of bringing us to a high place and showing us how great it can be, and then taking it all away so that we must rebuild on our own. Most people make a fatal mistake: they believe that when the initial rush is over, so is the relationship. They throw the baby out with the bathwater.

What if you knew that the romance was supposed to recede; what if you understood that life's message to us is: "Okay, now create that magic again, on your own!"? Assume that this design is the perfect plan in order to learn and grow in relationship.

An actor on the stage can work from their initial excitement of their role on opening night, but every night from then on they must recreate their passion and enthusiasm. They don't refuse to go on because they're not feeling it; they stoke their internal fire. I had a famous actor tell me the secret to his success; he pointed to his head and explained, "When the scene calls for tigers, I bring my own tigers!"

There is a natural evolution in love; the fantasy will fade in time. It is our job to recreate the romance. It absolutely can be done. There are challenges that go with that: first, most people can't get past the anger, pain and disappointment of losing the passion; second, people don't know that life is supposed to be this way; and third, they don't know how to recreate their excitement.

A NEW STRATEGY

In creating a new model for relationship, conscious loving, we start with the assumption that we are in an ever evolving system designed for us to learn and grow and achieve the love that we want. We have to be open to new possibilities. The opportunity here is to re-capture the magic, and to see with new eyes. If you could suddenly picture the relationship you are in filled with promise and possibility, it would always be magical. It would re-energize you to know that you have a constantly renewable source.

We are in charge of how our experience shows up. We have the ability to re-imagine it, to be excited and hopeful. We can take on optimism as a new strategy and use it as one of our tools for re-sculpting. Through the eyes of enthusiasm everything is possible. Through the eyes of optimism all challenges appear easy.

If you were moving into a house that needed a lot of work, you might give up, or you might go from room to room, imagining how good the house can be as you see new possibilities. You would deliberately be positive and work to see the best it could be. Of course you would. Our first job is not so much about changing details as it is seeing in new and empowering ways. Let's stop resisting the reality of the way it is and start using that reality to create and uncover what we want.

Imagine, for a moment, that we can feel about our relationship the way we felt in the beginning: at our absolute best, with our interest piqued and our joy in full gear. Here is the beginning of the exercise of reconstructing: Picture yourself and your partner at the peak of love. Take that in. Revel in it for a moment: allow yourself to luxuriate in those feelings. Now recognize this: that those feelings are still there. The proof is in the pudding; you can recreate those feelings. In fact, the excitement already exists, or you couldn't be experiencing them.

The feeling that we are enraptured by is called possibility. The excitement in a relationship is based on the amount of possibility it contains. A new relationship contains more possibility because it is the unknown. As we get familiar with each other, possibility turns into reality. Whether the reality is better or worse, possibility is used up and we lose that wonderful feeling.

What do we do now? We could get rid of our partner or start out new. We might patch together some concept of what we have so that we can limp along with the existing relationship. None of that is going to work, nor is it acceptable. We need to deliberately and systematically recreate the passion, the romance and the possibility. In order to do that, we have to know that possibility is there to begin with. We must rediscover those wonderful early feelings of possibility. We can begin by holding the assumption that those feelings are still there.

SEXUAL PASSION

When we do go about recreating possibility in relationship, the key is the mystery of all mysteries, sex. In the middle ages, sexual passion for anyone, even a spouse, was considered a mortal sin. The punishment for this transgression of desire was to burn for all eternity. Archaic as it is, we still have some of that mixed message in us, somewhere. We carry vestiges of primal guilt and fear, and we are reluctant to give ourselves permission to desire again. We have been programmed with a modern version of that middle-age baffling notion: sex is bad before marriage and good and permitted after. This mixed message certainly adds to the confusion and difficulty of passion. When searching for our passion this concept is another obstacle that must somehow be negotiated.

How do we rekindle the passion? Most of the sexual passion that is generated for each other is based on the fantasy we can create about our partner; we must recognize where that passion resides. The mind is the greatest sex organ there is. We get turned on, not by the physical, but by the mental game of sex. It is our imagination that fires up our passion. To the extent that we can fantasize about our lovers we are turned on. Our partners turn us off when they clash with the fantasy that we construct about them.

Continuing our excerpt...

T: I think what you want is to feel excited again; to feel possibility again... to be turned on again. If you could wave a magic wand, wouldn't you restore all the love, excitement, and sexiness to your relationship?

C: Of course I would, but I don't see any way of getting there.

T: First, you have to be able to imagine that again. Second, you have to use your frustration as a motivator to get back everything you lost. This is worth fighting for. Refuse to surrender this passion without a fight!

A: Are you telling her to get angry at me?

T: No, but passion is passion. It may start as frustration but it can migrate to desire and excitement. Any emotional fuel is a good start.

C: I have no idea where to start.

T: Do you have any sexual thoughts and desires? Ever? For anyone?

C: Yes, but I don't feel comfortable using thoughts about someone else.

T: Is there a movie star that you can fantasize about?

A: Hey, I'm not sure I like where this is going!

T: Do you think she might start an affair with a movie star?

A: No, but..

T: You are the man in her life. You are the one that she is going to be with. We are merely priming the engine. If we don't feed the fire, you two are not going anywhere. This is an exercise. Trust each other a little bit.

C: Okay, I've thought of somebody!

This was the beginning of giving each other permission to explore and imagine. With boldness and a little daring we can recapture our passion. How is your mental game? Have you been letting it slide? Do you give it the attention that it deserves? Most guys will practice a video game or their poker game more often than their sex game. Most women focus more on what they are not getting, rather than what they are not giving. Few women are savvy enough to give time and attention to how to seduce and turn their man on, though it is to there benefit to do so.

We wouldn't expect our tennis game to keep itself up without practice, but sex? That will magically take care of itself, right? Wrong. Like anything else, practice, preparation and determination will make our game come alive. If we are indifferent and inattentive to our sexual muse, we will get indifferent results.

Attention is the first step. Here is the process of re-energizing: Focus on the state of affairs between you and your partner; now picture it the way you want it to be; take an honest assessment of what you are putting into it. "Energy flows where the attention goes." Frankly, we give more attention to our golf clubs or dining room table than we do of our sex life. Picture being passionate and attentive to your partner again. See the vision in your mind's eye, and dwell there. Stay focused on that vision until you can feel what that feels like. Let the experience transcend the mental plane and travel to the physical. Energy can migrate from the mental plane to the physical through mere thought. Let your imagination run wild and allow yourself to enjoy it. Before long you will feel the beginnings of a quickening of your energy. In your mind, now direct that energy to your partner. It may be hard to refocus but gently bring yourself back to you and your partner. These are the first baby steps to being turned on once again.

I have heard all of the complaints: "It's boring. It's not the same as it used to be. He doesn't touch me right. She doesn't make an effort." Demand of yourself that you find the motivation to make this area work, because it will not work by itself. If you knew that you were going to get a million dollars to make love well, the next time you are with your lover, you would excel. If you knew it was the last time you would ever make love you would make it special and savor every moment. Don't permit anything to stop you from reclaiming your excitement with your partner. We all benefit when there is a healthy physical connection.

In Thornton Wilder's play, "Our Town," the main character is given the opportunity to go back and relive one day in her life, and she learns how precious and irreplaceable life is. She desperately tries to recapture those ordinary moments, the sweet and simple day-to-day times that we take for granted. We are in those moments right now and have the opportunity to savor them and to make them special. It is just our mental laziness that has seeped in. We let it all become too ordinary. It was the very comfort and joy of those ordinary moments in "Our Town" that was so special.

We have been given this wonderful instrument, the mind. The mind can and will recapture our passion if we apply our attention and energy and direct that energy specifically.

BRING YOUR "A-GAME"

Remember the beginning of this love affair, when you couldn't wait to unravel the mysteries of your partner. You were eager and excited. Your heart beat faster and your mind was on fire. Every opportunity to touch and kiss was a chance to excel, to show your "A" game. You ran toward each other, not because of who you two were and are to each other, but because of what you were discovering. You were each motivated by the pictures in your mind of having this person in so many ways. You were willing to be an artist and paint with fine strokes, because you were watching yourself perform. You were getting off on you.

It was your pride and delight in yourself that turned you on. You were thrilled to be with this person and perform so well; you were learning and growing in this exciting arena. You were poetry in motion, sheer mastery! Moreover, you had permission to be this master, because your partner didn't have a history with you. You were allowed to invent and reinvent yourself anyway you chose, and that freedom allowed you to be your best and totally uninhibited.

We no longer have the luxury of the unknown, but we are still faced with the challenge of mastery. We can deliberately choose to give this renewed passion our best effort. We can coach ourselves and bring all of our energy and creativity to the table. Sometimes we surprise ourselves when we go the extra mile; we make new discoveries, often discoveries that were just waiting to happen.

Empowerment means starting with the assumption that there is something wonderful there; it is our job to uncover it. Whether we are working in the area of career or money, or in this area of relationship, an enthusiastic effort is a great beginning. Of all the areas that we get fed and nurtured by, this is certainly the number one source of available energy, and deserves all of our focus and concentration.

LOOKING IN THE WRONG PLACES

If we go looking for an illicit affair, it is a part of ourselves that we are searching for. Affairs are exciting, not because of the partner we choose, but because we rediscover ourselves again. We are again delving into mystery and possibility, discovering and learning. The payoff of an affair is this; we are as excited as we used to be, as masterful, as attentive; we find our personal power again. The payoff is not the mess that ensues. That is only the price we are willing to pay to find this version of ourselves. It's an odd truth that "cheating" is really an attempt to find our true selves, and we are really not looking for another person, we are trying to rekindle the spark inside of us, to discover that person that we were when we glowed with love and possibility.

Listen to what people say when they are in the midst of an affair and you will discover what they are seeking: "I feel so young! I feel like myself again! I never knew I could feel this way again!" The motivation is all about recapturing our possibility. If you knew that what you are searching for is always available to you, without any of the mess and entanglement of an affair, you might hesitate to entangle yourself. Why give our power away to someone or something, when the solution is inside of us?

This is very simple, but not easy information. Nevertheless, it is true. The feeling we are looking for remains hidden in the one place we refuse to look: inside ourselves. We choose a partner to be the catalyst for this aspect of ourselves, but somehow that is no longer true. We look elsewhere because we can no longer find that part of ourselves in the partner we chose.

That energy and spark are still there. We have to focus on the mystery: how did I call that magic forth in my partner and how did they call it forth in me? The answers to this question are the beginning of finding ourselves and our personal magic.

The fact that we can fantasize about someone else points out that the excitement is within us. This new person is not creating those feelings and we should not give our power away by assigning that power outside of ourselves. We are the source of our sexual power and our desire, and we can direct it anywhere we choose.

Imagine that we can take all of our sexual excitement and redirect it toward our partners. That would be an awful lot of power and energy. Instead of being the creatures of instant gratification that we tend to become, we can cultivate our sexual energy and direct it where we choose. The news is this: it's our power and we can direct it anywhere we want at any stage of the game. Rather than give our power away to the new and unfamiliar, we can choose to own our power. Of course it is a challenge to re-energize our sexual relationship, and we have to be open to learning and discovering again. If we develop a pattern of relying on others for our sexual excitement, we will quickly need more and more stimulus for less result.

WHAT'S YOUR FANTASY?

One part of the equation of our sexual power is our sexual fantasy. Remembering that the mind is the real sex organ, the more we know about our sexual fantasy, the more powerful and mindful we can become. When we discover what turns us on and what turns our partner on we have gained power. The attraction between your partner and you was based on how your fantasies matched and interacted. You each unlocked a combination of responses in each other that created that atmosphere of attraction.

Every sexual fantasy is based on power and control, so to discover your fantasy you need to allow yourself to go there. It takes a little courage to really examine our sexual formula, and to do so we must throw out all of our concepts and judgments. Is it innocence that attracts you? Is it the ability to dominate? What is the power game that catches your fancy and turns you on? As you observe what turns you on you will find these answers. When you see what turns your partner on, you gain power in the relationship. When we can answer these questions we have the keys to rekindling passion.

Let yourself go there. To do so, let everyone and everything else out of your head, including society, religion and all of the outmoded concepts and judgments from your history. Remember that sense of joy and lust and power that turned you on. If you can feel even a glimmer of it through recollection, it's all still there to be rekindled. Feel those feelings again and when you do, deliberately direct them toward your partner.

This requires great patience. Recapturing the passion is a marathon, not a sprint. Choose to do the work, not for your partner's sake, but for yours. Recapture the excitement of discovery in yourself and in your partner, and re-awaken your power in the sexual arena. When we feel sexually powerful we are willing to engage in all areas of life. We deserve to be in a relationship that has passion and sexual excitement. We deserve a life in which we feel vital and relevant.

FORGIVENESS

One of the obstacles to recapturing our magic, is our past history. In order to really create beautiful music again, we are going to have to forgive our partners for all the real and imagined slights that we hold against them. Martin Luther King Jr. said "Forgiveness is not an occasional act; it is a permanent attitude." Take a scan of your emotional mindset toward your partner. If your mind goes to this incident or that, then something is left unresolved. We bookmark certain memories with emotion in order to resolve them in the future. If you think you aren't holding a grudge, think again. Every little slight creates distance, and when we put enough of these incidents together and we are facing a wide chasm.

Here are the five toxins that will eventually kill a relationship:

Blame

Disappointment

Disapproval

Disloyalty

Distrust

Blame is incredibly toxic and hard to release. When we say "It's your fault!" our ego gets involved and is invested in being right. We hold on to old hurts and nurse them, constantly referring to them and retelling them in order to keep the pain alive. We give our power away when we say "I am unhappy because of you."

Disappointment hurts. The message we deliver or receive is this: "You let me down." When we deliver this message we diminish our partners and ourselves. When we live under the tyranny of disappointment we experience ourselves as not enough or less than. Disappointment reinforces our negative feelings about ourselves and cultivates bitterness.

Disapproval keeps us trapped in our limitations, constantly makes us feel wrong in our choices and in our lives. This is a withering and toxic message that makes us feel constantly wrong. The deliverer of disapproval becomes righteous, and the receiver feels that he or she can never make the right choices.

Disloyalty is a signal to us that we are not worth fighting for or standing up for. If I am disloyal, my message is that I will abandon you. As the recipient of disloyalty, I am constantly reminded of my aloneness, even in a love relationship.

Distrust reinforces our worst instincts, causing us to doubt ourselves, our partner, and our world. The message of distrust is "You won't come through; you are unreliable." Distrust causes suspicion and distance. Ultimately, it reinforces a feeling of worthlessness.

All or some of these toxins are present in your relationship. They may be at the core of the secret hurts you are nursing. They are like pets to our minds, and we feed them and nurture them. These feelings are thieves that steal intimacy and sexual excitement. It becomes difficult to let them go, but for your sake, if you do want the magic back, you must let them go. Give up being right, give up being hurt, and get big enough and wise enough to forgive.

When we deal with other human beings we will get hurt. That is a guarantee. It doesn't matter that you were hurt wrongly; that pain only happened once. It is the reliving of hurt that creates the chronic pain, and that pain is self-inflicted. In our need to punish, we say "Look how much you hurt me!" We stay invested in being hurt and maintaining distance. Let go of pain and punishment for your own sake, so that you can declare an end to the suffering.

Know this: we will never be compensated for that pain. It will never be made up for. You can nurse and feed it all you want, and never gain anything from it. The past is a cancelled check. The only value in pain is in letting go. If we don't let go of all of these toxins and the behaviors that they create, we will suffer. If we do let go, we learn.

Let the magic be back. We are very stubborn creatures, and we can often mistake stubbornness for strength. Real strength is the ability to let go, not to hold on. How many people do we all know that have held grudges for years, taking a perverse pride in it, as though they have achieved something admirable? We know how foolish that looks from the outside, but inside we can convince ourselves that we are winning, that there is something to get. There is nothing to win but peace of mind. Our attachment to our pain is our biggest obstacle to releasing past hurts.

The antidote to those toxins is simple but not easy. Where there is blame, turn it to praise. Disappointment is replaced by positive expectation. Expect the best from your mate. Approval and praise can easily turn around the disapproval habit. We need to show our loyalty whenever we have the opportunity. It is a relationship builder and a vote of confidence that can shape our partner's behavior.

CHOOSE TRUST

If we fill our partners with loyalty and approval they will have the resources they need when the hard choices of relationship come up. The best advice for early relationship (and even later in the game) is to choose trust. We can find the evidence for either our trust or our distrust, so we have control through what we choose to reinforce. Trust creates an atmosphere of safety and ease, and isn't that how we would choose to show up?

DO IT NOW

Try this forgiveness exercise: Take a moment and close your eyes. Think about your partner throughout your history. The mind bookmarks our "injuries" through strong emotion. Let your mind think back on all the disappointments, the frustrations that you've had with this person. You will see that, like pulling a string, incidents and memories will come up for you. Now silently say the phrase "I forgive you." Say it over and over, like a mantra, until you can feel it.

If you have trouble doing this, make it up; go through the motions. Act for a moment as if you truly do forgive them. This is as much an exercise of the imagination as of reality, because, after all, those hurts only exist in our minds anyway. Let yourself go into that forgiveness, until you feel it in a heartfelt way. As you do this you will be surprised by what starts to come up and what you have forgotten or buried. Picture this person, and give yourself the freedom to feel released from all of that past hurt and rage. This is your mind, your territory. Allow yourself to embrace forgiveness, even for a moment, and watch the difference in how you feel.

If you allow yourself, you will change your relationship dramatically, simply by changing your own mind. Don't act as if you can't change, and don't tell yourself it's too hard. Give up your sad story and embrace the relief and release of forgiveness, for your sake. The point of this exercise is to release everything that you are withholding from your partner and all of the "reasons" you have had for holding back.

There is no reason good enough, no justification strong enough for us to continue our self-torture. You will be surprised at how much good will is trapped inside, behind those old hurts. Give yourself permission to let go. You will be delighted by the sense of relief you gain. It is a wonderful mental housecleaning exercise and an opportunity to take your power back from the past. Forgiveness is a muscle and the more we exercise it the stronger it gets.

PRACTICE GOOD WILL

When we see a baby in a stroller we experience feelings of warmth and pleasure. We feel a great deal of good will toward the situation. This feeling is available to us and we can summon it at will and apply it where we choose.

Let your relationship be good again. Who benefits when the situation gets better? Isn't it really you that gets to show up in the improved situation? If it were your room you would clean it, or your car, you would wash it. Why not take pride in how well our relationships run, how good it feels? Let the fresh air in, it's been stale long enough. After all, it is our air to breathe. We have bragging rights here too. We deserve the best possible relationship we can create, so let's allow ourselves to have it. We are doomed to be stuck until we learn what we are supposed to learn. Learn and move on. Be a pioneer in creating a new model.

We would all prefer to be in love with our partner again. It is more fun to picture your partner the way he or she was when you first met; the attraction and the excitement. We can dwell in this feeling, rather than the resentment. We can fill up on optimism, possibility, and hope. As we let this feeling surround us, we can surrender to it. It is just as easy to be captivated by joy, as by sadness. It is our mind; we don't have to let that mind control our experience.

We decide how we feel. We can cultivate a positive fantasy just as easily as we can indulge in the negative. Notice how powerfully we can feel: all those good feelings of warmth and attraction. We can allow every good feeling we have about this person fill us up. Similarly, we can dwell on the negatives and think only those thoughts.

Shuttle back and forth; think about your partner in your negative story, then bring those positive feelings up. Compare the feelings. What you will begin to notice is that we can bring these good feeling into the present. The mind will take whatever direction we give it, and if we insist on positive, that will become our dominant reality. The dog we feed is the dog that grows.

This is a way of rebuilding good will and re-affirming possibility in relationship. Directing our minds in this way will activate those positive feelings. It is manna in the desert; these positive feelings are starving for expression. If we really are in control of our own minds, then it is up to us to make choices that will empower and enliven us. Live in this positive space for a month; insist on this reality only. This action and these choices will transform the relationship.

CAN I STILL BE TURNED ON?

How do you recreate your sexual magic? First, you must know that it still exists. Here is an exercise to find your sexual power:

Get some alone time, and allow your mind to drift toward sexual fantasy. Don't push it or force it, but really let the feelings of excitement show up for you. Let whatever mental images come up in order to get turned on, and notice those images. Allow yourself to follow these feelings and impulses, toward your desire. Your mind knows where to go, so let it. These feelings will have a certain texture and quality that is stimulating. Notice what that is, what it feels like. See where your mind wants to go in order to be turned on. It may be a little scary at first, but go with it. Remember, this is not a sexual exercise, it is a mental exercise. Give yourself freedom and permission to fill that mind with whatever images it needs in order to reach that state of excitement. Give yourself privacy and the right to learn about you. You are in the land of imagination, so anything goes and it's nobody's business but yours. Notice the physical, mental and emotional changes that go on as you approach these feelings. This is a space that you need to get familiar with in order to reclaim your sexual power and apply it where you want. Take it in. Give in to this reveling, get familiar with this space. Give yourself permission to create, to succeed or to fail or anything in between. Allow yourself to feel the quickening of mind and body that this reveling creates. The mind knows where to go immediately when we decide to become sexually stimulated. Let your mind take you there, without fear or judgment. Notice your reluctance. Notice your considerations and resistance. These are obstacles to your reclaiming your sexual power. The exercise is complete when you feel your sexual energy stirring. You have succeeded when you feel the slightest bit of turn-on, but take it as far as you choose with absolute freedom and permission.

USING YOUR SEXUAL ENERGY

What is interesting about sexual energy is that it is also creative energy. It can be applied anywhere we choose. When we are "turned on" we can direct it toward romance, or a work project, or anything else that requires energy and enthusiasm. It does not have to stay "sexual" energy. Every project requires our sexual energy; we just don't think of it that way.

In *Think and Grow Rich*, Napoleon Hill discusses the transformation of sexual energy. He alludes to "flirting with the world" in order to get what we want. When we allow ourselves to get turned on by a project or our finances we are re-directing that sexual energy. We can transform sexual energy into new business and real money.

Energy is energy, and if we walk down the street smiling and get positive response, we get a lift of energy that we can apply to anything we choose. Think of yourself in mid-flirt: you are brighter, smarter, sexier, and more enthusiastic. You are attracted, so you are more attractive. We can move mountains when we are in this feeling.

Now, think about the first time you made love to your partner. Allow yourself to feel that excitement and let yourself enjoy it. Don't worry about the present, just luxuriate in those feelings. Really let the sensation build without any thought of what it means, or where it's supposed to go. You can feel an energetic shift just by holding these images. Come back to the present, bringing that feeling with you. Now think of your partner and notice how it feels. Notice the shift, even if it's a small one. Don't try to feel completely different about him or her, just try for a little shift. The way to transformation is small, incremental changes: evolution, not revolution. If you add even 2% more excitement to your relationship today, in less than two months it will be 100% more exciting.

Recreating the magic is more about changing our attitude than our circumstances. We change our mind and we change our world. See and feel the possibility of magic in your relationship. Take on optimism as a strategy. Deliberately believe you can renew the good feelings.

What is magic anyway? "An extraordinary power or influence seemingly from a supernatural source." That's how the Oxford dictionary defines it. We own that extraordinary power. It's our magic to play with and wield the way we choose. We can demand to have that kind of influence over the situation we are in. We must refuse to be at the mercy of the situation. Taking our power back means choosing our reality. Give up "giving up." Eliminate the toxins; practice forgiveness and renewal with an attitude of permission and adventure.

EXERCISES
    With all of these exercises, give yourself privacy, find a quiet space where you will not be disturbed, and do not judge.

EXERCISE 1
    Find a comfortable and quiet space to work.

Close your eyes and picture your partner when you first met.

Allow yourself to feel the excitement that you felt then, the sights and sounds and feelings, and drink it in for two minutes.

Open your eyes and think about your partner now. Compare your feelings to the feelings when you first met, without judgment.

Do this three times, each time bringing back more of that good feeling into the present.

EXERCISE 2

Allow yourself to muse on your sexual fantasies without judgment.

Give yourself permission to let your mind roam.

Revel in these fantasies for five minutes.

Bring your mind back to your partner with those feelings of excitement, letting yourself fantasize about your partner.

Do this exercise every day for a month, creating small incremental shifts.

EXERCISE 3

Think of all the real and imagined hurts from your partner.

Picture them, and fill in the blank "I forgive you for _____."

Continue until you really feel the forgiveness.

Do this every day for a week.

THIRTEEN

YOUR PUBLIC FACE

We've discussed the dynamics of relationship. We've talked about its origins. We have spoken of the different planes that we relate from. We have covered the different stages that a relationship must go through and what to expect from each stage. In our exploration, we have illuminated how we communicate and even how to fight constructively. Let's look at an aspect of coupling that we rarely focus on in relationship: how we show up in public as a couple. It may seem superficial, but the persona that we present to the world will dictate whether or not the world supports our love. As a couple we create a unique personality that is neither and both of us.

Excerpt from a session: Mary is talking about another couple and her experience of them when they get together...

MARY: I keep feeling excluded by L and J. When they are over to visit, I feel like a stranger in my own house!

THOMAS: Maybe it isn't you. Healthy love is inclusive, not exclusive. A good relationship has a certain texture to it, a feeling tone that signals you and lets you in.

M: but they really do make an effort.

T: I'm not talking about effort. It may be something that they are doing. Maybe they compete with you. Maybe they don't feel good enough. There is some subtext going on. You wouldn't feel excluded by real love, healthy love. You wouldn't feel awkward.

M: interesting...

T: If you want to measure the quality of a relationship, notice how you feel in its presence: excluded or included, comfortable or at ease, a little nervous or apprehensive... you can tell the dynamics of a relationship in no time...

M: I feel like I'm a third wheel there...

T: Yes. It clangs... in the presence of real love, you'd feel great! There would be ease there. You would feel like "This is nice! I like this..". almost like a warm bath.

M: That's how I feel that with my friend and her boyfriend!

T: Yes, they've got something good going, it's inclusive. They're not trying to hide or keep the world out. Real love loves company. It's user-friendly to the world. The other relationship is disguised as love, but it's really "you and me against the world." That's not healthy.

M: They seem like they're in love.

T: It's a little too defensive; it's a relationship designed to keep people out. It isn't very healthy and unless it changes there will be big trouble there...

How does the world perceive the relationship you are in? What is your public image? Is it "user friendly"? When you and your partner get together, you form a third entity with a personality all its own. It has qualities that you both have, and some that neither of you possess. You can be aware of it or unaware, but it still speaks volumes about you.

That cute banter that one couple engages in may be fun for them while it's boring everyone else to tears. What another couple perceives as a well-contained conflict may be leaking all over people in a way that they resent and are annoyed by. The opposite may also be true: you and your partner may feel awkward in a social situation, but the feedback may be that everyone finds the two of you adorable.

There is absolutely a "being" that the two of you create, with an image and qualities that interact with people and that people react to. That image creates a strange vulnerability that we are vaguely (and sometimes acutely) aware of. It's like being in the three-legged race at the company picnic: we will be judged by the company we are tied to.

There is an important moment of disillusionment in relationship that defines a new stage of awareness. Jackson Browne put it well in his song "Fountain of Sorrow." "... When you see through loves illusions, there lies the danger; and your perfect lover just looks like a perfect fool... " We've all had the moment. It is a necessary stage in the growth of a relationship. How you respond to this moment decides how you will proceed in love. Will you distance yourself, feeling shame and humiliation for having been fooled or will you take the opportunity to see what's really there? Will you look for deepening the love or for the exit sign?

TAKE A GOOD HARD LOOK

Short of putting on the "I'm With Stupid!" T-shirt, there is some use in this realization. Relationship is the opportunity to reinvent oneself. Being part of a couple is the opportunity to see what you look like from the outside in. What is it that others see when they look at the two of you? Do they see a controlling side of you that you aren't aware of? Do they see a nastiness that you've gotten used to? Get curious about this entity that you've created and what it says about you. The very asking of these questions will make you more aware of your public face.

Just so you know, all of your friends and family see your dynamics very clearly. Even perfect strangers see through our relationship in about ten minutes. It's only our tendency to "kill the messenger" that stops most people from telling us what they see.

Are you one of the following types of relationship?

The Bickersons: Constantly fighting in public as if for the benefit of others.

The Huggy-Bears: Forever displaying affection to the degree that it makes others uncomfortable.

The Intellectuals: Every discussion somehow reverts to a forum to display their mental prowess.

The Competitors: Never miss an opportunity to brag about themselves, their accomplishments or their children.

The Hipsters: They're in with the in-crowd and always on the cutting edge of what is hip and fashionable.

The Sportsters: Their identity is all wrapped up in their physicality. They probably jogged over and will bike their way back.

The Whiners: Always complaining, overtly or subtly. The weight of the world is on their shoulders and will soon be on yours.

The Travelers: always off to their next exotic destination and fully prepared to tell you all about it.

The Achievers: Always striving to reach that next landmark and claim new territory, with all of the bragging rights that entails.

The Partiers: always up for an occasion and ready to go the distance at partying. Lots of drinking and play.

These are some examples of the relationship identities that we fall in to. We can have an element of this one or that, but to become one of these identities is a pitfall of relationship. Look around you and see who you know that fits these categories and examine your honest response to them. Is it positive?

These personas are merely a lens to look through. They may shed light on the identities that we have created in our relationship. When we see these identities we realize that we are practicing a kind of shorthand in dealing with the world. Our routines take the place of our authenticity and we are in danger of becoming a caricature instead of our true selves. When we do see what others see, we have the opportunity to change these perceptions.

TRY IT ON AND SEE IF IT FITS

Once we identify how we show up in the world, there is bound to be a reaction. We may get embarrassed or sensitive about what we see. This is natural. It is not, however, the opportunity to attack our partners, but a chance to see ourselves more objectively.

There is a Portuguese proverb that roughly translates to "the tongue goes where the tooth aches." Simply put, we react to others with what we see in ourselves. What I object to in you is what I don't like in me. We often feel frustration with our partners and want them to change to accommodate our comfort zone. We may even blame them for the response we get in the world.

What if we take full responsibility for the quality that we don't like in our partners as our own? We can try it on for size and see if it makes sense as a part of us. Often we are really despising ourselves and projecting it on to our mates. Only by owning these qualities can we then begin to change.

Isn't it really our own helplessness and frustration that infuriates us? There is some deep insecurity or lack in ourselves that drives us up a wall. We, not them, are the source of the problem. We find it so hard to see ourselves that we must make our partners wrong again and again to cover this truth. Of course, everyone sees us making him or her wrong, whether we know it or not. Make no mistake about it, we are painfully obvious. Take on every negative quality in your partner as your own and then you can change it.

CRITICISM AND CONTEMPT

We spoke earlier about the toxic qualities in relationship. According to Malcolm Gladwell author of *Blink: the Power of Thinking Without Thinking*, John Gottman, a researcher in the psychology of relationship has discovered that the most corrosive and toxic qualities in relationship that lead to the end are contempt and criticism, in that order. While we might think that criticism would be the most deadly, it is contempt that does the real damage. Contempt is an attempt to exclude our partner from the rest of the world, giving them the experience that they are not "enough" or "good enough" to participate.

Haven't you seen yourself create distance from your partner? Haven't you felt that superior scorn that comes with all of its judgment and disgust? Of course you have, and it shows every time. We all know how to do contempt. We learned it in the schoolyard. Each of us has mastered the art of hurting as much and as quickly as possible, while appearing innocent. Because everyone does it, everyone knows this trait when they see it. The bottom line is this: we get away with nothing. We are seen all the time as though a bright beam of light is illuminating every action.

WITNESS WITHIN

In addition, we have our silent witness who is ever present. There is a part of us that we are accountable to: it watches, sees and judges. When the bible says, "Judge not lest you be judged!" they are talking about the witness within, not the rest of the world. It is we that judge ourselves for our actions. The world only bothers us to the extent that it matches our self-judgments. You may experience this witness as a bad feeling in the pit of your stomach when you do something questionable in your relationship. It may show up as regret or doubt. Either way, all of our actions are counted and seen and sooner or later we must pay the piper.

There is a great benefit to this "witness." It is an early warning system that we are somehow going against our own integrity. If you learn to listen to this inner voice and be guided by its actions you will ultimately have a valuable inner compass that can lead to clear right action in relationship. It takes a willingness to pay attention to the inner signals that are constantly going off. Master it and you will never go against your better judgment.

BEHAVE AS THOUGH YOU ARE TRANSPARENT

Nevertheless, we see ourselves at all times. Did you ever notice how well behaved we are when others are watching? Imagine taking that on, always. What if we decided to behave that well whether or not other people were present? We would certainly show up better. In fact, we might really like who we are. If absolute power corrupts, absolute accountability insures right behavior and right action.

It is a case of taking the opportunity to reinvent the self. Understand that you are transparent. Assume you are seen all the time. Let the silent witness guide your action and behavior. With inner vision and accountability you will suddenly get right results with unerring accuracy. With accountability comes certainty of right action.

TWO FORCES

To keep it simple, let's say that there are two major forces in the universe: entropy and the unifying force. Entropy is the tendency for everything to break down; the unifying force is an organizing principle, movement toward the highest order available. An example of entropy would be a teenager's room, a minute after you've cleaned it, an hour after and a day after. Notice the tendency toward chaos. The unifying force shows up in our desire for structure and order. We feel the unifying force when we decide to introduce order and clarity into any situation. To picture the unifying force, imagine the settlers of the New World through time-lapse photography.

When you start to clean your room you feel clarified. You can feel the power and the strength that it gives you. You begin to align with the underlying organizing principle, and you feel that sense of structure and order within you. If we follow this tendency in any area of our lives we will have guidance and gain power. We will know what to do and even how to be.

Moreover, we never stand still; we are forever going backwards or forwards, toward entropy or the unifying force, all the time. Those that try to stay in the same place will experience constant drift. One force or another is working on us, and even if we think we are standing still we are moving toward one polarity or another.

Try standing your ground and remaining still; you are moving with the earth on its axis at over 1062 miles per hour while the earth is revolving around the sun at 18.5 miles per second! It is an ever moving, ever changing universe and we are a part of that movement and change. Like a bottle in the middle of the sea we are subject to great forces.

So how do we use these enormous forces to our advantage? First, be aware that we are constantly changing or being changed. We can choose to direct that change or wait to be at changes' mercy. Embrace the forces of change and use the momentum in a direction that you choose. There is enormous force behind us! Decide how you want to change and create an intention to do so. It is a little like surfing: we can ride the wave, or we can fight it. We get much further going with the wave rather than against it. There isn't a question that we might change; we will change. Our only decision is how, and in what direction. Our tools for changing reality are these: intention, burning desire, and personal power.

Intention: Decide what it is that you want to see happen. "I intend to be kinder to my partner."

Burning Desire: Get excited about the change you want to create. Picture it, feel it, imagine all of the benefits of this change.

Personal Power: Discipline and practice build personal power. Reclaiming our power from all of the fearful and negative thoughts gains personal power as well.

The combination of these tools will create reality according to our desire.

CHOOSE YOUR NEW PUBLIC FACE

There's no escaping it—if we aren't getting better, we're getting worse. The good news is this: we don't have to magically wait until we are better human beings to act better; we can simply make new choices. The moment we start to behave in new ways, we become someone new. We are not obligated to that old version of ourselves, any more than our relationship is committed to its old way of being.

Create an intention. Consciously and deliberately redefine your relationship's public image. Let it reflect how you would like it to be and how you would like to show up in the world. Make a new recipe. Show up with thoughtfulness, kindness and consideration. Add some affection and playfulness. Allow your creativity to show up in this area. Break the old stiff mold that has held you back, and show up in a new way.

Why not change? You don't like the old patterns, and likely, neither does anyone else. You have no obligation to be the way you've been. Living in those older versions of your relationship is like wearing the clothes that fit when you were five years old. Upgrade the old program with a newer version that suits your needs and wants of today. Everyone will be grateful.

You can do this by consciously discussing it with your partner, or you can just make new choices. Wouldn't you be delighted if he or she showed up caring and considerate? What if she suddenly gave you the admiration that you crave, without any prompting? What if he made you feel safe in a whole new way? It can only be empowering and delightful. The world will notice and reflect these changes almost immediately. Energy begets energy: send out this positive energy and it will come back to you. Every construct starts with an intention.

Spend time picturing your relationship in the new way. Cultivate a real burning desire for change, for newness. We are allowed to have a better situation than we do, and we have the power to create it. Imagination is the workshop of reality. As we dwell on our partnerships the way we want them to be, we build good will and resources to create this reality.

Take your power back from the way the relationship has been. Don't let the past dictate the future. We are masters of our fate. We choose how we will be going forward. We are never obligated to continue to repeat the same mistakes or relive the old patterns. We are infinitely creative beings. I have seen couples reinvent themselves from the most drastic circumstances, simply through choices, hard work and desire.

Take on this project of reconstructing your relationship public image and watch how it empowers you to change for the better. Start with optimism and a real belief in the capacity for change. Transform the personality of this "entity" that the two of you create, and watch how it benefits you personally. The world will love and accept this new permutation and you will be proud of what you create. The hidden potential of relationship is its ability to allow you to reinvent yourself.

EXERCISE 1

Try to accurately identify how the world sees and experiences your relationship. Use the models given.

Describe how you would like the world to experience you.

List the qualities you would like to add to your relationship's public face.

Add one of these qualities for one week, and notice the difference.

Continue to add a quality a week, until you have transformed how your relationship shows up in the world.

EXERCISE 2

Create an intention to transform your relationship. Fill in the blank: "I intend for my relationship to look like _____, to feel like _____.

Repeat this intention every day. Look in the mirror and say it out loud.

Spend two minutes in the morning in reverie, allowing yourself to imagine this new relationship you are creating.

Let yourself feel the excitement and the joy this will bring.

Do this daily and note the changes as they come.

FOURTEEN

SHARED VISION

In the beginning of a relationship we are enraptured by a vision. In truth, it is that fantasy of the future that allows us to get excited in the first place. We take what we see and we project a future onto it in its most positive light. We then become enamored of this vision and future that we have imagined. We invest in this "reality" and proceed to insist that it be so, sometimes in spite of all of the evidence to the contrary.

Because of how we process our environment, what we call reality, is really an interpretation. The information filters into our optic nerve and gets translated through our neural synapses and scanned by our belief system into some recognizable pattern. The interpretation happens within us, however, not in the world. The result is what we call "reality."

We call this objective reality, but it is anything but objective. Looking at the process in this way, we become the co-creators of our reality. It is reality plus interpretation. Depending on our belief system, we can interpret anything almost any way that we choose. If I like your physical looks, I may assume that you are sweet and gentle; getting to know you may show me that you very different than my assessment. Looking at the exterior and assigning feeling or meaning to it is an arbitrary process at best.

That scowl on a stranger's face could be rage, or it could be chest pains. Our experience will be guided by how we choose to interpret our reality. The quality of a relationship is based on interpretation.

Excerpt from a session with Rosanne:

THOMAS: what's the sadness?

ROSANNE: I think my sadness is about Steven's idea of what this relationship is.

T: uh, huh...

R: and the truth of what I know it to be; I'm not really telling him that because he can't understand it.

T: You think he's not going to understand you?

R: He can't see me, and that's where I find the pain.

T: Why?

R: I find this often in my relationships; I know something that they don't know, or see it in a way that they don't. I find it painful that they don't know. This happened with my first husband. He thought everything was great while I was miserable. That makes me lonely.

T: I see, but he isn't going to get you, anyway. That is reality. In my life, right now, I'm in a totally different relationship than the woman I'm with... totally different experience. We are in two different worlds. So what! Isn't she allowed to have her experience while I have mine? You say you get lonely if you're not in the same experience as him. You could never be in that same experience. He's going to have his experience and his lessons and his interpretations of you, and you will have your experience. That doesn't have to be sad. That's just the way it is.

R: And he's allowed to have that? Why do I want him to have my experience?

T: Because you have a concept that relationship means walking lock step through life in the same experience. That's a very romantic notion, but if you try to create that, you will have a dead and inauthentic relationship. That's what people do; they end up deadening their relationship because they insist that they should both be having the same experience. "We think the same way, we like the same things." This becomes a prison of its own.

R: But you don't understand. He LIVES for me!

T: So what? Let him adore you. Live it up. Is that so painful? Besides, it won't always be that way.

R: (laughs)

T: Just because you're in a different experience of relationship doesn't make his experience invalid or yours valid. It doesn't make your way better than his. It just makes them different. Authentically, it could be no other way. Find the good in this the way that it is.

When we first fall in love everything is roses and sunshine. We experience the one we are with as absolute perfection. Every flaw becomes adorable and every tic endears us. He or she can do no wrong. This experience of reality is fueled by the vision, the moving picture that is running in our minds. "Previews of coming attractions!" The previews running early on are of epic and romantic proportions. I was working with a woman who confided in me that, five minutes after she met her man, she was picturing herself walking down the aisle with him. That movie contains a lot of promise and hope that excites us. It keeps us excited and engaged.

Our expectation of the future together inspires us and allows us to reinterpret the present through these rose-colored lenses. It is a powerful process: watch lovers laugh in the rain, while the rest of us are just getting wet. Because their mental pictures match, the couple are connecting in a big way. They live in the virtual reality that their inner vision creates.

FANTASIES ARE ATTRACTED TO FANTASIES

When our fantasies match we make a connection. We can meet someone who is very attractive but does nothing for us. On the other hand, we can find a person who may be not quite as "hot" but that we connect with in a big way. This is because our mental pictures or "movies" match up well together. Our fantasies match and they engage with each other, which creates incredible chemistry. This is our first shared vision. Suddenly we have a secret world that the two of us go to, where no one else is allowed. The two of us are creating pictures and scenarios that are titillating. Our fantasies choose each other, and we are the awe-struck witnesses, surprised and grateful.

Inevitably, reality moves in and replaces fantasy with the day-to-day business of relationship. We realize that we may not be riding off into the sunset. That extra ten pounds that made him look cute and prosperous now just makes him chunky. That adorable laugh of hers that was surprisingly loud is now just surprisingly loud. What to do, what to do? Bail out while the getting is good? That is what most people do, or want to do. When stripped of our fantasies and illusions we become dejected and even embarrassed and want to get rid of the evidence as quickly as possible. We took the "joy ride of love" and are now crashing into the wall of disillusionment.

Does that mean the end of all that's possible, or is it the opportunity to create? Can we salvage something from the wreck of these fantasies?

CREATE YOUR OWN SCRIPT

Here's a skill I don't think people are aware of: we have the ability to create our own "movie." We can script our screenplay, our story, our fable. We don't have to be at the mercy of pheromones, hormones and fantasies; we can deliberately build a shared vision that sustains and empowers us.

The potential of this skill is that, based on the reality we see and what we have to work with, we can create the best version of this relationship. This can restore good will and excitement. We can cast our partners and ourselves in some wonderful and empowering ways.

We have a government that, for better or worse, has mastered the art of "spin." The spin doctors understand that by interpreting the facts to meet their conclusions, they can create the outcome that they want. Whether we agree or disagree with the government's policies, we must concede that they are effective in achieving results. They understand that perception creates reality.

If I ask you to come up with the best possible story of your relationship now, what would that story be? Let your mind shift to the most positive interpretation of your partner and see where that brings you. You may notice resistance to doing this, but do it anyway. There are obstacles to change: there can be a tendency to not want to make love good again because it is so bad. Forge ahead. See her as the kindest person you know; cast him as the guardian of your safety. Dwell on this scene and let the feelings come. You will notice good will begin to arise immediately.

Don't be afraid to spin positively. Understand that if relationship is meant to end, it will. If it isn't meant to go on, no amount of positive interpretation is going to prolong it. However, if it is meant to end, there is still a positive story that can be told. "We've been together for two years and I have learned more about me in that time than ever before. Being with him has shown me how much strength I have. I am grateful for the experience." "I have done better in my career on her watch than ever before in my life."

You get the idea. Romanticize the relationship, deliberately. Make it an epic, a saga. Tell the grand story of the two of you, and how you fought incredible odds to get through your challenges. Let yourself feel proud of your shared accomplishments and the obstacles that you've overcome. If you retold your relationship as a childhood fairy tale, wouldn't it make interesting telling? Wouldn't you, as in every fairy tale, find great meaning and great achievement, even as you overcome monsters and challenges?

Think of the goals and dreams that you started with. You may still be fighting for some of those dreams. If you look at your relationship, and even your life this way, you will see more of who you are. In fables there is an incredible camaraderie among those on the quest. They become closer because they share the hardships and difficulties. They know the story they are in and the mission they are on. They rely on each other and recognize the importance of each other in the story.

Too often in relationship we become polarized. There is my side and your side and neither understands the other. Truly, the worst feeling in relationship is isolation, but often it is self-imposed. Instead of waiting for him to jump onto your page, get onto his, or better yet, create a new page, a new story that the two of you can participate in. Make it an adventure again, the way it was in the beginning.

When we achieve this point of view, we take our power back from the negative story that we have been in and we see it for what it is: just another story.

WHY HAVE A SHARED VISION?

Can you imagine IBM not having a mission plan? How about Microsoft? What if the telephone company simply drifted wherever it found itself, without direction or thought? How long do you think it would be before we have no phone service? Let's take the members of the Harvard Rowing Club. What if each one had an idea of the direction that they wanted to go in, and each one followed that direction? You could say they are merely expressing their individuality or asserting their independence, but is it going to work out?

Like it or not, relationship is a team sport. It is a joint enterprise that takes coordination and cooperation. The crew team relies on communication and shared vision to get them to the finish line. The large corporation needs clearly stated goals or it lumbers forward like a headless behemoth making random moves.

In the television show called the "Amazing Race" and in the show couples compete to finish different legs of a journey from one exotic destination to another. In a day they might be assigned to travel from Rio de Janeiro in Brazil to Quito, a small town in Ecuador, by plane, bus and boat. We're thrilled as we watch this mad dash from the airport to the bus to the boat, with every conceivable misadventure and mishap along the way. This seems like a show about travel and adventure, but really, it's all about relationship. What we begin to notice is that the couples with the best communication, the most trust and the clearest common vision are the ones who win. It takes good will and teamwork to cross the finish line.

The show puts a microscope on relationships so that any little crack or flaw is magnified, and it becomes the team's undoing. The couple with the strongest mental game has the best chance of winning. They are on the same page: at times they seem to act as one. It is clear to them and everyone around them that they are a team, not two individuals tugging in different directions. We laugh at the miscommunications and miscues of the losing teams, but we're really whistling in the graveyard. It is us that we are seeing and laughing uncomfortably about. We root for clarity, order and connection, and we laugh at misunderstanding and pettiness in the contestants. We instinctively know what works and what wins: shared vision and willingness to cooperate.

The same is true for every couple: we face extraordinary challenges. How we do is based on how well we connect. We also are faced with leg after leg of an often difficult and challenging journey. For couples in relationship the challenges may be about getting past the fantasy, or moving in together, but the challenges are no less real and fraught with danger. When there is a shared vision and a willingness to communicate, we are invincible.

HOW DO YOU CREATE A SHARED VISION?

Start by seeing your relationship as an "amazing race" of its own. See it as an adventure that you are in together. Capture some of the original joy that you had when you first found this "partner in crime" you are with. Decide to stop wandering and actually get somewhere. You had dreams and schemes when you first got involved; try to remember and recapture some of them and make these dreams your destination.

Tell the story of your relationship as an adventure. Write it down and you will see that it is quite a romantic tale. Give it some point, some direction. If you don't know where you want to go, make it up. Allow yourself to fantasize about where you could possibly bring this partnership. Talk about it, scheme, and dream again. What about that vacation house in Hawaii, or the country cabin you always wanted? Start putting something in front of you worth having, and talk about it. Maybe you as a couple will take on a cause, like world hunger. Remember, a company without a vision will fail, a team without a vision will lose, and a partnership without a vision will drift and dissipate.

It is important in business as well as in relationship to have goals and dreams. Spend some time discussing and making plans. Talk about the future. Talk about your hopes and dreams and what you would like to accomplish together. Common goals are the ties that bind and dreaming together about our future makes us stronger.

EXERCISE 1

Sit down and write the story of your relationship as a fable or an adventurous children's tale.

Project a wonderful future in this story.

Read it every day for a week and see how differently you feel about your relationship.

Invite your partner to do this exercise and share these stories with one another.

EXERCISE 2

Sit with your partner and separately make a wish list for the future.

Compare notes and put the list in order of priority.

Read it often or post it where it can be seen.

FIFTEEN

NURTURING: THE CARE AND FEEDING OF A RELATIONSHIP

WHAT ABOUT ME?

Isn't that always the question? "I always give and never get what I want. It isn't fair!" We're always feeling shortchanged or cheated in some way in relationship. We see what we give through our enlargement lenses and what we receive through our reduction lenses. It boils down to "I give everything and get little or nothing in return."

Can this really be the case? Is this what relationship always devolves to? I think it is a problem of focus rather than a dynamic in relationship. Because we don't relate to the bigger picture, or the "us," our concerns are all about "me." Of course, it is our favorite topic: start a conversation and see how long it takes a friend to turn that conversation to him. If it's less than 30 seconds, you have a good and attentive friend. Most people aren't listening in conversation; they're merely waiting for their turn. This is especially true in relationship.

So how do we get what we need and create effective communication within this system? How do we know what to give and how much, what to take and when? It would be nice to believe that we could give everything we can. It would be wonderful to fully expect to be seen and taken care of, but it just doesn't happen that way.

Here is an excerpt from a session with Louis and Patti, married for three years with two-year-old twins:

PATTI: Somehow I have become the maid, chief cook and bottle-washer in this relationship. I support him and think of us as "we" but he doesn't do the same. He expects me to do everything I do, and then take care of him sexually!

LOUIS: You're making it sound a lot harsher than it is.

P: Excuse me. I have been carrying the load here since I can remember and you are taking it for granted.

L: You knew the deal going in. I've had some things under development...

P: I'm glad to know that going to gym every day and going sailing with your friends is "under development."

L: How can I get anything done when you are so completely negative? You have never once supported my dreams. I need to do those things to keep my sanity.

P: And how long am I supposed to continue to support you and your dreams? You are way too comfortable.

L: You just want to be a martyr.

THOMAS: Time out! Clearly some deal was struck that isn't working any longer.

I am often challenged by the puzzle that couples present. There is a text to the conversation and a subtext. What are they really saying? It is tempting to assume that Louis is the bad guy and that Patti is being taken advantage of. I have found that despite the obvious, it is often the opposite. We need to look a little closer. Early on, some agreement was made that no longer fits the situation. No one is getting what they need and want here, and I could see that these were two very resourceful people that were capable of making the relationship work.

She is saying, in effect, "Why are you not coming through for me?" And his lament: "Why aren't you supporting my dreams?"

Start with the assumption that it is possible for each party to get what he needs here. Sounds simple, but most people believe the opposite. Remember the beginning when she anticipated your every want and desire: she still has that in her. He wanted to please you then, and somewhere he still wants to. It is up to us to provide a target for those arrows, to receive the love that is there.

Everything we give in a relationship and everything that we do is about us, we just don't always recognize it. We are selfishly motivated creatures, and that's not a bad thing. If I improve the atmosphere in my relationship, I breathe better. If I make it a more pleasant place to show up, I get to show up there.

We need to deal with the subtext in order to make sense of the text in any conflict.

MAKE A STUDY OF THEM

If you have a pet, you know every little nuance of its behavior. You are tuned in to its eating habits, its breathing, even when and how much it sleeps. If there is a change or disruption, you sense that instantly. You are utilizing your psychic connection to monitor them, always. Now compare that to the seeming indifference and disconnect that goes on in relationship. "Energy flows where the attention goes," whether it's to the cat or to our partner. This is the person you couldn't get enough of and were intrigued by. If we treated our pets the way we ultimately treat our partners they might starve to death.

Jump over your resentment and decide to recommit to knowing this person: their hopes and dreams. When was the last time you chose to be interested and intrigued by your partner? If you reach back into your memory, you will find that you know a great deal about this person. You know her secret dream, or his latest scheme.

What stops us from investing is our resistance, created by the belief that this interest will not be returned. Get over it. The reason to master the study of another human being has little to do with them. It is a relationship skill that will serve us all of our lives, and unless we master that skill individually, we as a couple are doomed. I can support someone's greatness, not because they deserve it, but because I have that power. When we are exercising that power we are getting stronger every time we do so.

SUPPORT THEIR GREATNESS

Did you ever walk down the street and see a fat dog? We cringe, knowing that it is someone's overindulging that is ruining this poor animal. They might argue that little Buffy gets everything she wants, but is that a good thing? Somewhere in there is a great dog, but its real needs are being ignored. Instead the owner's neurotic need to over-nurture is being indulged, and the dog suffers.

To be useful, caring has to be accurate. We can't just pour it on or turn it off indiscriminately. We can develop a light and easy touch, with the delicacy of placing a crystal glass on a crystal table. We must make a distinction between how we want to love and how the person we are with needs to be loved. Are you doing what you want, or what they need? It makes the difference between having a sleek Airedale or a fat mutt.

OBSERVE

To support their greatness we have to see their greatness. Put aside the story about him, your case about her. Let go of the resentment and see with fresh eyes. When we look at a child we have a willingness to see their potential. Look at your partner with those eyes. Be interested.

In art appreciation class they ask that we stare at a painting for a long time. As we do, aspects of the picture begin to emerge that were not apparent at first glance. Use your powers of attention and observation to see the masterpiece in front of you. Put in a little time noticing the details: "what is her biggest challenge right now?" "Where is he discouraged?" This attentiveness will pay off in gold. We all yearn to be seen and understood in relationship.

The simple act of observation will achieve this. We naturally become interested as we invest time in noticing. Spend five minutes thinking about your partner and come up with one interest that they have. Now do a little research. Read up on it or look it up on the Internet for another five minutes. Now take five minutes and discuss this with him or her. Your message will be clear: I care about what you care about. As we show them that they are worth our time, effort and attention, it will create a bonding and a positive feeling in the relationship, immediately.

Isn't that what we are all craving? To be seen and appreciated, valued and understood. If I am important enough for you to take the time to study, the result will be good will from me to you. This is a necessary resource to manage our challenges in relationship.

HELP THEM GROW

We have two choices in relationship: we grow together or we grow apart. The concept of helping a child grow comes easily to us, but not so much with an adult. We make the assumption that we are all grown up and so we tend to block ourselves from embracing growth in ourselves and others. The truth is that we will be growing and learning until the day we leave this plane, and we either do so willingly, or with great pain. In teaching a child we're careful to encourage them and support their efforts without shaming them with their lack of knowledge. With adults we are not so subtle. We tend to want to hit someone over the head with what they don't know.

Approach relationship with this simple fact: we are all still children emotionally. When we are gently nurtured we respond well, and when we are rushed or forced, we get scared and we don't take it in as well.

How do we help someone grow who isn't even aware that there is growing to do? Use that same skill set that you use with children: encouragement, positive feedback, gentle guidance. Put on your kindest, most supportive self and bring them to a new place, for your sake as well as theirs. After all, it is our own environment that we will be improving.

TRAIN THEM WELL

Whether we know it or not, we are teaching people how to respond to us from the minute we meet. You must know someone who constantly gets teased. This is no accident. That person is sending subtle and overt signals in order to get the response that they are getting. If we slowed down time, we could see all of the choices of behavior being made, including micro-expressions and gestures too quick for the naked eye, that result in that person corralling people into teasing him or her. We get what we create, subtly or otherwise.

We demand that the world treat us a certain way, but it is not always in conscious alignment with the way we want to be treated. If my routine is to be a victim, I will make the hundred little behavioral choices to get that result. If I choose respect, that is what will show up. We can gain conscious control over this process, by learning the decisions we are making, and having conscious intentions to create the results we want.

If we want to coax a cat out of a corner, we put out a saucer of milk and patiently wait. Little by little, the cat will come closer and eventually we will be able to pet them. Now, what if we are annoyed with the cat for taking so long? Every time it gets close enough, we will express impatience, and the cat, sensing this, keeps bolting at the last minute. It is we who create this whole set of behaviors: the cat approaching and the cat retreating. We can't say "Stupid cat! Doesn't know what it wants!" The cat is doing exactly what we are teaching it to do, no more and no less.

The fact that some of our signals are conscious and some are not matters not at all to the cat. It's all just stimulus that she's responding to. The same is true in any relationship. When we have a mixed agenda, we get mixed results. When we create clear intentions we will see that we get clear results that we want.

It is essential that we know what we are demanding, consciously or subconsciously. The answer to this query comes from the behavior we create toward ourselves in life. If I am being loved and respected, that is what I am calling forth. If I receive abuse, that is my tacit request being met.

TAKE RESPONSIBILITY FOR WHAT IS CREATED

If I am being ignored, I created that; if I am being cherished, the same is true. It is the good news and the bad news. While we certainly have the power to create the result as it is now, we also have the power to call forth any result we want. Any result.

Make new choices: support the good ones and starve out the ones that don't work. Find the talents and gifts that your partner has for relating and nurture them. Praise what works and stop responding to what doesn't.

A couple of years ago there was a case in court about a woman who had trained her pit bull to attack humans, and sure enough, that's what the dog did. She tried to make the case that it wasn't her responsibility that the dog attacked. Of course, she lost the case. If she had won first prize in a dog show, I'm sure she would have taken full credit, but she tried to distance herself from an unpleasant result of her training. We are responsible for whatever shows up in our lives, and the sooner we take that responsibility, the sooner we can change results to what we want them to be.

The couple in the example is not taking responsibility for the result. She chose to take the actions she took for her own reasons, because that is what she wanted to do. She didn't get what she expected from those actions, and she is filled with disappointment and resentment. Communication along the way would have prevented the situation from coming to this pass. Louis failed to make his agenda clear, to ask for and encourage her to support his dream.

Consequently, he shows up like a slacker. Through communication and examining both of their agendas, I got them back on the same page, with some caveats. They both agreed to ask before doing, to examine their own needs, and to be honest about what they were willing to give. Each had to look at their expectations and readjust them to reality.

AGENDAS

It is one of the most difficult truths of the conscious path to own responsibility for the situation that shows up around us, but if we are able to embrace it, there is enormous power in it.

What stops us from calling out the best in our partners? Maybe we want to keep the relationship in turmoil so we can justify having one foot out the door. We always have an agenda. Remember, human beings have an Agenda, a Hidden Agenda and a Secret Hidden Agenda. We can say that our Agenda is what we are consciously choosing. Our Hidden Agenda has more to do with the underlying desires behind our agenda. Our Secret Hidden Agenda has its origins in our history and unresolved patterns. When we understand these agendas, we know where our partners and we ourselves are coming from.

Louis' agenda is to build his company. His hidden agenda is to work as little as possible in order to get the maximum results, to parlay what he is willing to do into great success. Being in the financial industry, he has watched colleagues effortlessly cash in, and make fortunes. What is his Secret Hidden Agenda? Perhaps that agenda is to be taken care of, the way he never really experienced as a child. If this is his hidden motivation, and his agendas are in direct conflict, what results can he expect?

Patti's agenda is to be a success and live the lifestyle of that success. Her hidden agenda is to win the love, acceptance and appreciation that she wants from the world. She has always been industrious and is used to the world reflecting that in the form of approval. Her hidden agenda is to control her world and her environment in a way that she feels safe. Given her history and family background, this makes perfect sense, but if you don't know this about yourself, you will be controlled by it. We unconsciously try to bend our world to accommodate our agendas.

MAKE IT THE BEST
Understand this: until we create the best relationship that can be, we won't be able to leave it without regret. Our

lessons are our lessons and they will show up, even if we seem to pick very different candidates and different relationships. Make the relationship good, simply so that you can choose with clarity whether you want to stay or not. Is it enough for you, once you've created your best? We can only know this when we have brought it to its best possibility. Whatever the strategy and agenda, whether choosing to go or stay, the tactics of the moment are the same. Make it the best it can be, now.

LET IT BE YOUR SCIENCE PROJECT

We don't have to have an enormous amount of faith to resuscitate our relationships, just a willingness to see, to cultivate vision. You would be amazed at how much and how quickly you can change your environment, with a little application. The reason to improve can't be because our partner deserves it. We must do it as an exercise of our power, our ability to change our own reality. We are almost never at the mercy of the situation that we find ourselves in. There is always a great deal that we can do.

Be assured that you will end up in a relationship again with these same challenges and lessons if you choose to pass on these lessons. An old spiritual adage tells us that, by not learning our lessons as presented, we increase the difficulty tenfold for the next time we encounter these lessons. We can take on the project of improvement that our relationship requires with the same enthusiasm and zeal that we would tackle any other task. We are incredibly resourceful people and we can apply those resources to the benefit of our partnership.

Cultivate a vision that describes how the relationship you are in should be, and determine to create that vision. This is the proper use of our power. Change your circumstances because a good atmosphere is easier to work in. Flex your muscles for your own benefit.

Where to begin? Do everything you know to immediately improve the situation. Drop your hostility for starters. Put a smile on your face. Look for the positives instead of the negatives. Don't try to change the situation a lot; change it a little. Encourage her; praise him, subtly and overtly. Tinker with the energetic balance that has been created and come up with a new formula. You will learn a secret by doing this: you begin to like yourself better.

When we judge the experience of relationship, we are really talking about how we feel. By breaking the old framework of reality, we let in fresh air. We are no longer confined to the same tedious role and discouraging reactions. If we only do what we can do to improve the relationship, we will come up with many ideas. We've been given the answers in that place we fail to look: within. Follow that internal guidance system that knows what is right and wrong, and you will improve your situation intuitively and dramatically.

Louis and Patti had mastered a useless skill: the ability to blame a partner and make him or her wrong. Rather than hold a grudge and insist on how bad the situation is, determine to improve it, for your sake. Don't allow yourself to be weak to prove a point. You are not weak and you never were. To nurture means to teach, to cultivate and to feed. Bring out that side of yourself and start to heal both of you through healing the situation.

Here are ten actions to take right now that will improve your relationship immediately:

1. Practice forgiveness now. Give a "free pass" for the latest offense.

2. Be amused, rather than offended.

3. Compliment, compliment, compliment.

4. Pay attention to his/her interests and verbalize that attention.

5. Do three thoughtful things for your partner right now.

6. Drop your anger and resentment; drop your "case" about your partner.

7. Give exactly what you are looking to receive right now.

8. Drop all threats and ultimatums immediately and disclaim them.

9. Shower your partner with gratitude now.

10. Take on an attitude of optimism about your relationship and show it.

EXERCISE 1
Observe your partner objectively and re-imagine him/her at their absolute best.

Write a glowing description of this person from that best perspective.

Envision this new person for five minutes in the morning, or until you feel a positive shift in your emotions.

Read this description and do this visualization every day for a month and respond as though it is reality.

EXERCISE 2
Examine yourself for your three agendas: agenda, hidden agenda, secret hidden agenda.

Honestly assess how this creates anger and expectations of your partner.

Examine your partner's agendas.
Discuss with your partner.

EXERCISE 3

Practice the ten remedies every day for a week.
Observe the changes you create.
Discuss with your partner.

SIXTEEN

MAINTAINING RELATIONSHIPS: UPKEEP AND IMPROVEMENT

I have discovered that I have a good opening game in relationship. The man who shows up(me) is initially thoughtful, user-friendly and appropriate. For better or worse, I know how to begin to relate in love, but my middle game has always fallen short. Part of the reason for my journey into relationship counseling has been to make a study of me, while looking at the lives of others. Any counselor who tells you otherwise is either lying or self-deluded. Like you, I am always seeking answers.

In that quest, I have learned a great deal, and have learned to improve my middle game. We spoke of the stages in relationship, but to use this vernacular, let us frame it as the game that it is.

OPENING GAME

This is the stage of love where we make the big play. We show up with love and excitement. Our standards are clear, our hopes are up, and we have the energy and power to show up well. In this stage, I show up with a patience and kindness that I do not normally possess. I listen and I have a mastery of detail in caring for others. I yearn to be that man, but it does not come naturally to that degree and with that focus, except at this point in the game of love.

MIDDLE GAME

As we settle in to relationship, we let some slack into the sails. We are not trying to catch the wind, but merely to maintain what we have achieved. At this point, I have been known to show my impatience, though it can appear to be playfulness. I am less willing to attend to detail to the finest degree. The guy I was becomes harder to access, and I no longer have the resources that early relationship has given me. It may show up as an unwillingness to listen and a commitment to being right. Some fraying begins to show around the edges, and at this point I may be fighting disappointment in myself and the situation.

END GAMES

No longer being fed by the excitement of newness, I let more of myself show. I have less enthusiasm for the discovery of this new human being. The boundaries are down and I let my partner in to the level of intimacy usually reserved for family. Without the vigilance of new love, I have shown up in this stage with too much anger, and way too much impatience. This part of my game has always needed improvement. If I am not careful, I devolve to my worst instincts and am prone to defensiveness and protectionism. In the end game of love, I am my biggest challenge.

These are my relationship pitfalls and the challenges that I work on in order to keep relationship vital. It takes a willingness to look at parts of myself that I am not proud of in order to improve in these areas. I am not perfect, but that is not required of us. We are enough for the task when we take an honest assessment of ourselves and possess a commitment to change.

Through my work with clients I have had the opportunity to see reflections of myself in a variety of situations that are presented to me, and I have learned through teaching. Any forum that allows us to see ourselves is a chance at enlightenment. Look for the mirrors that reflect you and have the courage to see. When we dare to see ourselves, we will grow.

MAINTAIN YOU RESOURCES

The temptation early on in love, when our real and ostensible needs are all being met, is to divest ourselves of extraneous friends and interests. This is a tactical error. The support we've created in our lives is part of what makes us who we are, and to give up that support, means to give up a part of us. We gain power from our friendships and alliances; they feed us. When we fall in love, we feed on a higher stream, called possibility. While this seems more nourishing, we are actually running on imagination and using resources rather than replenishing them. It is the equivalent of running on fumes. Sooner or later we are going to sputter and flame out.

We can underestimate the impact of friendship at this time, because they just aren't as compelling as this new situation. Would I rather be "madly in love" or "hang out with the boys"? No contest, love wins it, game, set and match. Yet, our friendships, our hobbies, passions and interests are what make us stronger in the world. These are the many strands that make a mighty cord, and to give any of those sources up diminishes our power.

Why not surrender to love? Why bother maintaining? Because, without the power you are getting from other interests, you will soon run out of energy and resourcefulness to create and maintain the relationship you want. We do not have an infinite supply of octane. Without our streams of replenishment, we will be like Wiley Coyote, spinning our feet in the air, having sailed off the cliff.

Love is a game we play of escalating dice; it costs us more to play every turn. We need to be able to afford the game we are playing, and the coin of the realm is the energy we get from support in our lives.

KEEP YOUR INTERESTS

On Broadway in recent years, there was a show called "I Love You, You're Perfect, Now Change!" Unfortunately, this becomes the tacit message from many a partner in new relationship. We end up playing a cat and mouse game of outguessing our partner; playing the role that they need to see, rather than who we really are, and hoping and demanding that they live up to what we perceive as their potential. Neither partner should ever give up who we are. We are the sum total of all of our interests, our hobbies, our pursuits in life. To give any of them up is to give up a part of ourselves and our power.

Relationship is not for the weak or faint-hearted. We need all of the power that we have gained in life. Our interests make us fascinating and unique; they become the hooks that others attach to when they are drawn to us. Whether it is yoga or meditation or an exceptional interest in Proust or Kafka, each of our fascinations is like a facet of the jewel that we are. Never dull yourself or give up an aspect of the self that allows you to shine; we are the sum total of all that we care about and all that we do.

ESTABLISH A VISION

So much of life is a mental game. Whether we are speaking of romance or sex, or even of building a business, creativity starts with conception. "What man conceives, he can achieve!" This is not an idle statement. We create our reality through the vision that we hold.

As children, we are masters of the dream, but as we mature we are taught to "be practical." Tell a child at the beach that he is building a fortress to protect his treasure and he will immediately embrace that vision. Watch as he builds and creates, adding to the legend as he builds another wing on the castle. As children we have infinite resources to dream and imagine. We have to return to that power of dreaming, that "Imagineering," no longer with innocence but with intention.

For instance, see the relationship you want to create: have a plan and a blueprint for how it looks and feels. Immerse yourself in the pleasure of possibility. While being aware of the partnership as it as, have an eye on what can be. Let yourself see and imagine this love at its best. Be a practical dreamer, and invite your partner in on the dream.

It is not an indication that love must end just because it feels listless and boring. Re-imagine the partnership as fulfilling and exciting; visualize a new result. We can't reasonably abandon a situation until we bring it to a higher evolution, or we create huge regret in the future. If every attempt to enliven this relationship fails, perhaps there are other issues, but until we make the attempt to breathe new life into our partnership, we cannot know how good it can be.

CONTINUE TO LEARN YOUR LESSONS

Love is for lessons. We must reluctantly abandon the model that our partner is an endless source of entertainment and delight. Partners, lovers, adversaries and every relationship we are in, are all sources of lessons. From these alliances issue all of the lessons that we've chosen to learn on this plane. We give our power away when we proclaim that "so-and-so is not making me happy." Happy is not part of the job description. We alone are the source of our happiness and the source of our misery. Having said that, there are certainly relationships that have run their course and we must remove ourselves, but we can only do this in good conscience when we've played our side of the court and learned the lessons we've chosen.

The beginning of conscious relationship occurs when we start to examine ourselves through our partnerships. Why do I react with such impatience when my partner doesn't seem to understand me? The operative word is "I." I react. I perceive. I interpret; and in that interpretation lay many answers for me, and through me.

When we start with what we don't like about ourselves in our current situation, we begin the journey to personal power. When we blame, we give power away. We can't curse the arrows if we are busy creating the target. Every interface with people is a spiritual meeting designed to give us the opportunity to learn. The powerful question always is "What is there to learn here?"

TYPICAL LESSONS IN RELATIONSHIP
Trust
Kindness
Loving Yourself
Communication
Supporting Others
Commitment
Fantasy vs. Reality
Expectations
Attachments
Compromise
Respect
Compassion

Participation

I could probably write a book on each one, but as you scan the list, you know what each one means to you, and which ones resonate the most. Look at the relationship you are in and see through the filter of these lessons. When we embrace what we are trying to learn and to teach, we are doing the real business of relationship. Only then can love be fulfilling and something more than a two dimensional arrangement.

What is the lesson of trust? When we examine this issue carefully we discover that it circles around to how much I trust me. This is the truth of every lesson. The power lies in taking responsibility for how each lesson shows up and in cultivating that quality within ourselves. Our lessons will show up no matter how different and varied the partners that we pick. Respect, commitment participation, these are skills that we get to learn through the mirror that our partners provide.

MAKE THIS ASSET APPRECIATE

The "call girl principle" states that the value of a service is greatly diminished upon the performance of that service. When first seeking relationship we value it greatly; perhaps above all else. Having acquired love, its worth for us quickly diminishes. If we don't understand this principle we are at the mercy of it, but when we understand it, we can adjust. It is up to us to continue to find value in relationship. This means that our value points will change along the way and we must constantly seek and assign value.

We first value attraction and physical love. As we evolve we can start to shift to more enduring values. Partnership, companionship and communication are some of the bigger picture objectives of relationship that will provide real meaning for us. Love is a living entity that must have new goals and new challenges in order to stay relevant. It is perhaps our greatest asset, and yet few people understand that love requires thought and input in order to keep it healthy and vibrant.

Polish your love, nurture it, and make it something to be proud and excited about. Love will not nurture itself, so we must choose to see it as something of value and provide sustenance. Use your imagination and creativity to build your construct of love. It will pay you back in satisfaction and good will. When we have strong partnership we are stronger in the world. We have bigger stakes and more to fight for. Give yourself the advantage of experiencing love this way and it will return the energy tenfold. Love will provide strength and meaning and context in our lives.

COMMUNICATE

As we continue to fill in the big picture of relationship, I will continue to stress the necessity for communication. There isn't a challenge or an issue that cannot be managed through thoughtful dialogue. There is great satisfaction and security when we know that we can solve anything together. The knowledge that we have someone in the world who understands us, who is willing to work through challenges and issues with us makes us exponentially more powerful and secure in the world.

Communication is assumed in our relationships with our pets, our bosses and our world. When we nurture that same channel in love, we feel a clarity and confidence in all of our other dealings and interactions. When communication does not exist here, we feel weaker; isolated and alone. Reread the chapter on communication and master the art form. Nothing is more necessary and more useful than effective communication

THE HIDDEN RULES OF RELATIONSHIP

and it truly is the difference between a higher and a lower life form.

RESPECT

Webster defines respect: To take notice of; to regard with special attention; to regard as worthy of special consideration.

As I list the supplies necessary for this journey called relationship, I cannot overlook a commodity that shows up in great supply early, and yet seems to degrade over time. I am talking about respect. To respect our partners is to respect ourselves. When we respect others we are making deposits in an emotional bank account. We like ourselves better when we respect our partners, and we raise the quality of the relationship we are in. We dramatically improve our image in the world, and our relationship persona.

By respecting our mates we choose to be accountable to ourselves and the world. We gain power and prestige when we do so. Respect gives us moral and spiritual authority and empowers us for the inevitable challenges ahead.

We have little control over many of the circumstances we find ourselves in, but choosing to give respect gives us control over our experience. Let us regard our partners as worthy of special consideration, for their sake as well as our own.

PASSION AND SEX

We have spoken of the dance of mystery and discovery that is sex. As the enigma reveals itself and the mystery dissolves we lose the impetus to play. We act as though the puzzle is the delight and when it is solved the fun is over, but we can continue to seek levels of this miracle play that are not yet revealed. When we start with the assumption that there is much more to discover than the obvious, we rise to a new level of challenge.

Anyone can see the obvious, but it takes a visionary to see what is not so apparent. Oddly, if a rival becomes attracted to our mate, we see them with different eyes and we can recapture the attraction. Why should it take this kind of event for us to wake up to what is there?

We can deliberately look for and see new possibility, see a new attraction. Our imagination is our biggest sex organ and we are in control of stimulating it. We can get ourselves excited again. We just get lazy. If you imagine your partner as a stranger or see him on the street without knowing it is him, you will feel a thrill of attraction. The electricity is still there, we just have chosen to ignore it. In a society that constantly stresses the new we too easily become bored and indifferent to what we have. Real value is still there, but our vision often is not. We lose sight of what we have. I can take my antique Hamilton Watch for granted while someone else can admire it to the point of lust. I remember that feeling but I lost the vision and excitement of seeing it that way.

Maybe we don't know what we've got 'til it's gone. We need to constantly renew our perspective to see the value of anything that we have, including relationships. When we do, we reap the benefits. I still have this valuable watch and this beautiful partner and I can appreciate them and have that experience now. We are in control of our experience; we can recreate that experience at will. When we do, we have improved the quality of our lives and given ourselves back something of great value. Re-light the lights in this room again; Sex is a spiritual meeting on the physical plane that offers constant renewal.

FINANCES

The number one issue that creates conflict in relationship is money. Early in partnership we feel no need for this understanding. At the end of the day if there is no agreement in place, there will be inevitable clashes.

Will and Nina are in the second year of marriage and there are dark clouds on the horizon.

WILL: She spends money like water! I can't keep up with the bills. It's almost like she's doing it with a will, to see if she can break me.

NINA: That's ridiculous! If you paid attention to what it costs to run this house maybe you would understand that I'm actually doing a great job.

W: A great job of sending me to the poor house.

N: You were the one who told me that you never want to see me worry about money, that you would take care of me.

W: Okay, you win. I failed. I'm a failure, okay?

T: So what exactly is your financial agreement?

N: He promised to take care of me. He said I never needed to worry about money,

W: Yeah, I didn't know you'd take advantage of me!

T: So, the old agreement has broken down. Fair enough. Sounds like it's time for a new agreement.

As we build our relationships, priorities shift. Early in their courtship, Will felt like he could offer this and provide for Nina. As the landscape shifted through marriage and children, their needs changed. The old agreement, such as it is, does not accommodate those changes, and now he feels like he is being taken advantage of and Nina feels like she was tricked.

There is no intentional betrayal here. Literally, the old contract has expired and they haven't known how to create a new contract that reflects the changes in their partnership. This is a problem in dynamics, not an emotional issue, yet the problem has certainly created emotions on both sides. We worked together to create a new agreement that matched their current needs. This eliminated the hurt and resentment and gave the couple a new platform to operate from.

When we deal with finances we have to be realistic: take an honest assessment of circumstances and work out a new contract that reflects the present needs. We would not expect a twelve-year-old child to abide by the rules made for a six year old. Similarly, we can't expect the old agreements in finances to reflect our current situation.

DEFER TO THE SPIRITUAL

Like many people, I worked my way through college. Among the many odd jobs that I held, I drove a taxi in New York City. Despite my optimism, the wear and tear of the job got to me and it became a bit of a grind. Fighting traffic every day and dealing with disgruntled passengers was not quite the adventure that I hoped that it would be.

After one particularly trying fare, I was complaining to an old-timer about people being rude and taking us for granted. He said to me "You're looking at it all wrong. You think you are just driving a hack and plowing through traffic, but you are in a privileged position. You are the ferryman carrying people on one leg of their journey. As they make their way through, you get to ease their burden and maybe even give them wisdom and humor along the way. The way you're doing it, you are just a slave grinding out a job you hate, but I am an oasis, a part of their destiny. I have a chance to lighten their load and maybe even change their lives!" Needless to say, this was a decidedly different point of view for me. I realized that I had a choice, even in this limited situation. Suddenly I could make this job into anything I wanted it to be, even a position of privilege on a magical journey.

The old cabbie taught me that my experience depended very much on how I interpreted the situation. It could be terrible or wonderful, depending on my expectation. I could be the hack or the angel, all according to my choice.

When we look at the partnerships we have created, we always have a choice. We could look at this pairing we've made as a mistake or a disaster, or we could see it as a spiritual meeting chosen for our highest good. We could see ourselves as "stuck" in an assignation that has little meaning and no value, or we could assign dimension and purpose that encourages us and enlivens us. Which do you think gives us more power and a better experience?

It is no accident that you are with this partner. You are striving to learn and to grow and have chosen this person to assist you. Take on a new model. Imagine that you have lived a hundred lifetimes together, that you come together yet again to teach each other and to learn.

As we reach for the highest evolution of any situation we find ourselves in, we become more empowered. We heighten the situation we are in and raise the stakes of the game. Am I here to learn, finally, to let go of control of life? Did I choose this person in order to teach myself kindness? When we demand value from the situation that we are in, when we choose to assign meaning and purpose, we enrich our own lives and we see from a different point of view. This gives clarity and direction to our coupling and raises it above the ordinary. When we choose to see this way, we provide vision and charm.

Relationships are difficult enough, don't we need every advantage? Reach for the highest purpose and possibility in anything you do, and you will live with more quality in your life. Even if we assign meaning, we gain personal authority when we know why we are here and what we are really up to. Love can be routine or extraordinary, and that depends on how we choose to interpret it.

Take the relationship you are in and choose to see it as a meeting with destiny. Explore love from this point of view and watch how it transforms you, your partner and your present situation.

LOYALTY

Napa Valley is arguably one of the most beautiful locales in the United States. My fiancé and I enjoyed our visit to wine country and returned to our bed-and-breakfast for a romantic night. When we checked in, we discovered that the much anticipated hot tub and spa were closed for the night, earlier than advertised. Throughout the entire day I had been looking forward to easing into the tub and relaxing in the steam and I was disappointed by this news. I checked the brochure; I noticed that the spa was scheduled to close at ten pm. I looked at my watch and saw that it was only nine-forty. Given the amount of wine I'd had and the disappointment I felt, I decided to take action and talk to the manager.

My fiancée(now my wife) is by nature a very private person, while I, on the other hand, am anything but shy. She had no interest in a possible confrontation and did not want me to make a scene. Did I mention that I'm a native New Yorker? Wine had loosened my tongue, and I decided to talk to the manager.

I confronted him with the facts: the brochure promises one thing and they are doing quite another. I explained that as a patron of this B and B, I am entitled to what we paid for and I requested that he open the hot tub. He was having none of it. He apologized and explained that it was empty for some time and he decided to shut down early, and anyway, it would take twenty minutes to heat up, by which time it would be ten o'clock.

We had visited six vineyards that day and sampled the wine from each. I had a head full of steam and a belly full of wine and I was not giving in. To his credit he was trying to reason with me, but I was right and righteous and wouldn't be denied. As I went on with my alcohol-fueled presentation, I saw out of the corner of my eye that my partner, my lover, my wife-to-be, was nodding in agreement with him!

Exasperated, he opened his register and silently returned our deposit. "You are absolutely right and I want you to leave." That was all he said. Stunned, we left, defeated. No hot tub, no spa, no room for the night.

This led to a heated confrontation in the car, not about my ridiculous posturing, but about her "betrayal" of me with the proprietor. How could she, I demanded, possibly take his side in a confrontation in which I was completely right? Didn't she know that it was she, not me that caused our ejection by agreeing with him? That if only we had closed ranks and presented a united front he would have done what we wanted? It was a long drive.

What is the point, here? This is not a cautionary tale about the evils of vineyards and landlords. What she ultimately understood was that I needed her loyalty in that moment. Right or wrong, I needed to know that she had my back. I knew then and I know now that my "liquid courage" was not going to carry the day. Nothing of the events bothered me as much as her siding with the "enemy" against me. She could have chosen to take me aside and air her feelings and come to some meeting of the minds; she could have chosen to communicate. She admitted that she was angry with me for making a commotion.

By admitting where I was wrong, she was then able to see my point: that it is important to know that your partner is behind you. She did not show me that. It didn't matter that I was wrong: it only mattered that she didn't close ranks with me. We both learned something in this exchange because we expressed our feelings and points of view.

Sometimes when dealing with a partner, it is more important to be loyal than to be right. When we feel we have support, we can be strong in the world; when we don't feel that support, we are weaker. We have the right and even the need to challenge each other in private, but it is disempowering when we do so in front of the world. We unwittingly make ourselves strangers, rather than allies, and take away one of the benefits of partnership.

PARTICIPATION

We create bonds with the people at work when we perform tasks together; when we share lunch; when we go to the office picnic. Each shared experience creates the strand of a connection. When we have enough strands that bond becomes incredibly strong. The Indian chief shows the young brave that one stick can easily be broken, but many sticks are stronger than each individual twig. This is true of our time and experiences spent together.

Participation brings us closer. We don't have to be told in the early passion of love to spend time together. That is all that we want to do, sometimes to the exclusion of our duties and obligations. As we accrue memories and experiences we build a certain amount of equity in the relationship. We are creating a resource that we will rely on down the road, sometimes without even knowing that we gain strength from this bond. As we become familiar with one another we tend to take participation for granted. This is a strategic error. Participation is the grease that keeps the wheels moving, and when we apply less of it, we start to lose momentum in our lives together. We need that bond to feel a sense of common purpose and connection.

This is the result of not knowing the dynamics of relationship. The more we participate, the stronger we become individually. When we know this we have an accessible way to become stronger as a couple. If we choose to increase participation in any friendship we will become closer. The more this participation suits the needs and desires of an individual, the more powerful the participation becomes. Quality participation can make us invincible in the world.

Find ways to increase participation in your love life and you will discover a new way to renew and revitalize your relationship. Spend time together. Do things that you both enjoy. Make it your business to participate in a quality way at least once a day, and in a month you will have a deeper and more meaningful connection.

EXERCISE 1

Examine your history in relationship and write down your opening game, your middle game and your end game.

Take an honest assessment and see what needs improving.

Assess the stages of your partner's game.

EXERCISE 2

Look at your financial contract with your partner

Determine how it has changed from the beginning of the partnership until now.

Come up with a new agreement that is appropriate to your current situation.

Discuss this with your partner.

EXERCISE 3

Look at your relationship as a spiritual meeting, designed for you to teach and learn lessons. Imagine yourselves in other lifetimes, teaching and learning.

Determine what it is that you are trying to teach your partner.

Determine what lesson you are trying to learn through this partner.

Discuss with your partner.

EXERCISE 4

Make a list of the ways you and your partner have enjoyed participating in the past.

Make a list of ways you and your partner participate now.

Make a list of the ways that the two of you can increase your quality participation.

Discuss this with your partner in a no-fault way.

SECTION III

ENDING A RELATIONSHIP

SEVENTEEN

ENDING RELATIONSHIP WITH DIGNITY

"Happily ever after" is a nice fairy tale, but it has nothing to do with reality. Most people don't want to discuss the end of a relationship because they have a superstitious belief that this conversation will invite it in or bring on the end. The end is a real moment in relationship and, just like every other stage, ending can be done well, with dignity and respect.

When we look at the arc of relationship, we see that there is a beginning, middle and an end. We've talked about the beginning, the attraction and the fantasy. We've talked about the middle of relationship where reality sets in and we make our adjustments for it. Now let's deal with the end.

Because relationship is about learning and teaching, we are meant to walk our paths together for a purpose and for a specific duration. We don't know for how long, and maybe we are not supposed to know. This society struggles to know what happens after death, but perhaps what does happen is a deliberate mystery; it has great spiritual purpose in that it forces us to deal with the now moment. We aren't supposed to have the certainty of an assured future so that we can "go to sleep" in life or in love. The unknown inserts us into the present moment of our lives.

This is true of relationship. Try as we might to say, "'til death do us part," we know that this may not be so. We are dealing with the unknown, and we are not supposed to take that security for granted. When we are secure, we get lazy and can even become arrogant. If we live our lives as though

211

nothing is for granted, as though we might lose him or her at any moment, we will value them more. "Live every day as though it is your last,"; this is not a morbid philosophy. It forces an urgency and attentiveness to the moment. It creates appreciation and value for the experience we have right now.

We are reluctant to hold the possibility that this partnership is not forever, yet most of us have gone through the end in this area. We didn't enter love with the expectation that it would end, and yet it has ended on us and we have survived. Perhaps we can do more than survive. Maybe we can find real value and meaning in this event.

HOW DO YOU KNOW IF IT'S OVER?

I woke up that morning like any other, to a seemingly ordinary day. Yet I felt an odd detachment and a timeless quality that I had not experienced before. Suddenly, I knew. Despite all of our struggles and desperate conversations, I felt the certainty that this relationship was over. I could see the two of us in my mind's eye, our battles and our struggles, as though from a far distance. I was filled with an overwhelming sense of compassion for the two of us, and a sadness for having to go through everything that we'd gone through. Later I would be devastated and the tears would flow, but now there was only a detached pity.

There are moments in life that take on a surrealistic texture: being at a funeral; leaving home for the first time; the end of a relationship. Time stands still and we see ourselves from a distance, going through the motions but strangely detached. It ends, not with a bang, but a whimper. You wake up one morning and you know it's over. It isn't over because of all that has happened, but you have a certainty that its time has passed. Suddenly, everything is different. It isn't an awful feeling, just a strange one. Once you have experienced this feeling you will never forget it.

We believe that relationship ends because of conflict, or that it will end in the heat of battle, but it rarely does. Fighting doesn't end a relationship; it merely makes the experience of relationship painful. The end sneaks in while we aren't looking. The wearing away of good will and the gradual death of the fantasy ultimately kills the love, and we have nothing left.

The end does not come because of the one big offense that is committed; it is the weight of a hundred slights that breaks the back of relationship. The daily and ordinary meanness that we dish out takes its toll, and soon there is nothing left to fight with. We lose our purpose and our direction; we lose the will to go on.

In the beginning is the fantasy: we have an idealized image of the person we are with. As reality moves in, that image is constantly being adjusted, but we are desperately fighting to hold on to the good that we originally saw. We are capable of doing enough harm to each other and that image, so that, ultimately we can no longer piece the picture back together. We lose sight of love. Unless we vigilantly remain light on our feet and adaptable throughout the stages of love, we lose our vision. This sensation can be filled with ennui or boredom. It is the death of love.

NOW WHAT?

Some of us desperately hold on, even when we know it's over. We fear change that much. Often, holding on becomes a matter of pride and ego, rather than common sense. Lovers hold on for years sometimes after the natural life of the relationship is over. Often, the grieving process starts before we have left and we can feel the different stages of separation even in the midst of relationship.

Grief is comprised of the following stages, whatever the loss we are dealing with, but not always in this same order:

Denial: The stubborn refusal to accept the end.

Anger: We become furious with ourselves and our partner for this failure.

Bargaining: We scramble to make concessions and attempt to patch together solutions.

Depression: Sadness descends as we begin to feel no possibility of resolution.

Acceptance: We come to a peace with the reality that it is over.

And if, in fact, love is over, how do we leave? Paul Simon wrote a great song about the subject, "Fifty Ways to Leave Your Lover." "Just hop on the bus, Gus. Make a new plan, Stan." Sounds simple but we are not always prepared for this eventuality. The idea that everything that we've worked for has come to naught is too much for the mind to immediately accept.

REGRET

Regret comes in life from not doing everything that we can do. We are infinitely creative and we can always think of something else to try. At some point we must decide that we are done. When the building is on fire, get out. You can figure out what caused the fire later. It does no one any good to stay in a relationship that isn't working. If you've come to the point where you know in your heart that you are done, you've got to take action. Have no fear; if love is not meant to end it

214

will not end. If it is over, nothing will salvage it. If you can consider taking action with dignity and kindness, then you know you are ready to leave.

This moment bears self-examination. Here's a litmus test: "Does leaving seem right when I am considering everyone's best interest? Can I leave with clarity? Will it be empowering and be the right move for both of us?" Leaving because you are angry will come back and bite you. Trying to get even will result in creating your own misery, and you won't end anything; you will just create more misery. When you can separate your good from theirs, and see that this is the best for him, or her, and you, then you have given the situation the right consideration.

OBJECTIVITY

I know how difficult this moment is, but you can face it with power and dignity. It is the time to communicate. You need to have conversations, perhaps many of them, in order to come to a dignified meeting of the minds. Before this dialogue you need to be as clear in your own mind as you can reasonably be, that this is what you want.

Take an honest assessment: do you see yourself with this person in the next year? The next five years? Are you building or simply trying to hold ground? Is there enlivenment in this situation for you and your partner? Have you honestly tried everything you know to do before declaring the end?

Talk to your confidantes, not in order to hear their opinions or suggestions, but in order to hear your own thinking. Like every other stage of relationship, this stage should be approached with care and thought.

FEAR AS A MOTIVATOR

Just as it is wrong to stay in a loveless situation because of fear, it is also a bad idea to leave, simply out of fear. Obviously, if you are in danger, get out, but if you are in fear of the responsibility of a partnership, you need to reassess. Relationship is not supposed to entertain and amuse us. As in any business partnership, there is real work to be done. It is a certainty that the work that shows up in this relationship will show up for us in the next one, because we have our patterns and lessons that follow us wherever we go. We can't duck our lessons by leaving the situation; we carry them with us. Many people have the impulse to leave as soon as the real work of relationship shows up. Running away only delays the process of our learning.

Any fear that we have is internal, though we may have externalized the situation. Be more afraid of not learning your lessons and having to repeat them over and over again.

We choose our partners in order to learn and to teach, and that means that our lessons must show up sooner or later. When we accept this, the work is no surprise. When we refuse to accept what we have chosen we are only deflecting and delaying the inevitable.

CLEANING UP THE MESS

Leaving in conflict is not a good idea, but sometimes the conflict will not resolve by staying. How do we go about ending it cleanly? Start with the golden rule: "Do unto others as you would have them do unto you." How would you want to be treated at this time? What would be the most loving and compassionate way for you to be handled in this space? Leave your anger behind: anger is usually a cover emotion for pain or fear. To the best of your ability, resolve this anger. Try the ten-year test: what will all of these issues look like ten years from now? How much of it will matter, if any?

In the lyrics to the song "The Way We Were" there is an interesting reference: "... What's too painful to remember, we simply choose to forget... " You will remember differently when time has passed and the pain is no longer present. Oddly, most of what seems so important now will not even be remembered, so be sure the stakes are really as high as you are making them.

All of the real and imagined hurts will fade away, and in their place will be a historical perspective. Maybe you will understand why you picked this person and chose to learn what you did. Maybe you will see your behavior in a whole new way and have a deeper understanding of you and your motivations. You may eventually see yourself in this relationship as young and foolish, or headstrong and willful. You may see your partner more objectively and understand what was not working at the time and even why it didn't work. You may even see why you loved each other. As we look back on our younger selves we see how naïve we were in the past. You can be sure that the same is true now. Our knowledge is still incomplete.

In any life decision, we need as much clarity and vision as we can find. Reach for that clarity. Put your anger aside for now, and decide that, if this is the end, you are going to handle it masterfully. Find that reserve of kindness in you that you save for puppy dogs and children and exercise that kindness in this situation. View your partner with great compassion and visualize a healthy outcome. Few moments will affect us more deeply than this time. This is a rare opportunity; relationship doesn't end every day. If you end it well, you will pay fewer prices and take the opportunity to learn.

Keep in mind that this person is someone that you loved. Even if you were dealing with an animal, you would seek to end it humanely. The other point, of course, is that your internal "silent witness" is watching. The "you" inside will not let you off the hook if you are cruel. Make it a point of honor to approach the situation with perspective and compassion.

WHEN IS IT NOT OVER?

"The opposite of love is not hate, but indifference." We've heard this before. Feelings run high because we still care, despite what we think or tell ourselves. Don't be so ready to throw out the baby with the bathwater. Too often we are ready to pull the trigger in order to avoid our own pain.

We say, "It's over!" in order to be in control, so that we won't hurt so much, but we inadvertently put ourselves into the experience of the end of the relationship by doing so. We unwittingly create the very feeling we are trying to avoid. Declaring it to be over when it is not doesn't make it so. It only creates havoc. On the other hand, when its time is done, there is little we can do to change that. Don't be eager to embrace the relationship being over when you are merely looking for control.

Relationship is not a concept; it is an action. It also has a timetable of its own. When it is meant to be over, it is. When it is meant to continue, love will find its own way, regardless of our conscious intentions.

We choose to relate, to understand, to empathize with our partners. When we stop choosing to relate, there is an emotional disconnect. When we can no longer choose to relate, it is over. If you are angry and choosing not to relate, that is different than not being able to. Make the distinction: be honest with yourself and try to take the action of relating.

The worst pain you will experience at the end of a relationship is regret. The regret comes from not trying when we could have made a difference. It isn't pain or anger that signals the end of a relationship; it is indifference. Anything other than that feeling means you still care in one way or another. Don't create what could be a lifetime of regret by not trying when there is still some feeling and passion present.

HOW DO I TRY TO RELATE

Tai Chi Chuan is an ancient Chinese martial art. It's a fascinating technique within this practice requires you to empathize with your opponent; by so doing, you disarm them. When your opponent feels that empathy, he or she will drop their defenses. To relate to another person means attempting to empathize: to know the experience of that person sitting across from you. How hard are you trying to know that experience? Are you so busy building your case that you are unwilling to consider what is going on over there? For the sake of effective communication we must find that empathy within us.

Let the light in. What is it that you would have to be experiencing in order to be doing what he or she is doing? What is the emotional pain that must be there? Try to gain some distance and perspective. If it were a movie you were watching, what would you know about their character? You would see their motivations and all of their reasons for their behaviors and actions. You would understand completely. Use that understanding and deliberately choose to relate, the way you understand that person on the screen. Knowledge and insight can only increase your understanding of the situation.

We show a great deal of compassion toward the characters on our favorite TV show, but too little with the people in our lives. How often have you sat in the movie theater with tears streaming down your face for an imaginary character, while holding a grudge against your "loved one" sitting next to you? Choose to relate. It isn't dangerous, and it won't compromise your position. If anything, it will clarify whether you should leave or stay and why.

YOU CHOSE ALL OF THIS

On some level, consciously an subconsciously we have made a thousand little choices that add up to the reality we now find ourselves in. When we own this we gain great personal power. It is the good news and the bad news: we created this reality. When you start to wonder why, consider the opportunity that the situation is for you to learn.

If you really are at the end of your relationship, your freedom beckons. Possibility is around the corner, and it should be enlivening. And if your freedom is really at hand, why not learn whatever you are supposed to while you are still in the situation to learn from? You could refuse to learn, because, after all, you do have free will, but why waste the situation? It took a long time to create this relationship and it is going to take a long time to recreate this scenario.

We create relationship in order to learn the lessons we chose. Why not exploit this moment and use it for what it is worth? Remember, you chose this situation to learn from. You made the choices to get here, and I don't just mean that in a metaphysical sense. If you could slow down time and visit each moment of decision that got you here, you would recognize each of your choices and you would own them.

If you want to enjoy the next stage of your life, you would be wise to learn from this one. Do everything you are meant to do here, finish this task before you start another. You will never regret doing the work you need to do now in order to create a better future.

OUR RELATIONSHIP LIFE

Whether we stay or move on, we are always working on our relationship life. This situation is not the fault of your partner. It is your next lesson in the arena of relationship. We can be certain that we are improving our relationship lives by bearing down and learning what this situation presents. Learning is never for the benefit of others, though they may ultimately reap the harvest, it is always designed for our improvement and advantage.

In a spiritual sense, this soul of yours chose to learn from this person in just this way. Relationship on a spiritual level is always an agreement based on pure love and cooperation. You and your partner chose each other and made a spiritual pact to learn and grow through participation with each other. Further, you chose it to look this very way. You are always in control whether you feel it or not.

MAKE A PLAN

If we want to get to San Francisco from Los Angeles, we'd better have a road map. It would only be dumb luck if we happened to find the exact route. It is a strange form of insanity to decide to "wing it" through one of the most important transitions in our lives, i.e. the end of a relationship. I think that is about as clever as trying to "wing it" in outer space, and we would probably get the same kind of results. Do not be afraid to get conscious about what you want and what you are trying to achieve. For everyone's sake, get clear about what you are doing.

We don't have to know immediately and exactly how we want it all to play out, but we do have to have some specific ideas. Get clear about what you do know. The obvious questions to ask are the same as those questions of a reporter:

When am I leaving?
Where am I going?
Who am I going with?
Why am I leaving?
How am I going to achieve this?
What will this look like when it is fully accomplished?
What do I hope to gain?
Is this permanent or temporary?

You won't have the answers to some of these questions, and some you will know clearly. Start with what you know. You need to know your own mind; you need a roadmap, otherwise you will be led by your emotions that are subject to change, minute by minute. Feelings and emotions have only one message for us: do something! When we act from our feelings we are creating behavior designed only for the relief of those emotions. Then we are led by the petulant child within all us that demands instant satisfaction. This is too important a moment in time to leave in the hands of a willful child.

The obvious benefit of getting clear about what we are up to is that we do get to know our own minds. The subtle benefit is that we will see how serious we really are. It is useless to play with the idea of leaving, because, while it feels like an empowering thought, it actually puts us into the pain of that experience. Knowledge is power. Have the courage to know what you really want, instead of playing at it in order to satisfy some temporary feeling.

HAVING THE CONVERSATION

Once we are clear in our own minds we are able to communicate effectively. Clarity allows us to speak without the vagaries of our fears and doubts. This is never a conversation that should be had out of anger or vindictiveness, especially if we want it to be effective. The moment is important and we should give it its due. Be clear that this is not punishment or an attempt to get even. Make a distinction between a "clearing the air" conversation and an "it's over" talk. When we are clear about where we are coming from, we can be truly compassionate and even receptive to our partner's point of view.

When you are stating that it is over, this is not a negotiation, but a declaration. The goal should be to impart this information with clarity and compassion. Expect it to be an emotional conversation and allow for that. Be prepared to drop it and come back to the talk at another time. Allow this person that you have loved to have his or her reactions, without any judgment or defensiveness. When you are clear that this choice is for everyone's highest good, there will be no guilt or regret. This conversation is an opportunity for you to show up with dignity and compassion. Take pride in how well it is handled, how clearly you present yourself and how lovingly you can deliver this difficult truth. If you do manage this you will remember the conversation and be proud of it for the rest of your life.

Bear in mind that you are delivering news that likely is not welcome. Have some empathy; in your haste to get the words out, don't forget the experience of the person sitting across from you. It is likely to cause great pain and shock, and you have to account for this. Give time and space. Be willing to explain. The hardest part of this conversation is the actual beginning. Resolve to make a good beginning, and be flexible. Set an agreeable tone. Give this moment the importance and attention that it deserves.

AND AFTER?

Logistically speaking, after the talk, be sure that you have someplace to go. Give your partner some space and room to recover. Make an appointment to talk later on, but for now, create some distance. You will both need that space in order to regain balance. There will likely be the need for follow-up discussions. It may take three or more conversations to establish what you want. Even in the dissolution of a business, there are matters that need to be dealt with.

Be clean and fair. Have an idea beforehand as to the disposition of things, and remember the golden rule. Karmically, we want to be as clean as possible, because we will carry this event with us. The Law of Karma says that if I am slapping you in the face, I am really hitting myself. Take this to heart. If you really want to separate, give your partner little reason to continue to engage. Remember, no shame, no guilt and no blame.

If we manage this transition with thoughtfulness and care, we will create some emotional equity for ourselves. The "watcher within" is taking note of our behavior and our choices. We are accountable for all of our actions. Determine that you are going to be proud of how this transition is accomplished.

SELF MAINTENANCE

Even if this breakup is your idea, you are going to have reactions. Don't be naïve enough to imagine that you will feel only relief when you finally make a break. Don't mistake the feelings of nostalgia and sadness that must come up for regret, either. It is a good idea to download to friends, to talk about it, not in order to be right, but in order to let out the emotional torrent that will be in there. Don't look for truth in your ranting, just let it out. You will have rational and irrational thoughts. Allow your emotional instrument to go through the changes that you have created.

Journaling is also very useful at these times. Don't edit your writing or even monitor it much, just pour it out. You can always look back at it later (you might not want to), but for now, simply use the release that it is. My take on the end of a relationship is this: deal with the pain when you must. Talk, write, cry, scream and pour it out. When the events are not present for you, let the feelings go.

Stay busy! It isn't avoidance to keep yourself engaged in the world, it is self-preservation. Deal thoroughly when you must and don't deal with the pain at all when you don't have to.

The recovery time for a breakup varies with each individual, but it is reasonable to expect a time of recovery. As with all mourning, the pain will not be constant. You will have times when the issue is not present, and this is natural. Enjoy these times. Even when dealing with death, the grieving is not an ever-present event. We are human beings with rhythms and patterns, and we blink on and off, just like the rest of the universe. Take the times when the grief is not present and use them to make yourself stronger.

Oddly, sadness at the end of a relationship is a concept: to feel sad we must be in an idea, rather than an experience. When you truly get present all concepts disappear, including the sadness. Ask yourself "Am I in the experience of loss right now? Is anything hurting me right this second?" The answer is no; without the concept of loss you are absolutely fine. Use this idea. When we are present, there is no pain and no fear. There is no loss in the moment. Emotions are a function of time and when we stay in the now, negative feelings don't exist. Determine to stay present to your experience and you will not be in pain.

LEARNING THE LESSONS

Just because we don't have to suffer, doesn't mean we aren't choosing to learn. The whole point of why this partnership didn't work is that there is something to learn. The sooner we embrace this the quicker our lives will work the way we want them to. There is a fine line between taking full responsibility for what has happened in the relationship and taking the blame for it. Responsibility gives us insight and wisdom; blame and guilt give us pain and avoidance.

How do we live in the assumption that everything that has happened has been our choice, and that these choices have created the situations we have found ourselves in? How do we take responsibility without taking on blame? Tricky business, this. Yet, according to Freud, we choose everything that happens because we think it will result in our pleasure, or in the avoidance of our pain.

PATTERNS

For example: You made the choice to stop listening to her, because you couldn't hear her, and didn't understand her. You didn't like that feeling, so you began to avoid it, and her. This resulted in her feeling abandoned and disconnected, and perhaps trying harder for connection. But you chose these circumstances. There were other choices available, such as getting into a conversation about your communication, but you decided that this would be too uncomfortable. You didn't want to feel like a fool, or didn't like how you thought it would make you look or feel. You made a choice, which had consequences. Choices become habits, and habits create patterns. This disconnect between you became a pattern of non-communication.

Another example: You have a concept of what he must do to "prove" he loves you. You decided that, to show his love, he must call periodically (this arbitrary time changes with the individual, whether it is once an hour, a day, three days,etc.), To satisfy your concept he must sit in rapt attention while you go on about every detail of your day. In your construct he must declare his love in very specific ways, and if your secret formula is not met, he doesn't love you. You have chosen a formula based on what you have come to believe that has nothing to do with reality. He could love you 'til the cows come home and still be unable to express himself according to your formula. Your choice has made love unworkable. When he fails your test, you take it as proof that he doesn't love you, when, in fact, it is only proof that he isn't psychic; that he doesn't know your pattern. You could choose to react organically to the relationship, instead of being ruled by your "secret" formula.

Compare notes with your friends and you will hear their "secret" formulas, too. We see it all the time. We all have friends whose patterns we recognize as unworkable. When our formulas don't match, we conclude that our partners are crazy, or that they are being totally unreasonable.

There is great power in examining our choices and underlying patterns, and if we are ever going to learn how to make relationship work, we must identify these patterns and beliefs. Self-knowledge is power in a relationship; it is also the necessary wisdom to ultimately make partnership work.

POSITIONS

Look at the positions you have taken in your relationship and you will learn more of your lessons. When a politician has a position on an issue, you hear his point of view and the action he will take in that area. "I believe in clean air and a healthy environment!" This is position should indicate action. Of course, we are talking about politicians here, so all bets are off. Yet, we, like politicians make "campaign promises" early on in love.

What are the positions you take in relationship?
"I don't believe in saying 'I love you.'"
"I demand respect."
"He needs to show me that he loves me constantly."
"I need my independence."
"I don't indulge in public displays of affection."
"I come first in any relationship."
"I am the 'fixer' in my relationships."
"My partner must come to me."
"My money is my own."
"He must call me every day."
"She must get along with my friends."
"My family comes first no matter what."

All of these are positions that will create behaviors and attitudes. They all require defending, and all are potential disaster. Each one represents rigidity in each of us, and we can make choices that become more important than the person we are with. Is love worth giving up in the name of concepts? Even if we don't give the person up, we do create a little more distance with each acting out of a position.

We don't throw people out of our hearts all at once; we do it little by little. Examine your positions and see what you are really trying to achieve by them. Maybe you already have what you are looking for, without having to default to a position. In any case, automatic behaviors create a deadening relationship, whereas, new choices create enlivenment.

Some lessons will be learned in relationship, and others will be learned by the loss of one. To insure that you have as little regret as possible at the end of a relationship, learn everything that you can from the situation. Don't be afraid to take responsibility, you are responsible whether you know it or not.

REGRETS

Mary came to me after her relationship had ended. She felt that she and Greg were not sexually compatible and she didn't want the struggle that this implied.

MARY: Greg was almost perfect! He really had everything I wanted in a guy.

THOMAS: So, what happened?

M: He made it clear that he would not do some things in bed. I felt that one of the things he wouldn't do was a deal breaker. I couldn't imagine a life without that sexual pleasure and I felt that I couldn't do that to myself.

T: Did you try and work it out?

M: He said that he wasn't going to cave on this one. But now, I'm not so sure. I was just so offended! Now I wish we had discussed it more. I just have the nagging feeling that we might have worked it out.

T: Any chance that you two can revisit this?

M: Oh, no. We've both moved on. He's already dating.

The biggest pain at the end of a relationship is regret. Regret comes when we take action that works against us or don't take action when we could. It also comes from not learning what we should have learned. We can insure as little pain as possible in love, by rolling up our sleeves and determining to learn and grow through the entire experience.

The measure of a person's power is their ability to see truth. When we take on what belongs to us in the form of lessons we are living in truth. Ask the question: "How did I create this situation?" If you are in a conscious relationship, if your partner is wise, they will be vigilant as well. The bible says "the truth shall set you free." When we are in the truth about our lessons and taking on responsibility for our actions, we are free. Suddenly we have an unerring road map to clarity and happiness in our partnership. We all have that internal guidance system that pings when we are in truth about ourselves. Learn to listen to that inner voice.

Ruthlessly examine yourself and your motives. Don't rewrite history, either in your favor, or against it. Too often, our pain and sense of loss will tempt us to see what isn't there or to rationalize so that we come out the hero or the victim. Stay within the idea that this is a no-fault situation, and simply do your best to understand the facts. Take responsibility, not blame. Look for clarity, wisdom, and understanding. This may be a hard time, but not necessarily a bad time. Take the opportunity to end the relationship with love and dignity. In every love situation we are given the opportunity to improve our relationship lives. All of these actions will keep you from having regrets, and insure that you learn what you need to in order to create your next, healthier relationship.

Make a determination that this will be an extraordinary experience of growth and change in your life. Renew your life dreams and plans and take the energy that this time gives you to build and grow. Determine that this will be a great time in your life; a time of healing and discovery.

EXERCISE 1
Make a plan before having the discussion with your partner.

Write out your plan and let it include steps to be done before and after your conversation.

Be clear about what you will do after this conversation.

Have an opening, middle and a conclusion for your talk.

Include what you both will do before, during and after, in your plan.

Read this plan three times before beginning any conversation.

EXERCISE 2

Close your eyes and picture yourself having this conversation.

Picture in detail how you want it to go.

Picture the beginning, middle and end of the conversation, and see each part working out.

Picture his/her having considerations and "hear" these considerations and respond.

Take at least ten minutes to do this; if it was worth being involved, it's worth spending time to end it well.

Stay with these images until you feel comfortable having the conversation.

EXERCISE 3

Make a list of your support team during the breakup.

Make a list of activities to engage in during this time.

Start a journal and write in it every day.

Deal with the feelings when you must, using your team, and stay busy when the feelings are not present.

Look for what you can change and improve in you at this time.

EIGHTEEN

NOW THAT IT'S OVER

The deed is done. With parting comes a combination of relief and confusion. You've finally escaped, but into what? Facing this new challenge brings doubt and second-guessing. "Was I too hasty? Did I act too soon? Should I have left this relationship?"

The good news is this: It isn't the actions we take in life that we regret; it's the actions we don't take. However, the fight for clarity is a race against time. We must outstrip the feelings that are going to descend before the seeds of doubt take root. Resist the constant impulse to rewrite history. Before long, regardless of whose choice breaking up was, you will feel like the victim. You will start to experience the end in a whole new way, as though it happened to you, rather than you being in your power and making a choice. I am always amazed at how quickly the mind changes the story, to the point where it becomes unrecognizable.

A suggestion: Write down the events as they happened while it is still fresh in your mind. Otherwise, you will forget and you will struggle, and the story will become a vague mess wherein you feel strangely guilty and responsible.

Feelings have a virtual reality of their own. We see through the filter of those feelings and interpret reality according to that filter. What we think has occurred quickly becomes obscured by our latest set of feelings. We continually retell and recombine the facts until we are not quite sure what has transpired.

STAGES

The loss of relationship represents a huge event within the mind. It is a loss as significant (and sometimes more powerful) than the death of a loved one. Arguably the grieving process is longer and more complicated than when dealing with death. Death, though painful, contains closure within it. The most common emotion felt at the end of a love is the sense that there should be more, that this ending was somehow not enough or is incomplete.

As we spoke of in a previous chapter, there are stages to mourning a relationship. In *Death, the Final Stage of Growth,* Elisabeth Kubler-Ross describes the process in five steps: denial, anger, depression, bargaining and acceptance. You can probably relate to one or more of these stages, even now. It is not uncommon for more than one stage to show up at the same time.

Denial is an odd duck because, intellectually we know something has happened but we are not relating to it emotionally. It can show up as a spacey feeling, a sense of being out of it. We will be able to recite the events chapter and verse, but we will feel little connection to it. There is a surreal feeling, as though we are witnessing someone else's life. We start to rationalize and tell ourselves that maybe it is not over. Maybe this is just another fight. The feeling tells us that it can't possibly be over, not that quickly and simply.

Lisa and Bob have been broken up for 2½ months. She is still struggling with the reality of the situation:

LISA: We've gone through this before and he always comes back.

THOMAS: Have you gone through it for this length of time?

L: Never this long. This one is a doozie! I am going to really give it to Bob when he comes back this time.

T: What if he isn't coming back this time?

L: We've gone through too much for it to end like this. He'll be back.

T: We don't know that. I think you need to take the opportunity to look at this as though it really is over.

L: That would be like betraying him!

In this case, Lisa is practicing self-deception and self-nurturing. It is my job to gently land the reality of the situation for her, while preserving this very important instinct for survival. This is a natural stage. Our minds are trying to wrap themselves around this cataclysmic change. Lisa is aware of this reality somewhere in her psyche, but is not yet ready to deal with the implications of this event. Without ripping away the veneer of her cover story, I need to give her a version of reality that preserves possibility while dealing with the truth. It is a delicate bit of surgery. We will revisit Lisa at the next stage of grief.

At some point we find ourselves in the stage of anger and some form of bargaining. We start to make deals with life: "I will accept the breakup as long as I get a better relationship in the future," or "the next time I get involved it's going to be for life!" We list our demands to the arbitrary unknown as though we are in a negotiation.

THE HIDDEN RULES OF RELATIONSHIP

Lisa comes in six weeks later, a very different woman.

LISA: I always knew that I was compromising in this relationship. It was never quite right, but I was willing to do the work because I believed he was worth it.

THOMAS: And now?

L: Frankly, he would have to do an awful lot to make up for this. Unless he comes back with a ring, he'd better not show up at all. I deserve better than this!

T: What have you been up to? How have you kept busy?

L: Well, I took your suggestion. I reconnected with friends, and they all say the same thing. I deserve better. Better treatment, better results.

T: I agree. Unless you are being loved and honored, you shouldn't be in this situation.

L: Well, It's going to take an awful lot to convince me to come back!

Notice that Lisa is now in a position where she is valuing herself more. Even through her anger and her bargaining, she is clear that she needs more. She is becoming strong enough to acknowledge the real possibility that Bob, and what he brings to the table, is not enough. She is starting to acknowledge her needs and wants in this relationship, even as she begins to accept the real possibility that it may be over.

Bargaining fails as the veil falls from our eyes. We become incensed by the idea that we have worked so hard, only to find ourselves here. It isn't fair and we are filled with rage. Some times the stages come all at once, and sometimes in the order that we need them to show up.

Lisa came in two weeks later, very emotional, very distraught.

LISA: What was it all for? (crying) I was the perfect girlfriend. Now, I have nothing!

THOMAS: I want to remind you that these are just your feelings of the moment. It is not going to feel this way forever.

L: I can't believe I did all of this work and I have nothing. I turned myself inside out for this man! How can life be this unfair? At least when I was with Bob, I had something! Now I have pain!

T: We talked about this. You weren't only working on your relationship with Bob. You have been working on your relationship life. You are learning what you need to learn in order to create the love relationship you want. I know you're hurting now but I promise you, nothing is wasted. The universe is a perfect accountant. You can't do all of this work on relationship and not have it pay off. Having gone through this, you will never settle for a love that doesn't give you what you want. I know that it feels like a high price to pay right now, but you are building a future that you will like.

L: Really? When will that show up? When I'm fifty?

Within the pain and suffering the anger begins to emerge. This is a useful and powerful emotion that gives us the energy to rebuild. This emotion is a mixed blessing; it is useful because we no longer feel helpless. It puts us in that aggressive space, which can be difficult to negotiate, and care must be taken not to become bitter.

When we don't choose to contain the anger to the subject at hand, we can let it leak into other areas. It feels good to flex the muscles after being so confined for so long, but we intuitively sense that it is not the final outcome.

It is certainly a relief to feel like we don't care or hurt the way we did, but at the end of the day it doesn't always feel productive. We have a tiger by the tail and we are not sure what to do with it. Keep in mind, even as we feel this general sense of anger that it is specific to the area of relationship. Resist the need to be bitter; as with each stage, this will change as well.

Eventually the futility of this bargaining gives way to depression. We are no longer holding on to a sense of possibility in this situation. The newness of action has worn off, leaving us feeling deflated. "What's the point?" is a very common feeling at this stage. Remember, this is all transitory. We will not stay in this place of depression, either. Depression is that stage where what we had is gone and we have not yet created anything to replace it.

Six months after the breakup Lisa came in feeling listless and defeated.

LISA: I really don't know how much more of this I can take. I actually had a date the other night and had to end it early. I don't think I'm ready for anything new. I can't focus, I can't concentrate.

THOMAS: You know, you are working internally to resolve the past, and you might not feel like participating right now. Force yourself to get out there when you can, and indulge yourself when you can't get out there. This is not any final outcome. You are resolving what you need to. You aren't going to stay in this place either.

L: If I just knew that I'd feel good again, I could put up with anything.

T: You're in the stretch run. You're going to wake up one day and feel totally different. I guarantee that you will look at this time and even laugh.

L: Well, I'm not laughing now. I don't know the last time I heard myself laugh.

T: Give it time and keep maintaining. If you knew that you are exactly where you need to be in order to get everything you want, you would willingly pay this price.

L: I'll have to take your word for it.

I could feel the weariness in Lisa as she longed for an end to this painful time. The pain can be overwhelming and seem as though it is endless. In a real way, the worst of it is passing and she will begin to heal in earnest. Even though Lisa seems bitter, she is still hearing me, as I give context and meaning to her suffering. She needs to know at this point that the suffering is not all for nothing. When the pain passes, as it will, what will remain is the reality that she is doing all of this work in order to create a working relationship, one in which she can get what she needs and wants. She is working on her relationship life and learning necessary lessons along the way.

The final stage, acceptance, arrives with grace and dignity. Acceptance is the act of taking responsibility for our lives and our circumstances. There is great power in this simple act; it is an unremarkable shift that changes everything.

It has been eight months since Lisa and Bob broke up. She arrives with a decidedly different energy.

LISA: Well, I have to say you were right about one thing.

THOMAS: What is that?

L: I can honestly say that it doesn't hurt anymore. I know what happened. In fact, I'm clearer about what happened then ever before. I can't believe how much power I gave away to Bob and that relationship. I wasn't admitting it, but I felt like I was nothing without him. I'm almost embarrassed for the woman I was.

T: Don't be embarrassed. We all give our power away in relationship. Until we know better, we think that we are supposed to behave that way. The problem is that when love leaves, it takes our power with it and we're left with nothing.

L: I see that now. I didn't like the person I was very much. She was such a fool!

T: (laughs) Welcome to the club! Love makes fools of us all, but the real fools are the ones that refuse to learn what you've learned. You have just experienced a master class in love, and you will never make the same mistakes again.

L: Great. I'll make new ones. What is love supposed to look like now?

T: How about this model: real partnership and mutual respect? You can be madly in love and still not give your power away. You can build and grow together and still be relevant in the world. There is a great model for you to follow that will give you everything you want.

L: Sign me up!

T: Your ticket has already been bought and paid for. All of your determination to learn and grow through this will pay off beautifully.

Lisa is a success story when we look at the outcome, but at any given point it might look very different. She went on to create a far more realistic relationship based on her needs and personality, and she is still thriving in it. She got her payoff because she was willing to go through these stages and look for her power and her growth. It wasn't a meteoric arc straight to happiness, but a long tenuous road, but her determination saw her through it.

All or many of these stages can be happening simultaneously, so don't be thrown if you are feeling some of this and some of that. There is no hard and fast rule on the order of our growth. Acceptance, like the dawn, sneaks in on little cats feet. You find that, having spent all of the other emotions, there is now a part of you that is truly ready to move on. This doesn't mean that you like what has happened; only that you are no longer in denial. You are no longer holding on to any illusion that the relationship will continue. By accepting, we can now move on. By moving on we are creating a new space, one that real love can grow in.

There is something to learn in each of these stages, and a freedom that will come from working through them. Emotions have a virtual reality of their own, but we need to be vigilant in order not to buy in to these "realities." Grieving is a journey and we must be committed to getting what we can from this journey. When you don't know what else to do, learn and grow.

WRITE IT DOWN
One of the best tools for coping during this period is journaling. We get to peak in on our mind and discover what we feel through our writing. *The Artist's Way: a Spiritual Path to Higher Creativity* by Julia Cameron suggests a method called "morning pages" to unlock the mind.

The purpose of these pages is to recover a sense of safety in the world; by writing our truth we discover what it is that we want in the world. We are reconnecting with that creative part of each of us and giving voice to the inner self. The exercise gives freedom and permission to let out everything we are feeling and thinking, without editing and without judgment.

A powerful variation on this theme would be to give yourself permission to write in the morning about your experience with the pain and struggle of the end of this relationship, from that same non-judgmental space. Allow yourself to say everything that you need to say about the experience that you are going through. Talk about the loss of relationship. Vent the anger and the pain, the guilt and your fears. Reveal yourself to yourself along the way.

You give yourself a sense of being heard through this exercise and an opportunity to stay in touch with your personal journey. If the purpose of this breakup is to learn, then this is a useful tool to do so. You will discover and uncover feelings you didn't know you were having, and will be surprised and moved by what comes out of you. This is a time to truly value yourself, and this is a meaningful way to acknowledge that inner voice. Release without judgment and you will experience great relief. Let it pour out of you without worrying about how it sounds.

This is an exercise "for your eyes only!" Keep your privacy so that you feel the freedom and permission to say anything that you need to say. You may grow to love this exercise. Let some pages accrue before you decide to read them back. Let this dialogue grow. This is a way of truly taking care of you through a difficult time. Perhaps it is the opportunity to provide the nurturing that you didn't receive in your love relationship.

KEEP TALKING

It's important that we have the opportunity to verbalize our experience along the way. We need a sense that someone knows what is going on with us. This is a huge opportunity to connect with the people in our world with news that deeply concerns us. To be heard is one of our basic human needs. To know that we are known, to trust that we are seen, these are as essential at this time as the air we breathe.

How do we manage this effectively? Be sure to spread it around. Don't wear one person out with your tale; rotate your friends and family so that they don't get "used up." Yes, they love you and care about you, but no, they cannot keep hearing the story non-stop.

Part of effective pain-management is to find resources and use them judiciously. If you talk to a best friend one day, talk to your mom the next. Don't overtax your resources. This is a chance to try talking to new people. You may be surprised at who steps up and who does not in this time of crisis. Often, people form indelible bonds at times like this. To share this kind of intimacy is the opportunity to make a friend for life.

Include the people you share with in your conversation. Listen as well as talking. Let them participate with you and share their experiences and knowledge. Nothing is more off-putting than an impenetrable stream of words coming at us without a break. Create dialogues, not monologues. Listen, go slow and don't try to tell everything at once. Pace yourself (and them) and really try to communicate your experience. The art of making friends is within the sharing of intimacies.

In our effort to tell our story it is essential that we listen as well. Often, life is speaking through the person we are talking with, and life has many messages of wisdom. Take in their experiences and even their mistakes. When we connect on this level, we are no longer alone and we are utilizing the spiritual aspect of connection.

STAY BUSY

When you are in the midst of your feelings, go with them, express them, and write them down. Manage your feelings in all of the ways that we've spoken about. When you aren't in the sway of your emotions, let them go. Keep yourself busy and occupied as much as possible. Get out of the house. See a movie, share a meal. Go to a party you don't want to go to. Don't do this because it will be fun or exciting; it probably won't be. Do it because you are changing your energy. Put yourself out there in the world because you will feel marginally better when you do. Cultivate habits that you have wanted to build during this time. Go to museums you've wanted to see. Fill your time and get busy.

This is not cheating; it is simply using your time wisely. You can't sit around and grieve all day, day in and day out. It isn't useful, or even real. Pain, like most sensations in life, pulses off and on. It doesn't flow in a steady stream. Like the universe it clicks on, and clicks off. You will have times where you are absolutely pain-free, and you should make the most of them. Make hay while the sun shines; have a good time when you can. Build up some emotional reserve for the times when you are in your feelings and must deal with them. Deal when you have to deal, and do so thoroughly and as expressively as you can; talk, write, cry, relate. When the feelings aren't present, give yourself a break; play, laugh, enjoy life. We are creatures of many colors; don't try to be all or nothing. Make your rule of thumb for pain management at the end of a relationship this: I will deal with the pain when I have to, and I won't deal with it when I don't have to.

THE FUTURE

The most painful exercise that people go through at the end of a relationship is musing about the future—theirs and their partner's. The following are some of the most painful questions we get stuck on:

Will I ever be with someone again?
Is this the last relationship I'll ever be in?
How will I meet someone in the future?
Will he/she meet someone new before I do?
Why aren't I over this yet?
Who is ever going to love me?
Will I ever fall in love again?
Am I too old to start over?
Will I ever want to love again?
Will anyone ever want me again?
What are they doing now?
Is she thinking of me?
Does he still care?
Is he already dating?
Is she in love already?

These are the thoughts and mental pictures that prey on us in our weakened state. We are not a position to think about creating anything new when we have just ended a relationship and neither is our ex-partner. We shouldn't even try. At this point in time, we are not equipped to think positively about relationship, nor do we have the energy to create one. We are in the midst of a very deep process and the reasons that this love didn't work haven't been sorted through yet. Turn these painful thoughts away at the gates of your mind. Refuse to think them or be ruled by these images.

We have to focus and learn what there is to learn. We can think about rebuilding with intelligence only when we discover our destructive patterns and habits. It is useless to put futile and unnecessary expectations on ourselves. We have only one job to do, and that is to master the situation we have just gotten out of.

There will come a time when we are ready, willing and able to create a new relationship, including doing all of the work that that means, but this is not that time. Our fear makes us demand too much from ourselves. The impatience we feel is the fear that we never will love again. This fear has no place in our thinking right now. Refuse to deal with that question; it isn't the time. Turn these thoughts away. It is your mind and you have dominion over it. You do not have to entertain any thought that you choose not to think. Literally refuse to think these thoughts. Hit the delete button.

Each of these questions has a hidden desire beneath it. "Will I ever be with someone again?" This question contains an underlying request. If we turn each painful thought into the actionable desire that is beneath it, we make that thought useful. "I want to love again in a way that works for both of us." This is the actionable desire underneath the original thought.

Take each toxic question and find the desire beneath it. You will have your roadmap for the future. In addition, the desire is a higher vibrational rate than the original nagging question, and the higher thought is more capable of bringing better results. You will resonate to a higher frequency and feel and think better.

LEAVING OR LEFT

The order of our feelings at the end of a love relationship is going to be different, depending on whether we are the initiator or the recipient: are you the one leaving, or the one who has been left?

It matters a great deal; if you chose to leave, the demons that attack first are feelings of doubt, regret and uncertainty. There may be a growing concern that you made the wrong choice, or that you left too soon. The reasons for the decision fade long before the feelings of doubt remain and continue to attack. You may well have to fight a rising dread that you made a terrible decision that has left you with nothing. The guilt and fears of this position can grind you down and take away your resolve and peace of mind. You may try to assuage that guilt by reverting to your anger, but more often than not, this creates a deep conviction that you are somehow wrong. Being left creates its own set of dilemmas that we will address following this discussion.

What is the solution to the dilemma created by leaving? We could live in guilt and uncertainty for the rest of our lives but perhaps there is a better way. The answer to managing this set of feelings is in three parts:

Be vigilant: make sure that you do everything you can within the situation to resolve issues, while still in the relationship and after. Handle this parting with simplicity, honesty and respect. Own what is yours.

Be vocal: let people know what is going on as you go through it; share what you can of the details and developments. Look for what there is to learn.

Be accurate: write it down along the way. Keep a journal throughout to accurately reflect the choices and reasons that you are making these decisions.

All of our feelings are just a signal that something inside needs to be healed. Feelings are not a reflection of reality. Feelings are actually a result, not a cause. An event happens; a deep drama ensues within, with indictments and judgments, trials and convictions. Thoughts and ideas form.

This is the compelling drama of feelings and that drama wants to ensnare you. Don't buy into it; the only purpose of these feelings is to learn. Pain is a signal to heal, whether it is in the ankle or in the heart.

What is there to learn from guilt and regret? Guilt, like all negative feelings is based on fear. It is the fear of punishment, by God, society or you. The definition of sin according to the American Heritage dictionary is this: "A condition of estrangement from God resulting from transgression or disobedience." I like this definition because it clearly displays that "sin" is a condition or state of mind resulting from some action, and that there is no independent punishment for that action.

The state of mind of sin is its own punishment; it is separation, in this case, from God. Our own "sinful" acts that cause us guilt and regret create the state of mind: fear of punishment. They separate us from ourselves. We lose the safety of "right action" and we live in fear of punishment, and that fear is the punishment. Guilt is its own punishment. Don't believe the illusion of guilt.

So what can we learn from the feelings caused by leaving? That there is no "punishment" for the action we've taken. The punishment is an illusion. In this universe we live in, there is cause and effect, but nothing as judgmental as punishment. If we tell our troubles to the stars will the stars move for us? The stars do not care about our little drama, and are not looking to punish us.

Responsibility is the opposite of guilt; it is the willingness to take on the consequences of our actions and live with those consequences. Responsibility is a "running toward," rather than a "running away." The real lesson behind guilt and regret is this: when you embrace responsibility, guilt and regret melt away like the illusions that they are. Regret is the fear that we have made the wrong choice. If we believe in destiny, there are no wrong choices. There is only the mystery of why.

Why was this choice perfect and why was this set of events meant to be, and for everyone's highest good? By living in this question, answers will be revealed. It is a model that, when we impose it onto the situation, we will come to new insights and understandings. In short, we will learn.

If you are the one being left in relationship, if all of this was not your idea, feelings of worthlessness, abandonment and despair can attack first. Anxiety, or fear of fear, often comes up. It is easier to leave than to be left, because we are embracing newness and change and moving into it. When we are the one being abandoned something is being forced onto us. We haven't ostensibly chosen these events. There are feelings of helplessness and rage. We feel invalidated and cast aside. How do we manage this?

Choose it: Determine that this breakup is what you have chosen and find real reasons for these choices.

Keep your dignity: Don't beg. Refuse to be pathetic. If he/she is meant to come back, they will. Take the opportunity to redefine yourself.

Fill your life: Get busy. Get social. Talk, reestablish friendships. Take on new hobbies and interests. Become the person you want to be. Don't isolate.

How do we combat the feelings of self-loathing and judgment? The first order of business is to take on that I have chosen this destiny. On a higher spiritual plane I decided that this is the perfect move in my life for my learning and growth and happiness. This is a way of taking our power back from the situation.

Notice that when you take this position on, you feel a sense of relief. It can seem facile to say that you chose this ending, but in a spiritual sense it is absolutely true. When you embrace this point of view you understand relationship in a new way. It really is a spiritual agreement that two people make in order to learn and grow together and individually.

Imagine that your two hearts, minds and spirits have come together to teach each other, and that when that teaching is done, you have agreed to move apart. The purpose of a model is to illuminate. Don't get into an argument about whether or not this is true; take it on as a premise, a model for learning.

This model will allow you to see why you would choose a situation like this, and ultimately reveal what there is to learn from it. We try to "be realistic" in these situations, to "take our medicine" and face reality, but we have to know what reality means. There is a higher reality that we are always engaged with and it reveals more truth and purpose than day-to-day, conventional wisdom. You will reach the end of suffering when you find purpose for that suffering.

We chose this on some level, and made the thousand little choices that brought us here. Meditate on this. Take the time to find out why you chose this reality. You will learn that you have very good reasons for not continuing this relationship;

you will even discover that, given the chance, you would make those same choices again and again.

Without the constraints of the old model, we are free to reinvent our lives. Just as new relationship is the opportunity to reinvent ourselves, so too, the end of love gives that same opportunity. Who would you most want to be with perfect permission? What does it look like in the world? How does that make you feel? Give yourself the freedom and permission to take on new energy and new interests. Some of these interests will stay with you for life and some will fall away. No matter. What is important is taking on the new, even as we learn what we need to learn.

SELF-NURTURING

Don't reach for hope right now; it is too painful. Hope is actually a negative emotion masquerading as a positive. We "hope" the situation will get better, despite our expectation that it will continue to be bad. If we expected good news, we wouldn't need hope. Avoid painful tactical errors. We have no control over our circumstances; we only have control over our experience.

Hope is an incredibly deceptive emotion. While it seems to be positive it is actually based on negative assumptions. I hope that the situation works out only because I actually suspect that it will not.

We wouldn't need the windup of big positive emotion if we actually believed in the situation in the first place. If I am hoping that "she comes back to me," I am already living in the experience that she will not be coming back, and I am using hope as some kind of superstitious talisman to lure her back.

Hope is the emotional equivalent of magical thinking: maybe with enough hope added the situation will reverse itself. Think of the last time you hoped for something. Didn't you apply hope because somewhere you suspected the worst?

Hope creates attachments which, in turn, generate great emotional pain. We can only be hurt by that which we are attached to and hope is the culprit. The fact that Hollywood has put a pretty pink bow around it and created songs with "hope" as its central theme, does not give hope any magical power; it merely makes hope yet another narcotic to keep people inert and stop them from taking effective action.

Better to face the uncertainty of the unknown than the saccharin sweetness of narcotizing hope.

Don't strain yourself and imagine you should be in a different place than where you are. Assume that you're exactly where you're supposed to be. Put one foot in front of another and deal only with what is right in front of you. Don't worry about the future; there is already a version of you in the future handling whatever needs to be handled. Just take care of you in this moment.

That is a simple concept, yet, how many people actually know how to take care of themselves? We are not taught to self-nurture. How will we know what we need in this or any other situation? We can find a useful model that will give us insight into what we need: imagine a hurt child. Picture this child after the hurt, and what is it that they need the most? A child would need warmth, understanding and compassion. That hurt child would also crave a feeling of safety.

Ultimately, we want some understanding of what happened and a way of dealing with it for the future. We are that hurt child, and the sooner we start to nurture ourselves properly, the more quickly we can work through the pain. All of our childhood patterns show up at this time. This is an opportunity to gain a window into our own psyche. We can take this task on as the next piece of work in the business of life. We can determine to do a masterful job of taking care of ourselves during this breakup.

The future will come; it inevitably does, and with it will bring new opportunities and change. This is truly a limited situation. Despite how it may feel, we will not stay in this dark place, so, in a way, it is a rare chance to master the skill of nurturing ourselves. That makes this time incredibly valuable. Our happiness in life depends entirely on our relationship with this inner child, and this is the rare chance to dramatically improve that relationship.

Most people tear at themselves at this point in time because of the pain, but we can choose a different strategy. We can choose to find the real value here, and as we do, the pain passes quickly. This time is not the opportunity for self-judgment, but for self-nurturing.

Take this time, because it is no accident, nor is it a mistake. Our Higher Self and life have conspired to put us here, in this moment. Through great effort and pain we have brought ourselves to a place of possibility for incredible growth. Recognize the real value of this time and you will quickly find the way out of suffering.

Along with the opportunity to self-nurture, it is also a rich time to connect to others. As I have said, you will be surprised to see who steps up, and who doesn't. The art of making a friend has everything to do with sharing intimacies, and this is an opportunity to share on a heartfelt level. The people that you connect with at this time can become friends for life because of the nature of what we have to share.

Don't expect people to seek you out, however, and don't make it a test. People have enough in their lives to deal with, so they won't necessarily come find you. That doesn't mean they don't care.

This is a time for courage, and putting yourself out there. Do not look for solutions or answers from people, just let them be there. You may even have something to teach them. It can be important to tell your supportive friends not to try to fix you or help you, or even give you advice, but simply to be there and listen. It is a real art, and you will find some people are better at it than others.

TRY NOT TO JUDGE OR BLAME

We are analytical creatures; we love to break things down and scrutinize the details. This end of relationship time sets the mind spinning. We go over the "evidence" and render our interpretations endlessly. We make "case" and "counter-case," assigning blame and responsibility alternately on others and ourselves. The problem with this analytical process is this: the moment we get into the details of our situation, we lose the bigger picture.

Given that a breakup is one of the biggest events in our lives, we are going to need as much clarity and objectivity as we can get. Judgment, by definition, breaks down the whole into smaller parts, as we seek to reinforce a point of view. Notably, the point of view is often there first, and then we attempt validation through judgment.

Ask yourself where you would be best served: by concluding that it was his or her fault? Will it help to assign blame? It can give us some emotional satisfaction to arrive at one position or the other, but that rarely reflects clarity. Taking responsibility for the situation means being willing to know that each party has a share in the responsibility for what has happened, and that every person involved came together to make this result. Fight for the biggest picture you can see, because that one picture holds the most truth and insight.

HOW LONG?

"Okay, I'm willing to go through this, but I want a time limit!" Who can blame us for wanting an end to suffering? No one wants unending pain. It is too much for the mind to bear to think that pain will go on without resolution.

It may not seem true now, but this is an incredibly valuable time. Know this, this too will pass; when we look back on it, it will have passed quickly. As we look back on our past we see that it all worked out perfectly somehow. This is true of the future as well, even if we can't experience that in the moment.

Use the time, get everything you can from this period, because, whether you are realizing it or not, the pain is changing everyday. When we look at the pain moment-to-moment it looks like a constant stream, but we have moments where there is no pain. That is the nature of pain; it hurts, then it doesn't. There are even moments where we laughed and had fun, through the pain. Don't be guilty or ashamed of this; it is natural for pain to have a pulse and a rhythm. The way to get through this time most quickly is to determine to learn what we need to learn.

Roll up your sleeves and get busy. Don't wait for the feelings to come and get you; go after them. Know that every negative feeling is an illusion, and determine to bust through that illusion to the truth and insight underneath. Underneath every negative thought there is a positive desire. Do your best to identify the underlying desire and you will defeat the pain, every time.

We can be victims or we can be in our power. Each position is equally open to us. Make a choice, and decide to manage the pain, powerfully and efficiently. If it were a pain in the knee we wouldn't moan and sentimentalize that pain. We would handle it as quickly and with as little drama as possible. Can you imagine romanticizing your knee-pain? "I miss the way it was, it's so sad!" "It used to be perfect, and now it's all ruined." I don't think so. We go to a doctor, get it wrapped and get it handled, without nostalgia.

We can be sloppy and indulgent or we can choose to be sharp and efficient. We can't afford indulging in negative thinking about the future; it will just take away our resolve. Unless we have a crystal ball, we do not know what the future will bring. We aren't supposed to be worrying about the future right now. We can determine to take pride in how well we handle this time and how quickly we get through it. Make an intention to recover quickly, to learn everything needed to learn from the situation, and to change what needs to be changed. You chose this challenge: now choose what you've chosen.

EXERCISE 1

Buy a composition notebook and start a journal for this time.

Write in it every morning when you wake up. Pour out your thoughts without editing.

Use this journal every time you want to express anything about the relationship. (Or anything else)

Keep this journal for your eyes only.

Don't read it, just write in it.

EXERCISE 2

Make a list of friends and family that are resources for you to talk to.

Call or talk to at least one of them a day.

Listen as well as talk.

Rotate them. Don't use them up.

NINETEEN

MORE MAINTENANCE

Elaine has been out of her relationship for two weeks. She left Dave because he wouldn't commit.

ELAINE: I'm so bored! I don't know what to do with my time. It isn't so much that I miss Dave. He ran like a thief when I suggested moving in. I just miss the relationship thing. What am I supposed to think about?

THOMAS: Thinking may not be your friend right now. Why not make a list of everything you've wanted to do that you haven't had a chance to?

E: But everything I think of, I think of doing with him.

T: Do you think that he's thinking about you?

E: He's off with his friends having fun and getting over me.

T: Then clearly you need a new strategy.

Ending a relationship certainly brings a mixture of relief and pain, and yet, somehow we must go on. As time goes by, we find new tricks and strategies to get through. All the advice in the world doesn't seem like enough, and, at the same time, it's all too much. Because we are no longer engaged in this all-consuming activity called relationship, we have a lot more time on our hands. We have to manage ourselves and our time in a whole new way.

MAKE THIS TIME COUNT

Hard as it is to believe, this is a unique and special time. Eventually we will see this time differently when we look back, and we will want to have done some things differently. We can give this time meaning: we can take on something new or something that we have been meaning to get to and haven't gotten around to. Start painting, or start writing, or go after that career move you've been thinking about. You need a challenge that is as big as the loss you are experiencing.

There is an energy that is unique to the time, and we can use this energy now. We have the resources to take on a challenge that is as strong as our emotions. Loss brings a force that has momentum and power. We can let it consume us or we can use that energy to drive us.

What I proposed to Elaine was, "Be a slave to a purpose." Immerse yourself in a pursuit that is bigger than you, I told her, and let your only problem be that you don't have enough time to do everything you need to for that pursuit. You have a drive now like no other, and if you think of it as energy rather than pain, you will see it correctly. You need the purpose to go with it. Don't even worry about whether that purpose is your ultimate goal. Pick a direction and go! Take on something that you have put off until now. It is important to give your life meaning and direction right now, even if the direction is arbitrary. If you don't aim yourself in some direction, you will dissipate. If you do find a purpose, you will make something good and real happen. Movement creates direction of its own. Just move. Do it now!

This is not the time to worry or think about creating relationship again, there is time for that later. Don't bother about the size or importance of what you take on, just dive in. You will find clarity and direction as you go. Maybe it will be the pursuit of the greatest dream in your life, or perhaps just a useful and powerful distraction. Either way, an essential part of self-nurturing right now is to find a passion and a direction and immerse yourself in it."

TAKING YOUR POWER BACK

As we immerse ourselves in a purpose and direction, we will find that when we do dive in some interesting changes occur. As we get involved in the details of a new enterprise, we discover that we start to feel better. There is a reason for this: we are starting to use our personal power in a new and productive way. It feels good to stretch our muscles as we begin to realize that we are still relevant in the world. We take our power back from everything that we have given that power away to, and we find resources within ourselves that lay dormant.

Gaining personal power is a fascinating process. Power accrues with attention to detail. We fan a small flame within us and little by little that fire starts to grow.

Here is more of what I told Elaine: "Elaine, be intensely interested in whatever you choose to do. Make a study of what you are up to; decide to learn and master the area. As you grow, so will your power. Your sense of self will begin to heal, little by little. You may regain your humor, your clarity for a minute or an hour or a day. You will notice your mind starting to work better. These are all the signs that your power is returning.

As you gain authority and knowledge in this new area you are interested in, you gain stature in the world. Your identity starts to reshape and reform and you feel like you again. It doesn't matter where you look to find your personal power, it only matters that you get involved. You could start to refinish furniture or take a course in real estate. Take up a hobby of boating or coin collecting, or start to volunteer and visit the sick. Find something that engages you and watch as you change and grow."

HIGHER PURSUITS BRING HIGHER RESULTS

This recovery time at the end of a relationship has unique challenges. Often we are tired of being in our own skin; we become weary of that same internal monologue. Focusing on others at this point can be easier and more accessible than focusing on ourselves. There are payoffs for getting involved in improving the world and becoming a humanitarian.

When we reach out to other people, we actually feel useful. This is a huge antidote to that "useless" feeling at the end of a relationship. When we get involved we travel an arc from "nobody wants me!" to "I'm making a difference!" We start to see ourselves as contributing and adding value to the world. We can run the spectrum from helping a friend out to counseling troubled youth, and every bit of that service will make us feel better and more powerful. We begin using our energy constructively, and the most important person in the world will notice: you.

Be of service. Service is a powerful way to get out of ourselves, out of our own heads, and into the world. It is energetically, emotionally and spiritually "right action." Imagine that for every hour of service performed, one day of suffering is eliminated from our mourning period. A tremendous and valuable shortcut, service can cut down the grieving period dramatically as we re-sculpt our identity and sense of self.

LEARN, LEARN, LEARN

The end of a relationship is painful because we experience our powerlessness in our situation. We experience a breakdown between our intention and our ability to manifest that intention. We no longer control our experience and so, we are controlled by it. Nothing is more frustrating than being faced with our own helplessness.

The antidote, of course, is to learn whatever we are meant to learn and change what we can change in our lives. One enlightened part of us has bothered to set up the situation as a way to learn. Another part of us feels as though something bad has happened to us. Often, the personality does not know what the higher self is up to, and when we experience this disconnect, we feel like victims. Take it on like this is your choice, even if you're not feeling it. Choosing to learn, taking on the responsibility for our circumstances puts us back in our power.

The rush of emotion can often be overwhelming, and blinds us like a light too bright to look into. It will pass, and it is best to notice these emotions without believing what the feeling seems to be telling us.

Emotions have a virtual reality of their own. We see "evidence" that accompanies the feeling. We begin to believe these feelings as truth when, in fact, they are only opportunities to learn. When we see through the filter of our feelings it looks like a very compelling reality, but we must look for the objective truth.

I have watched people rewrite history according to whatever feelings they are feeling that day; they reinterpret the events of their breakup to accommodate these feelings. It feels accurate, because they are matching the feeling to some arbitrary reality, but that is the pain talking, not truth. Dare to look at your fears and see what they are trying to tell you. Are they saying that you will be alone from now on? That you will never love again? What is the bottom line of those fears? Does it mean you will never have a good experience again? Can that really be so? What is the underlying desire beyond those fears? Look at the worst possibility and look at the best outcome. Reality is somewhere in there, but not likely at either extreme. Fear, by definition, is not truth. Here is a useful acronym: F-E-A-R: False Evidence Appearing Real.

The reality we experience through fear is an interpretation of the future. The underlying desire is always positive. We want love and companionship; we want to believe in a future that holds real partnership and comfort. This positive message is the reality beneath the feelings and the message that those feelings hold.

Ninety-five percent of what we fear never happens and the other five percent will not be the experience that we've anticipated. When we examine the past we will see that this is so. So little of what we concern ourselves with actually happens, and when it does, the experience is not what we expected or anticipated.

Worry is an attempt to control life; we feel that if we can anticipate and second-guess life, we will somehow be armed against it. Being in the truth means that we choose to face the unknown and have no control over it; this is harder for us to deal with than any scenario we can imagine. However, when we manage fear-based thinking, the unknown becomes a place where all possibility exists: finding new love, meeting new challenges, making your fortune, etc. To dispel its power, notice the habit of worry, but don't believe in it.

This time is an opportunity to learn how to treat ourselves with care and with love. There is a tendency to indulge in self-judgment during this time; determine to go easy on yourself instead. Judgment blocks us from seeing the bigger picture.

We can be proactive and make the deliberate choice not to judge ourselves and all of our actions in the relationship and out of it. If being in relationship is an opportunity to reinvent ourselves, the change of being alone is that same opportunity. Decide who you want to be from now on without obligation to the past or the way you were within the relationship. Take on being powerful and decisive in life.

Elaine needed some direction and a new way of thinking. This is what I told her: "Make a list of the qualities you want to add to your life and your personality and start to integrate them. Look at your circumstances and deliberately take on a positive spin. Take on that you chose this situation for your good and for your growth. Tell a new story about yourself and tell it like it is good news.

Don't fall into the trap of morbidly grieving. It isn't real and it isn't productive. Nobody, even under the worst circumstances, is in pain 24 hours a day; we are just not wired that way. Pain, like everything else in this universe, pulses on and pulses off. There is nothing to learn by trying to hold on to the pain. Deal with it when it is present and let it go when it isn't."

CHANGE EVERYTHING

The Chinese character for the word "crisis" contains within it the symbol for opportunity and the symbol for danger. Which do we choose in our present situation? When we wallow and dissipate we are courting the danger. When we choose newness we are embracing opportunity. I often recommend the following strategy: change everything you can possibly change during this time. Change your wardrobe, change your eating habits, change your hair, change where you play; change everything. Take on the opportunity to try new hobbies, new interests, new hangouts and new friends.

Leave the dead past in the dust! Adopt an identity of change: you will lose nothing. Everything of value will sustain, and everything useless will fall away. You are no longer beholden to being who you were. It didn't get you where you wanted to go, anyway. Take permission to become. Chances are, you didn't like that version of you anyway.

Let the winds of change blow through your life like a rush of fresh air that clears out the old stale habits and the old self. Declare yourself emancipated. It is liberation day and you must celebrate it.

Yes, there will be pain at some point, and we will have to deal with that pain, but this time shouldn't be defined by pain. At the end of the day, it is about the new and exciting possibilities that have opened up. Don't be ashamed or hesitant about being positive and optimistic about this change. Let the world see you as excited by the challenge. Put yourself and the world on notice that this is the chance that you've been waiting for and you are going to make the most of this opportunity.

ACT "AS IF"

There is a technique called "acting as if." It's simple enough; we take on the premise that we want to create is already true. We commit to the choice. We've all done this at one time or another in our lives: think of the job interview when you acted as if you weren't nervous. Remember that first date when you acted confident and behaved, as if you knew what you were doing. We use the magic "as if" in order to enter the world of new possibility.

This is a very useful technique because it calls up something new in us and gives us permission to be the way we would want to be. Now, I'm not suggesting that you act as if you are an Indian heiress or the CEO of IBM, but I do suggest that you practice acting as if this breakup was your idea. Try on for size that you are delighted with your circumstances. Take an hour a day to live the premise that you are free by your own choice and thrilled with the freedom. Be enthralled by your circumstances; not because you actually are, but because, when you take this on, it will become true for you, little by little.

Ask yourself Goethe's immortal question: "How would you live if you knew you couldn't fail?" Think about that for a moment and let yourself feel the way you would feel. Imagine that everything you touch turns to gold and everything you attempt works beautifully. This is not an exercise in self-delusion, but rather a taking on of possibility. To live into this premise calls forth the winner in you. When you try this exercise, the feeling will be familiar to you. Why? Because you have that version of you inside: the "you" that can't fail. We all have an internal "winner" within. We can summon up this version of us at will. This exercise empowers that "winner" within.

Nothing succeeds like success. Why? Because when we operate from an atmosphere of success there is an expectation of success, from the world and from ourselves. We don't have control over outside circumstances, but we do have control of our inner experience. Change your premise and you change your life. Assume success, love and possibility. Your instrument will respond to whatever you feed it: Act "as if."

BREAK THE HABIT

In his book, *The Organization of Behavior: A Neuropsychological Theory,* Donald O. Hebb presented a theory of behavior based on the physiology of the nervous system. Hebb reduced the types of physiological evidence into a theory of how habits are formed: the Hebbian learning occurs because "cells that fire together, wire together." Take the example of a billboard advertisement that shows a particular car alongside a beautiful woman. Two sets of brain cells will fire in response: the brain cells that control sexual arousal and the brain cells that recognize the car. After repeatedly viewing the billboard, these two unrelated sets of brain cells become physically wired together simply because they have fired together again and again. Eventually, seeing the car by itself will cause the arousal brain cells to fire and the prospective buyer to feel "turned on." This is the evolution of a habit.

Now imagine all of the cells that have been wired together in this continuous association called "relationship." The pain/pleasure loops, the nostalgia loops, the family and friends associations go on and on. It explains why, at the end of a relationship, everything reminds you of him or her. The physical process of ending a relationship demands a breaking all of those associations in order to make new ones.

A powerful truth about these neural connections is that they do become weaker when they are no longer stimulated. Eventually these synapses "unhook" from each other. The good news is that physiologically, we can break the connection. The quicker we make new habits and associations, the quicker that connection will be broken.

This explains why the pain is often sharper for the person being left than the one leaving: he or she is left with all of the old stimuli that continue those cells firing. It also explains why the "geographic cure" or moving away can provide enough new stimuli to keep the old connections from firing. Practically speaking, this is a most compelling reason to make big changes and keep yourself moving forward.

We must take on the physiological task of retraining our neurons. We can create new pleasure associations and new neural patterns that transcend the old. Neurologically speaking, it is not a good idea to continue to dwell in the old patterns, but rather, to create new patterns as quickly as possible.

MAKING NEW HABITS

According to the Trans-theoretical Model of Learning, the five stages of creating a habit are as follows:

Pre-contemplation: Denial of the issue
Contemplation: Acknowledgement of the need for change
Preparation: Forming an intention to change
Action: Affecting change
Maintenance: Repetition of action affecting change

Stage 1 is a kind of denial of the issue based on ignorance or perceived lack of need: "Why diet? I won't feel any better." At the end of relationship it may be the unawareness that our old habits are causing agony and need to be changed. We are lost and are not connected to any action for change.

Stage 2 begins when there is a dawning awareness that something isn't working and needs change. It is a period of pondering and acknowledging. The thoughts begin to occur: "Maybe I do need to get out more." We become aware of a need.

Stage 3 is all about creating an intention to create a new set of behaviors and circumstances. This stage involves preparing to do so: Contemplating buying the gym membership or going to a nutritionist; these are the thoughts associated with this stage. At the end of a relationship this may show up as a determination to become more social.

Action is the keyword for stage 4. I actually go to the gym or attend the classes that I signed up for. It is the stage of trying it on for size; not yet a habit, but the impulse is much more than just an idea. I make a coffee date with a friend. I join a meditation group.

Stage 5: maintenance. We repeat the behaviors and actions that we have created. The brain starts to create new patterns and responses. We have new associations for pleasure and fulfillment. This is the stage that the action migrates from conscious repetition to automatic behavior. Our neurons actually promote these actions and seek the fulfillment of these behaviors.

This is how we create change on an essential level. Creating a habit is a powerful process to identify and master. Simply put, we can embrace every area in which we desire change and apply this process. The evolution of habit is simple and inevitable: ignorance, learning, planning, doing, habit.

In this transitory stage of life, we can see how to apply this process to great effect. This is the time and the means to changing our social life, our physical life and our emotional life. The process starts when we choose to change. We introduce new patterns through the planning and the execution of this process.

How long it takes to create the habit depends on what we are trying to create, but many elements of our lives can be changed very quickly. We begin by imagining how we want your lives to be and then we take action and begin.

CHANGE YOUR LIFE IN 21 DAYS

Many experts agree that it takes 21 days to make a habit or break a habit. The maintenance or final stage of creating a habit can be the most challenging. We generally have the resolve to start but we need follow-through. A strategy to handle maintenance is required.

When I am trying to cultivate a habit I spend some time imagining the results. I will write down my goal. I recognize that it is important to declare myself to the world, to make myself accountable. In addition, I will write down reasons for changing. I will refer to this list every day. There are days when this list will inspire me and days where I am going through the motions, but I understand that I am building new neural patterns. Much like doing the scales on a piano, it is not required that I am thrilled by the process every time, only that I accomplish the task.

I set small achievable goals within the habit I am trying to instill. I visualize the bigger picture, but I only require that I put one foot in front of the other. I don't judge my results; I manage my expectations. Every step toward my goal is progress and I give myself the approval I need to continue to go forward with good will.

Learn how to self-coach through change; anticipate pitfalls and encourage yourself. Forgive yourself for you shortfalls and gently bring yourself back to your path. Be patient and loving with yourself. It matters that you master the task, but it also matters how you treat yourself along the way. Emotionally, we are children and it is essential that you treat yourself as lovingly as you would a child. Talk to your support team and let them know what you're up to. Make yourself accountable to your new habits and patterns. Just knowing that your supports know what you are attempting will give you strength.

Avoid the toxic nay-sayers; there are always those people who are ready and willing to knock us down. We need all the resolve we can get. Take two minutes in the morning to picture yourself succeeding at this new goal. Really see yourself doing it. You can even find pictures that represent the success you want and put them on the refrigerator or around the house. Don't be afraid to be corny; the reason some actions are corny is that they are tried and true. Reward yourself for succeeding and pat yourself on the back for doing so. If you get discouraged or fall off the wagon, forgive yourself immediately and thoroughly (as you would with a good friend) and get back in the program. Do all of this and you will create change.

Fatigue, boredom, depression and stress can all make it difficult to stick with your program. But having a relapse isn't as important as how you deal with that relapse. If you are so devastated by failure that you call your good intentions into question it will make a habit change more difficult for you. If you allow for an occasional relapse and treat the setback as nothing more than a slight misstep that teaches you something, then you are on the right track. Be excited about changing and taking your power back from old habits.

Our lives are our own to shape and invent in the way that we choose. Make this an important time of change.

EXERCISE 1

Find a quality that you would like to add to your personality.

Create a mantra that you can repeat to yourself; a personal cue that describes the change you are creating. (example: I am absolutely patient.)

Use this quality in every social setting that you can experiment with. (a party, card game, etc.)

EXERCISE 2

Choose a reality that you want to create.

Act "as if" this is already so, whether it is confidence or beauty or whatever you have chosen, in every setting in your life.

Notice how the world reacts to this behavior.

Notice your response to the exercise.

Repeat daily for at least 21 days.

EXERCISE 3

Find an area in your life that needs a new habit or routine.

Research what it takes to create that new habit; find a gym, research a diet, for example.

Prepare to take action. Join the gym; stock your pantry with healthy good.

Take action. Go to the gym every day; begin the diet.

Maintain this habit for 21 days and notice how it makes you feel.

SECTION IV

CREATING RELATIONSHIPS

TWENTY

THIS BUSINESS OF LOVE

If I want to get from New York to Boston, I'll consult a map. I'll do whatever preparation is necessary in order to have a smooth trip and get where I want to go. Surprisingly, when it comes to creating relationship people are willing to "wing it." They either don't prepare or have some concept that stops them from getting organized and preparing to create what they want. They want to "fall in love" or be "swept off their feet" or "knocked out" by the experience.

There are very few things I would like to "fall in" and love certainly isn't one of them. That notion isn't a romantic concept; it's a childish illusion. If I were driving without the map, I would end up lost in Rhode Island, scratching my head. Why is it that we expect that love will show up miraculously when we hold that expectation for no other area in life? Does anyone give any thought to how we're going to get there?

GET ORGANIZED

Rather than wait for love to take us we can actually make a plan to create love. Consider this: it is insane to expect to get what we want in any other area without any planning. It is not only ill advised, but delusional. Who are we kidding?

Every major area of accomplishment takes thought and execution; could this be the one area that amazingly takes care of itself? The answer is a resounding "no." If we want to build a business, a partnership, let's say, we would take our first step, not be waiting across a crowded room for a business partner to show up. "Across a crowded room, I saw my future CEO." We don't rely on "magical thinking" to risk our hard earned money and effort on a chance endeavor. We are hard-nosed and practical.

We demand to know what qualifies a person as our business partner. We would probably have a list of qualities that the candidate needs in order to fill the bill. We would research and talk to people we trust concerning what they see. With great care we would approach the interviewing and selection process; checking and second-guessing and researching every step of the way. But for a life partner, we abandon all reason and start to build a relationship with a random person that we happen to have an attraction for.

Hmm, what's wrong with this picture?

GOOD REASONS, BAD REASONS

A good relationship is an accomplishment, like getting a good education. It takes care and nurturing, planning and execution. It is also a high-ticket item that one has to be able to afford. As an endeavor, relationship is going to cost time, effort, planning and emotional good will.

The first order of business is to make a determination: "am I ready for a relationship?" Here are a couple of lousy reasons to create relationship:

"I think I should."
"People will think I'm strange if I don't have a partner."
"I'm bored."
"I'm lonely."
"I am tired of hearing from my relatives: "Are you still single?"

All of these reasons may motivate us to start a search, but they leave us unprepared for following through. No area takes more commitment and presence than relationship. Don't, I repeat, do not enter it casually. This impulsive action is the way that people end up entangled with the wrong person, sometimes for life. Love is not a cure for boredom, or a band-aid for how we show up socially. Neither is it something that we "should" do, for any reason.

This brings up the question: "Are there any good reasons for pursuing relationship?" So here are some good reasons:

"I am ready to find a partner to build with."

"I know what I want in life, and I want a partner to share with."

"I want to learn and grow and explore love."

"I'm in the right time and place in my life to create love."

"I am ready to challenge my love lessons."

Relationship is a feature that requires abundance in our lives. We must have so much fulfillment that it can spill over into supporting a love relationship. Don't look to relationship for what it can give you; be prepared to feed and care for it. Love will not fill in the missing pieces; it will only shine the glaring spotlight on our deficiencies. When we are in our power first, we attract someone at the power level that we are living within. Being at our best, we will attract the best; being at our worst attracts that as well. The law of attraction is indifferent to positive and negative, it simply attracts. That which seemed to be an answer to our problems will quickly turn into an unmanageable nightmare.

WHERE TO START

A good relationship begins with being in a good place in your life; it begins with liking yourself and feeling secure in who you are. Know yourself and know where you are emotionally, socially and in every other way. Wanting love with all of your might is absolutely useless. We must be ready for the work and commitment that love takes.

Being a good public speaker or high wire artist both have something in common; when done well they appear effortless. We sense that this can't be the case; in fact, it takes great concentration and timing. It is the culmination of the mastery of a skill that we are witnessing when we see excellence. Anything worth achieving requires dedication and skill. Relationship is an area that greatly benefits from our willingness to develop skills and to work for the results that we want. Don't be seduced by how easy it looks. You get what you pay for: when you do the work and you will get good results; let the work slide and you're on a slippery slope.

Answer the following questions honestly: Do you like where your life is right now? Do you feel like you are in your power? You are going to attract only those on the same level and in the same space as you. This means that if you are coming from a weak and needy place, that is the quality of the choice you are going to make in relationship. We get our mirror reflection. Make sure you are where you want to be in your life, or at least headed in that direction.

MAKE A ROAD MAP

If I want to get to my desired destination, I make sure to have a map. This translates directly when we are speaking of creating relationship. You must prepare for the journey. Know as much as you can about what you want in a relationship. You cannot just declare that you want the best. "The perfect match," is not quite descriptive enough to define what we are looking for.

If being outdoors is a central part of your life, it might be wise to pick someone with that preference. If you love to exercise, look for this in a partner. We can't just fling open the doors and take all comers, or somewhere down the line there will be incompatibility and conflict. In our neediness we may accept anyone, but in reality we do have strong preferences and requirements. So often we see friends stuck with incompatible partners. This is the result of a lack of planning and foresight. Our needs will choose for us while we are busy focusing elsewhere.

MAKE A LIST

Make a list of qualities that your partner should have. Of course, you must be flexible, ultimately, but start with your clear wants and likes. If I don't create an image of what I want, I will get some unacceptable default result, usually picked through unconscious neurotic need rather than discernment.

In making this list, give yourself permission to ask for exactly what you want; age, type, interests and hobbies. Define your search physically, intellectually, emotionally, spiritually and financially. It is important that your future partner have a compatible spiritual understanding to yours, and that they be on the same page as you in as many areas as possible.

Obviously, there must be some chemistry, though we rarely marry our best lovers. Remember the original premise of marriage in the middle ages: It was a mission to secure the financial future of the family. Considering that money is the number one issue that couples fight about, this is an area to be aware of when you are making your choices.

Give yourself permission to truly express your desires. We must let ourselves know what we desire. This exercise is the beginning of your roadmap. Start the process of choosing rather than taking all comers and hoping that you find a match. Express your desires and put them on the list. Desire is the light that lights our path.

AM I WORTHY?

As you are making your list, the process will bring up a variety of feelings. You may feel unworthy: "Who am I to ask for all of this?" The answer to this question is that you are the central character of your play. You are the being that you have been charged with caring for and providing for.

It is often surprising that people are so willing to act like extras in their own movie. We have been so beaten down and diminished by life that we dare not ask for what we want and need. Nevertheless, you are truly the star of the show and you need to embrace that.

Who else is going to give you what you need? The world follows our pattern of self-nurturing and matches that pattern. Self-nurturing is a stage of growth and personal maturity. You must get determined and excited about getting what you want in a relationship in order to manifest that reality. Creating love is an important stage of growth, and of taking responsibility for our lives.

The process of finding love isn't rocket science; it is a matter of being clear and being organized, and being entitled to having what we want in life. If you don't initially feel like you deserve love, then decide to get it anyway. Create love and then determine that you are going to earn it. Decide that you are willing to give whatever it takes to create the kind of love relationship you want.

THE POWER OF GIVING

I have a friend who would agree that he isn't the handsomest guy in the world; he is not the smartest, nor the richest. But he absolutely gets anyone that he sets his mind to into relationship with him. He is willing to do whatever it takes. He has mastered a set of skills. He finds out what his prospective love partner needs and what she wants; what she dreams about and what she hopes for. He explores her preferences and learns what she likes and doesn't like, and without giving himself up, he provides everything for the woman of his choice. He gets into relationship by making himself indispensable.

He nurtures and supports her interests: if she is an artist he may get one of her paintings into a show. If she is a singer, he will get her into the studio and cut a CD. Whatever her area of interest, he will shine the light on her and her potential greatness.

He is willing to give powerfully and accurately in a way that is very compelling. He knows that giving is the most powerful force on this earth, and he knows that giving accurately can be irresistible.

THE THREE KINDS OF GIVING

We hear people say "I gave everything, and still didn't get what I wanted!" Your results depend on the quality of your giving. Most people give very little or give inaccurately. They haven't taken the time to master the art of giving. There are three types of giving that we need to discuss:

~Ordinary Giving
~Informed Giving
~Kingly Giving

Ordinary Giving: I want to impress you, so I decide to give you a present. I give you this book that I just read, and that I absolutely loved. In doing so I give you something that I like. I get a pleasant acknowledgement, but little more. I may be taken aback when you aren't bowled over by this gift. The problem is that I loved the book, but I don't know how you feel about it. I gave you something that I wanted and enjoyed; this is called "Ordinary Giving." It is still giving and to that extent it is powerful. I extended myself and expressed some caring and thoughtfulness, but it is not the most influential kind of giving.

Informed Giving: The second example goes as follows: I noticed you admiring my new notebook. You comment on the material and the pattern. I go out and buy a notebook just like it for you. You are delighted, because I gave you something that you wanted. This is called "Informed Giving." "Informed Giving" is incrementally more powerful than the first kind of giving or "Ordinary Giving" because I am giving you something that speaks to your wants and desires. I now have gained power in the relationship. The obvious benefit to this giving is that we see our power in action and we influence our world.

Kingly Giving: The third kind of giving is called "Kingly Giving." The example for Kingly Giving is this: You need to take a test that will cost you a thirty-dollar application fee, and I notice that you don't have the thirty dollars for the fee. I decide to give you the money for the test. In this way, I have given you something that you need. In addition, to be considered Kingly Giving, I give you the money in a way that doesn't shame you or burden you emotionally. This is by far the most powerful form of giving; Kingly Giving is the act of giving what is needed, no more, no less, without obligation or shame. When we master this skill we learn the art of giving and we cultivate a means of making ourselves indispensable in people's lives. When we are building a relationship or any friendship, we can practice these forms of giving and master them to great effect.

Giving is power. Giving is influence. It is a way of interacting with our world that allows us to be at cause, instead of being at effect. Giving is a muscle that we build; it makes us stronger and more interesting. Our presence is welcomed when we give appropriately. We get love and appreciation for our efforts. Giving is the quickest way to gain control of any situation and to influence the outcome. In addition, when we give we gain personal authority in any situation that we find ourselves in. We can randomly give in a clumsy and ineffective way, or we can master the skill of giving accurately and powerfully.

ABUNDANCE

We may believe the scarcity argument: "Oh, there are too few good ones out there." Go outside at night and take a look at the incredible array of stars and see if you can still believe in scarcity. Scarcity thinking keeps us settling for less than we want in every area of life. We live in a smaller, less interesting world when we take on this thinking.

We willingly make way for others to get what they want through our un-entitlement when we buy in to this argument. It is an abundant universe! There is plenty for everyone. There are six and a half billion people on this planet and you only need one to make a match. Start thinking clearly and accurately.

EXERCISE 2

Make a list of everything you desire in a partner.

List five reasons why you deserve this person.

Read this list and these reasons out loud every day for at least a month

Notice how you feel before, during and after this exercise.

EXERCISE 2

Find a person that you want to deepen your relationship with.

Practice all three forms of giving, starting with Ordinary Giving and advancing through Informed Giving and Kingly Giving.

Notice how your target person responds to your giving.

Notice how you feel when you are giving in these different ways.

TWENTY-ONE

PROCESSES

CONCEIVE IT

We can create the reality that we want to create. We do create the realities that we are surrounded by. Every invention and innovation was first conceived and created in the mind. "Whatever the mind of man can conceive and believe it can achieve" quotes Napoleon Hill. We need to conceive the possibility of getting exactly what we want. When we believe it, we build from that belief.

Create a blueprint for the reality you want to create. Start to construct your own field of dreams. "If you build it they will come." The obstacles that arise when we attempt to conceive are the issues that we need to work through. Don't believe the mind when it tells you that you can't, or that what you want is impossible. Your mind is really saying that you are afraid, and you don't want to face your fears.

The prospect of getting what we want is far more frightening than the opposite. We are inured to failing and losing; it is our conditioned state of mind. We can certainly say that it is our "comfort zone." We have an identity that does not want to change. When we reach for the stars, the biggest obstacle is within. This identity wants us to turn back and to give up. Dare to insist on getting what you want despite this identity and challenge your comfort zone.

We create our blueprint through that marvelous factory for reality, the imagination. Like Thomas Edison, catnapping under his porch and dreaming up such wonders as the ticker-tape and the light bulb, we must let our minds take flight and soar. When we trigger the imagination we picture, we imagine and we allow ourselves to feel the emotions that creation brings. Picture yourself having the love that you desire in your life. As you do, you feel the emotions stirring and the excitement building. This is the energy of creation.

Fantasize and daydream, allow the mind to play in this arena. You have achieved the right chemistry when you feel enthusiasm. Let yourself believe and conceive. These are the tools of creation; use them accurately and you will be filled with the inspiration necessary to bring fantasy into reality.

WHAT YOUR SUBCONSCIOUS IS CREATING

If you've made your list, you now know who you want, or at least the qualities that you require in a mate. Let's take the next step to implement your plan for creating relationship. You, and your mind, are the projector and life is the screen. Your mind will project whatever you believe subconsciously. You have been programmed to hold certain expectations about relationship and you are going to live into those expectations.

If you think subconsciously that you don't deserve to be loved and cherished, you won't be. If you believe that "a good man is hard to find" he will be. You are the author of your reality, and that programming will dispassionately create exactly what it is trained to create.

We can interact with our subconscious mind and create our own programming. The mind responds to repetition. Whether you are a student of piano, endlessly repeating scales, or an adult who is deciding to create some new possibility in your life, the mind will accept your programming with the same objectivity. Through constant repetition, the conscious information eventually moves to the subconscious as a more efficient storage system. The premise of the repeated information is accepted and acted on as truth.

Create positive expectations and use the mechanism that the mind is; it will follow whatever instructions we program in. Imagine your ideal mate sitting across from you. Feel the feelings that this image brings. Invest in those feelings and have a positive expectation that you will create this reality. Repeat and invest, like a child doing musical scales, and this will become your subconscious basis for action.

CHANGE YOUR MIND AND CHANGE YOUR LIFE

Though we may have faulty programming creating our relationship results now, we can change that programming. The subconscious is highly suggestible. It is also highly changeable and adaptable. We can rewire the mind through affirmation, meditation, visualization, hypnosis and a variety of other methods.

Affirmation is simple: I make statements about the situation I want to create as though I have already achieved what I want. "I already have and enjoy a loving and fulfilling relationship!" The mind will accept and act on whatever premise we present; therefore, if I affirm, "I am successful" the mind starts to respond in the following way: I start to think, feel and act as though this premise is true and I am successful. I start to make choices from this premise.

The process of learning is achieved through constant conscious repetition. Whether we are learning a new skill or a new language, we consciously repeat and assert the information until it becomes second nature; the information grows too large to process consciously and so it starts to go below consciousness and enters the subconscious mind. Since the subconscious is the unseen rudder that steers us, constant affirmation changes how we make choices on the deepest level.

Hypnosis addresses the subconscious mind but in a different way. In hypnosis, the conscious mind is set aside and the hypnotist speaks directly to the subconscious. In effect, he becomes the conscious mind making conscious choices. He is then able to give suggestions directly to that part of the mind. Through suggestion and the introduction of new ideas to the subconscious, we start to change our blueprint on that essential level.

Many people have had great success in changing their lives this way. Self-hypnosis is a similar process, but we create the suggestions that we are guided by. Self-suggestion is the constant, positive prompting of the mind toward the goal we hope to achieve. As we continue to prompt the information filters down to the subconscious and we are directed from this location.

Visualization is the practice of creating pictures and images that contain the reality that we want to create. I close my eyes and "see" myself finding that special someone, and feel everything that that makes me feel. The mind will accept any premise that we present: that is why we can go to the movies and suspend our disbelief. We have no trouble accepting that aliens are attacking the world. (Some people accept it a little too much!) We react with fear and anxiety as though these events are really happening. When we practice visualization, we experience the movie that we are attempting to create. We know that the mind is locked-in when we start to experience the feelings and emotions associated with our visualized reality.

Use this method for a set period of time; ten minutes in the morning, before you start your day, every day or ten minutes at night before going to bed. By presenting a specific set of images to the mind, we align the subconscious with these conditions, and the mind accepts the premise as reality. We begin to make choices, experience emotions and create behaviors that reinforce this reality.

Meditation is a method that allows us to tap in to the power of the mind. The true meaning of meditation is observation. If you were to meditate on the topic of your love life, you might sit in quiet contemplation, with your eyes closed, and simply observe the thoughts and feelings and patterns that come up. As your mind reveals its thoughts, you simply observe without judgment. The muscle we are exercising when we meditate is "conscious awareness." We become clear that we are not our thoughts, our feelings and our patterns. We gain the freedom to create new patterns as we are no longer obligated to our history.

You may be surprised at what you see within yourself as you meditate on this topic. Past hurts and old patterns will make their way to the surface, as you simply watch, and breathe, without judgment or interpretation. Through this process of unearthing and accepting a new clarity is achieved.

All therapeutic healing is the process of mining the subconscious, and bringing it to the surface through conscious awareness. We are driven by these thoughts, feelings and patterns when they are below the surface, but we enter the realm of choice when we become consciously aware. By making a practice of sitting and observing, without interpreting or identifying, we can create the powerful changes that we want in our lives. As little as fifteen minutes a day of this simple practice can give you an objective point of view about the past and the opportunity to make new choices. All of these methods have power in them; some will suit your mind better than others.

I teach and practice a method called the "Paradox Process"[1]. It is a simple and direct way of accessing the subconscious and changing what I want to change through a series of exercises. Discovered by Rodger Bell in 1985 as a simple alternative to conventional meditation, the Paradox Process is a transformational tool designed to be accessible and user-friendly. I have had the privilege of co-developing The Paradox Process with him from its inception, and I have always been impressed with its simplicity and effectiveness. This technique is a command language for the mind. Through a direct set of exercises, we identify, accept, understand and transcend whatever the painful issues are that we are confronted with.

The Paradox Process uses the principles of computer programming in order to "deprogram" our negative feelings and patterns. Simply put, we identify the issue that we are choosing to work on, and then observe and clear the emotional charge contained within that issue using the techniques of this process. Insight always replaces the negative feelings, and so we gain wisdom through the work. In addition, we no longer buy in to the "virtual reality" that the upset created, so we take our power back from the issue. As we master the Paradox Process, we become powerful and gain wisdom and clarity about our issues.

Whatever your method, you must have a practice or discipline to learn and grow. If we don't choose to learn from our past, we are doomed to repeat our lessons over and over again. Socrates, in 399 B.C. said, "The unexamined life is not worth living." Whatever your belief system, religion or

---

spirituality, start to understand what makes you tick; become curious about why you make the choices in your life.

The mind is a tool that we are given to use, and much like the body, through exercise we make it stronger. If we leave the mind to its own devices it will revert to old painful patterns. The mind is always created some reality or other. If the mind is negative it will create negative realities. When we choose to direct the mind positively, the mind can and will create the positive realities that we choose to create.

THIS BUSINESS OF LOVE

These are all fantastic tools for creation, but we have to be clear about what we are creating and objective about the new story we want to find ourselves in. We can approach any area in our lives with logic and a level head, but the minute love is involved, we become the worst kind of fools. Suddenly we indulge in magical and superstitious thinking and clarity goes out the window. Captains of industry, capable of steering multi-million dollar corporations can't manage a single little enterprise called relationship. We give our power and our sanity away in the presence of love.

Let's look at it logically: The process of finding a mate is really a candidate interview for a specific job. For any other position we would write a job description and map out the requirements of the job. Let us approach this area with the same can-do attitude that we approach any other enterprise. When we take this approach it will go a long way toward defining what we want and it will empower us to see the task objectively.

There may be that indefinable something that goes into a love relationship, a "secret sauce," but most of it is thoroughly definable. We can get clear about what we want and need from a relationship. When we've reached the limits of that search, then we can worry about what magic is necessary.

Take on every step of this job search that is in front of you to do. This is a job. Don't let a sense of un-entitlement you're your choices. We hold a positive expectation about every other pursuit or task in life, so let us approach this area with the same enthusiasm. Be excited, think positively, and expect the best. When interviewing to fill a job, we don't begin with negative assumptions.

CHANGE THE STORY

If the thought of this pursuit brings up negative feelings and reactions, you have a story going on in your head. This story tells you that this is difficult for you, or that it just can't be done. You have qualifiers within the story as to why you will fail. This is backed up by history and examples. There is a full-on PowerPoint presentation on the topic. This is a form of self-hypnosis and auto-suggestion. We must challenge these expectations; they will become self-fulfilling or at the very least make it much more difficult to achieve what we want.

This negative viewpoint is merely the mind's exercise in creative writing. We have the ability to rewrite our story, to bring our story to the conclusions that we choose. We are always manifesting exactly what we choose; it is essential to change this negative story immediately.

Begin with the obvious; stop being negative. Refuse to go there. I jokingly tell my clients to give up complaining for lent, but I'm not kidding. The one task that will dramatically and instantly change reality is to refuse to think negatively. Try it for twenty-one days and create a new habit.

Here's what that exercise would look like: The instant that you find yourself entertaining a negative thought, stop in your tracks and immediately change that thought. You can change it to a positive thought, or simply change the topic, as you would when a friend is being negative. We wouldn't allow a friend to tell us that we would fail at something we are attempting, so we don't need to tolerate that thinking from our own mind. If your mind is chattering on in a way that is negative and unsupportive, change that thought immediately. Thoughts don't end there; thoughts create feelings and feelings create our experience. If the feelings are negative, the experience will be negative as well.

The mind is the factory that creates our reality. When we truly understand how the mind works, we will not let the mind randomly create what it wants, based on its feelings and negative patterns. We will not settle for anything less than creating what we choose to create.

EXERCISE ONE: AFFIRMATIONS

Pick a topic to focus affirmations on: creating relationship for instance.

Take five minutes in the morning; find a quiet space and start formulating positive statements as already accomplished fact. i.e. "I am in a loving and committed relationship that is leading toward marriage and family." Try to make between five and ten statements.

Repeat these statements until you feel your positive emotions responding to the affirmations.

Use the affirmation that is most representative of what you want throughout the day. Do this for thirty days and notice how it makes you feel.

EXERCISE 2: VISUALIZATION

Choose a reality that you wish to create.

Find a quiet time and space to visualize. In resting position, close your eyes and allow yourself to picture that reality. Fill your mind with images of the experience that you intend to call forth.

Allow yourself to experience the emotions that this reality will bring up. Don't try to be too specific with your imagery, it is more important to feel the feelings of this reality than to see the details.

Stay in this visualization for between five and ten minutes, allowing the emotions to fill you.

Refer to these images throughout the day and connect with the emotions that they create. Do this for thirty days.

EXERCISE 3: MEDITATION

Find a quiet space where you can close your eyes and focus.

Pick a topic that you want to meditate on.

Focus on breathing rhythmically as you take a journey through your history of this issue. Allow the feelings and emotions to pass through you without identifying with these feelings.

Stay in this state of quiet observation and allow everything that wants to come up pass through you. Allow a sense of peace to flow through you as you travel the timeline of this issue: past, present, and future.

Stay in this space from ten to twenty minutes, remaining the observer.

Do this every day for a month.

EXERCISE 4: STORY

Pick a topic to manifest.

Write the story of the easy, effortless creation of this manifestation.

Include the simple steps you took to make it happen and how it felt every step of the way.

Read it aloud every day for a month.

TWENTY-TWO

YOUR MANIFESTORS

In order to speak intelligently about manifestors, we must first accept that we have responsibility for the way that our lives show up. Let's take on the model that we create our reality, not necessarily because it is true, but because it will allow us to speak in terms of manifesting. Let's agree that we take on this premise. This allows us to explore how that is possible. We can look at the elements that factor in to this creation process.

Let's look at it logically. We have visual senses that interpret the color and light that we see into images that we recognize. We have aural senses that translate the vibrations we hear into sound. We have tactile senses that translate touch into some recognizable form. Our minds perceive the reality that we experience and we interpret those perceptions into discernable patterns. We have feelings and emotions through which we determine positive or negative intent. Everything we experience is an interpretation. We call that interpretation reality, but it is strictly subjective. You may interpret the look on a man's face as sadness, whereas, I may see it as anger or even gastric distress. We will have dramatically different experiences based on our unique interpretations.

The Rashomon effect is the effect of the subjectivity of perception on recollection, by which observers of an event are able to produce substantially different but equally plausible accounts of that same event. Each of us is capable of creating a very different experience of reality using the same events and the same circumstances, because we each have a very different internal experience. To that extent we create our experience of reality based on the interpretation and meanings we assign to the events in our lives. We have enormous control of our experience based on the filters that we choose to pass our experience through. In a very real sense we have to concede that we are the co-creators of our reality.

While living in the question of whether or not we create our circumstances, we certainly can't deny that we are in charge of the experience that we have within those circumstances. How we interpret our experience dictates the feelings that are created. Happiness and contentment, for instance, are the products of experience, not circumstances. In a literal way, we have control of our own happiness.

BUILDING BLOCKS OF REALITY
Here is the short list of manifestors:

▼ Thoughts
▼ Feelings
▼ Actions
▼ Perceptions
▼ Choices
▼ Interpretations

All of these thoughts, feelings, actions, perceptions and choices, and interpretation of the events of our lives become instrumental in shaping, not only the present event, but all similar events. There is a chain of command to creating what we want, and we have great influence over it, when we know that this chain of command exists. We have control of our reality when we start to alter these manifestors. We literally change our lives when we change these manifestors.

We have been programmed since the time we were children to behave in certain ways and hold specific beliefs: "Be a good girl!" "You're not a nice person!" All of this programming goes into the subconscious very directly when we are young. We have no defenses against these beliefs. The perceptions these beliefs create alter the choices we make. We modify our behaviors and actions according to our belief system.

The trouble with programming is that it goes largely unseen. How many of these hidden beliefs and perceptions are operating right now? Are you responding right now to a programmed belief that you are not good enough? The only way to tell is by the results that we are getting in life. When it "doesn't make sense" that I can't accomplish what I want, there is a hidden influence in play. That unseen rudder that steers our lives, the subconscious, with all of its antiquated programmed beliefs is busy making choices for us. We can reprogram that subconscious mind. We can change our manifestors from the ground up. We can master the controls of these manifestors and steer our lives directly toward the results that we want.

THE LIAR MIND

These are challenging ideas. The very thought that we can change the mind is unthinkable to some. It challenges conventional beliefs at an essential level. This idea is not voodoo or metaphysics, yet trying to get some people to accept change is like pulling teeth.

The problem lies in the fact that the conscious mind doesn't know what the subconscious is doing. I confront this all day long in my practice: I will say point blank "you are fighting yourself, you don't really want relationship on some level," and I will get answers like "That's ridiculous! That's all I want!" They truly do not see that they are their own biggest obstacle. The choices that they are making are counter-intuitive to the results that they want to achieve. It isn't as though their denial will get them anywhere; in fact it ensures that they will stay in the dark.

We believe this conscious mind of ours. It is a glib and facile liar, but we want to believe it. In fact, the conscious mind is blind as a bat and constantly misguided. The following is an example of how the conscious mind works: You slip on the stair and hit your shin; your mind immediately looks around for some explanation, something to blame. It doesn't matter if it is truth or not to the conscious mind, only that the explanation somehow fits the event. You spy what appears to be a spot of wetness. "John spilled soda on the stair again and made me slip and hurt myself!"

This is a tidy explanation, with cause and effect, blame, a story line, and even possible action to take in the future. The only problem with the example is that it is a total fabrication based on the limited information given. You will confront John with the righteousness of someone who knows what happened and you will be totally wrong, but the conscious mind has satisfied itself that it has gotten to the truth. Viola'! Score another point for the "liar mind."

Because the explanation is tailor-made to the feeling, it's always a perfect match. We feel like we are telling the truth because our feelings are validated, and our perceptions are answered. When we watch a child explaining how the lamp got mysteriously broken, it can be cute. When the stakes are our lives and our happiness, it's a little less charming.

Your conscious mind is a practiced and skilled liar. It gives topical explanations based on what it observes and concludes, and often the explanation has little to do with reality. The mind rationalizes everything, not according to the truth, but always to our advantage, using the material at hand. "Billy made me break the lamp!" is not just a simple deceit. It is an interpretation of events for the advantage of the teller. Little Johnny gets to deal with the event without the impact of a full frontal blow. He shades it to a glancing shot and gets to manage reality in a different way. If that's what we're up to at age six, imagine how sophisticated that mechanism is by the age of twenty-five or thirty. Many years of practice make for a well-oiled and totally unreliable "liar" mind. Conclusion: Don't believe your mind.

PERCEPTION IS REALITY

What we begin to see as we examine these mechanisms is that what we perceive is what we create. This is good news and bad news. The reality that we are creating is the direct result of our perceptions. Conversely, when we change these perceptions, we change the choices we make and the reality we create.

One powerful way to change our perceptions is to deliberately hold the highest possibility for any situation we are in. If I say "imagine yourself rich and happy right now," most people can indulge in that thought. By forcing a perceptual change we re-route our experience of reality. We automatically make different choices based on the new perception. Our feelings change, our thoughts change, our choices change.

We want to be able to trust our minds but it is unreliable at best, if left on its own. Because it is filled with old programming and beliefs, the mind is not dependable as an accurate reflection of reality. If we can't believe our own minds, whom can we believe? Should we defer to some higher authority to tell us what reality is and what isn't? This could prove inconvenient when we are trying to figure our lives out at three in the morning. It is never a good idea to give our power away so thoroughly, anyway. A better idea is to take control of this mind. Learn what is operating now and then choose new premises from which to act.

We have a constant reflection of our inner beliefs and choices. The reality that we find ourselves in is the reality that our manifestors have created, so far. We need not believe our internal beliefs, and we should be suspicious of this mind, but as observers we have a bird's eye view. As we begin to deliberately change our minds to the beliefs and choices we desire, our old programming will make itself known.

CHANGE IT NOW

If I were to go about changing that old programming with an eye to changing the reality that I find myself in, I would begin to change my beliefs in the area where I want change. I would start simple. I would make a list of those beliefs, just to see what I am dealing with. If the area I want to change is relationship, and finding a good one, I would start with all of my beliefs about love. Suppose my mind is holding the thought: "It's hard to find a good partner." This is not a reality; it is a belief. Similarly "all the good ones are taken," "I'm too old" and "I don't have anything to offer" are also beliefs. Next to each old programmed belief, I would write the opposite. I would embrace the highest possibility in this area. For instance, next to "it's hard to find a good partner" I might write "Love is all around me and I will find the right partner." I would choose to believe that I am already in the process of creating what I want in relationship. I would deliberately retune my manifestors and discipline my mind to hold these new beliefs. These beliefs in turn would begin to create new thoughts and new feelings, and my perceptions and choices would alter accordingly.

Take an honest look and determine what beliefs are ruling your relationship area. Be sure to make the distinction; identify them as beliefs and not as reality. As you begin to see these beliefs that you are holding as true, you will start to understand the choices you are making, based on these "truths." Next, write down the opposing positive belief next to each negative belief. "My perfect match is out there waiting for me," "I have everything it takes to create a great relationship"; these are examples of creating positive beliefs.

It is not required that you believe these new beliefs, but ask yourself this: which set of beliefs do you think is more likely to create what the reality that you want? It's not hard to guess: the dog that you feed is the dog that grows.

When we feed this set of beliefs into our system, we start to think and feel differently. The mind starts to function in the realm called "possibility." New choices are made and new actions are taken. Remember, beliefs create perceptions, choices and actions. These are the bases from which we interact with life. We are not engaging in a process of self-delusion; by understanding how the mind works, we feed it the proper fuel to get the results we want.

When we change our beliefs and perceptions reality must change. We make new choices on an essential level. We take action that matches the beliefs that we hold.

▼ Thoughts: "My perfect match is out there walking toward me as I am walking toward him."

▼ Feelings: As I embrace this I feel hope and excitement.

▼ Actions: I dress for this new reality; I get in shape and look my best as I prepare to receive my ideal partner.

▼ Perceptions: I see the world working for me, not against me. My world now has love and possibility in it.

▼ Choices: I choose to smile, to be excited and optimistic. I participate in the world, knowing that love is coming.

▼ Interpretations: I see myself as relevant and lovable. I see my love as a potential partnership.

These are the changes that you can make, now. Nothing has to happen in order for you to make these new choices. Better feelings, perceptions and a better experience is immediately available. Don't wait.

REPROGRAMMING YOUR MIND

The mind doesn't make a distinction between what it now believes and a new belief that we present. We can read a novel or see a movie and suspend our beliefs about reality. If we can accept the premise that robots are taking over the earth in *The Day the Earth Stood Still,* we can certainly embrace that our ideal mate is out there for us. We all know that those robots aren't real, (well, most of us, anyway) and yet, our palms still sweat at the description of automatons coming to get us.

It is not required of us that we believe our perceptions in order to respond to them as real. We are unique in that way. We can, with the full knowledge that it is not real, indulge in sexual fantasy and become fully aroused by those mental images that we conjure. We have the unique ability to embrace "beliefs" without believing them.

HEALTHY CHANGES

There are physiological changes that occur when we start to perceive ourselves as successful in love. There are new ways of thinking and new thought patterns. We feel younger and healthier when we embrace these new premises. Living in the realm of possibility allows us to feel our full potential. We literally get smarter and prettier and more powerful. Our immune system gets stronger. We are inspired in our work and in our lives. We are friendlier and easier to get along with. As the endorphins course through our system we gain a sense of well being. We have less physical pain and less stress in our lives.

When we live in possibility we live more fully, with a greater sense of satisfaction in our lives. We like ourselves better and we enjoy life more.

Try it yourself: close your eyes and picture yourself absolutely adored by someone fabulous; picture that you are the center of their universe. Let yourself feel their love and desire, their respect and admiration for you. (Don't tell yourself that you can't do this; if you can watch a movie, you can do this.) Picture the whole world applauding you for achieving what you want, approving of your love wholeheartedly. See them smiling at your happiness. Take these feelings in; aren't they more fun, more enlivening than believing that you won't have what you want or that you can't create love in your life? Feel yourself relaxing and feeling lighter; a burden has been lifted. And the truth is: Of course you can do this.

This exercise is a small demonstration with great implications: it means that you can control your experience. If you had even a moment of excitement during this exercise you improved your experience through your will and your power. If you can change your experience by one percent, you can change it one hundred percent.

DON'T BELIEVE IT, JUST DO IT

Take on new beliefs because they change you; not because they are true. We are self-fulfilling prophecies, all of us. What prophesy are you fulfilling now? You can present any premise to your mind that you choose, and you will live by that premise. You already are living through a set of beliefs, you just haven't been aware of it.

It takes courage to change ourselves. We have to dare to leave our comfort zone and try something new. When we've had enough, when we are no longer willing to settle for being shortchanged by life, we will embrace change. But you can be proactive and choose change before life becomes too painful to bear.

Make a list of the beliefs that you would like to operate from. Take the list of new beliefs that you have created and recite them everyday, like a mantra. Every time you find your mind reverting to the old beliefs, turn your mind back to the new ones. Be vigilant with your mind and refuse to think in the old ways. At first this may be a lot of work, but you don't see the work you are doing now, suffering with the old beliefs. Be honest with yourself and acknowledge that you have been waiting for the opportunity to change. This is that opportunity.

CHANGE YOUR PERCEPTIONS

As we believe, so we will perceive. When we refuse to interpret reality in those old tired but familiar ways, we demand a new perception. We demand an empowering perception that we can and that we will win. Ask any Olympic athlete where most of the work of winning is done, and he or she will tell you that the real battle is in the mind. More than most, athletes will recognize the power of the mind to win or to sabotage us. They are rigorous in continually working with and changing their perceptions to the positive and the possible. They visualize and picture themselves winning and succeeding, continually creating that powerful message to the mind.

The Speed Skater will "see" himself crossing the finish line first. Watch as the bobsledder goes through every turn of the course in his mind before the race. We can take on this model in our own lives. See yourself as a "winner." "See" love coming your way. This is not all that is needed for change, but it is the first action to take. Right thinking creates right action. "See" an abundant field of possibility in your choices for relationship. "See" yourself loving and being loved.

SET UP YOUR DAY

Take two minutes in the morning to set up your day in the following way: picture you facing all the challenges of the day and winning each challenge. "See" yourself getting that new account and closing that deal. Visualize yourself talking to that girl that you've wanted to approach. Go through every turning point of the day and "see" success. Picture it, feel it, and fill up on those feelings, and watch how it affects your choices and your day. Our real battlefield and our first victory is a victory of the mind.

REFUSE TO THINK NEGATIVELY

Nothing is more withering than a negative thought. It deflates us and leaves us unhappy and unmotivated. Here's an alternative: rather than being at the mercy of your negative thoughts, try something new. During the course of your day, refuse to think negatively. Recognize that this is your mind and you are the captain of your ship. Take control of your mind. Don't let negative thoughts "think" you and use you. If it were a friend talking to you that way rather than your own mind, you would immediately walk away. Don't put up with this negativity from within, either. Why let your mind say something to you that you wouldn't let a friend say? Don't let yourself be spoken to that way, not even by you.

When you find yourself being run by negative thoughts, stop those thoughts immediately. We need to acknowledge the truth that we are being poisoned by toxic thoughts.

Picture the mind like a computer, and the thoughts are pop-ups that appear on the screen. These pop-ups contain the worst possible messages about us, about life, about the outcome of our lives. Picture this message popping up: "You're a failure!" "Nobody wants you!" "You can't do it!" These are the kinds of messages that we are receiving from this negatively programmed mind, and worse.

DELETE

Here's an exercise for you. When these "pop-ups" appear on the computer screen you hit the "delete" button. The moment you recognize a negative thought in your mind, silently say "delete." Sometimes it takes hitting the "delete" key a few times to get rid of the message, but be vigilant. Send the message to your mind that you will not be accepting these unsolicited negative thoughts any longer.

As you do this practice vigilantly, you will re-program your mind (literally creating a new program) to always delete these negative thoughts. You will have effectively created your own pop-up blocker. It takes twenty-one days to rewire your neural network, so do this exercise for three weeks, and you will create a new habit. You may be weak at this in the beginning. Control of the mind is a muscle people rarely exercise, but you will quickly gain strength and very soon you will automatically eliminate your negative thoughts.

If you want to take this exercise a step further, after deleting the old pop-up, create a new, positive thought that supports and reinforces your goals. For instance, change "everyone gives me a hard time and a hassle" to "everyone cooperates with me and loves to do so." Before long the positive thought will become your reality. The new thought you choose will now make your choices. We have an internal dialogue in our minds for each topic of our life: money, politics, religion, relationships. Make a list of your ideal choices and most positive thoughts about relationship and let that become your internal dialogue, your roadmap to reality.

WHY CHANGE YOUR MIND?

If we have a perception that a ring of fire surrounds us, we will be careful where we step. If the ring of fire is an illusion, then we are stepping around phantoms. We look like madmen. When we discover that we don't have to be run by this set of programmed negative beliefs, we experience a freedom and possibility that we didn't know existed. It is liberation day when we see through the illusions of our negative thoughts and feelings. Suddenly, all of the work of managing and defending against these negative thoughts goes away. The emperor has no clothes. All of that negative thinking is a network of lies and interpretations, and we won't be run by those lies anymore.

Are any of our beliefs true? How can we tell what is the truth? This is the point in which each person's beliefs and creativity comes in to play. Hindu philosophy believes that all that we see is the illusion of duality or Maya. Good and evil, right and wrong, black and white, are all illusory. The objective truth lies in seeing through the illusion, and mind without illusion is objective reality. We are living in a dream. When we embrace this knowledge we have tremendous power over the outcome of that dream.

A tenet of the basic Christian philosophy is that we are made in the "image and likeness" of god. God is everywhere and contained in everything we see. Inasmuch as god is a creator, and so are we creators. We surrender to our creator and through supplication and prayer God will provide all that we need.

In every major religion we have a means of interacting with the Universal and shaping our lives. We have the concept of surrender or accepting reality exactly the way it is. We have the concept of us as creators of our reality.

While these philosophies have been instilled in us from an early age, we have never been taught how to use this truth and how to use this knowledge creatively. The promise of these ideals means that your life can be exactly the way you choose. In this sense, you have been choosing your life all along. When we choose and create without any conscious direction we are at the mercy of our programmed beliefs. When we take responsibility for our choices we choose with discernment, power and accuracy.

Most people, when they hear the idea that we create our reality tend to feel guilty. They look at their lives now, and they feel responsible for how the events of their lives have shown up. It is true that we are responsible for our lives, but that doesn't mean that it's our fault when life goes wrong. We do create our lives; our lives have shown up the way we've chosen them, but we have not been awake, or aware of our choices. We may not have recognized these outcomes, but we have made the choices that led to them.

When we make different choices we will inevitably create different outcomes. We must refuse to settle for less than what we want. It is within our power to create a relationship that honors us and serves us. As we become aware of the power that we have to choose, we begin to choose more carefully.

As we take on the model that we create our reality we can be inspired by the freedom and the possibility that this truth allows. We also recognize that everything that we've chosen is for our and everyone else's highest good and chosen in perfect spiritual cooperation.

HOW TO ENFORCE THESE CHANGES

Learning is the process of constant repetition. Whether we are learning a new instrument or a new language, the process is the same. Through constant repeating of phrase after phrase, the knowledge goes from the conscious mind to the subconscious. The conscious mind doesn't have the capacity to store the information and so the information goes below consciousness. Eventually, we know these patterns "by heart." The choices and patterns become automatic and our subconscious mind does all the work and makes our choices for us. Our behaviors become automatic.

What an elegant system: imagine creating all of these positive relationship patterns and having the subconscious mind do all of the work. This is where action originates.

In fact, this process is already ongoing. The fly in the ointment is that the subconscious is using its old negative programming as a blueprint for choices. The mind will accept whatever premise we present, and it will operate from that premise, positive or negative. If we don't present the new, the mind operates from our default programming.

We can use this very mechanism to change our lives. Use the "affirmation" process. Make a list of how you want your relationship to manifest for you and repeat it every day. State this scenario as already accomplished fact, so that you are affirming what you will get, not what you want to receive. Say "I already have a loving, caring relationship!" rather than "I want to be loved." Make it a five-minute litany and repeat it every day, without fail. Within a very short time the mind will respond to this new information, rather than the old patterning. Be objective even if you encounter resistance. If this process was the learning of an instrument or a language, you would not let your feelings or interpretations get in the way. Assert yourself with your mind. Make it do what you want it to do.

CREATING REALITY: THREE STEPS

The process of manifestation is simple. The way to create any new reality is through intention, burning desire and personal power. You need only these three steps to call forth anything in your life.

1) Intention: State clearly and powerfully what you want to achieve. State it as positive, filling in the phrase "I intend____."

2) Burning Desire: Cultivate excitement and belief in your intention. Visualize what you want to create and feel the emotions that this creates.

3) Personal Power: Take your power back from all thoughts, feelings and concepts that are standing in the way of getting what you want.

Clearly state your intention to create the relationship you want. Create an intention that reflects your true desire. This intention should allow you to see the reality that you want to create. It should be simple and actionable. Fill in the phrase: "I intend _____"

When you've formulated your intention you begin to cultivate burning desire. We achieve this through the factory for reality, our imagination. Picture yourself receiving the very object of that desire. The tools for burning desire are visualization and imagination. Visualization is the process of producing your own movie that contains the experience you want. Spend five minutes in the morning being immersed in that movie, staying in it until you actually feel the emotions that this reality creates.

Don't worry about the details of your movie. There are some details that you just can't know yet. It is more important to connect with the feelings that this visualization creates than nailing down the details. Revel in this exercise: let yourself enjoy the emotions. Let this visualization lift you and carry you through the day.

Personal Power can be achieved in several ways: The first way is to take your power back from all of the negative thoughts and feelings that stand in the way of achieving what you want. Refuse to believe the negative. When these thoughts come up, delete them and deliberately choose the opposite thought. Cultivate some practice to handle the negatives in your life.

A second way to cultivate personal power is through attention to detail. One technique for applying attention to detail is through affirmations; by making statements, in a positive way, that describe exactly what you want in the way that you want it, as already accomplished fact. Again, if it were a language, you would be exact in your thinking and practice. Hit all of the right notes. Be that exacting in what you are creating.

A third way to gain personal power is through the practice of giving. We have discussed the three ways of giving, and each one will increase your personal power incrementally. When we reach a threshold of personal power, what we desire becomes reality.

Do these exercises, even if you feel foolish. Drink the cool-aid. Is it better to be smart and cynical, or to feel foolish and get everything you want? Determine to change your thinking; get rid of the old negative programming and introduce new and exciting ideas and possibilities into your mind. Remember, your mind will respond to whatever thinking you practice. State your intention, and then create the thinking that supports it, and repeat this thinking, like a litany, for twenty-one days. Do it as if your happiness depends on it, because it does.

BLUEPRINT

If you are building a house, it begins with a vision. You create an intention to build. Once you have a blueprint, you start building, brick by brick, in an organized way, until the structure starts to appear. Building a relationship is no different: create your vision and start to build the mental structure that supports it.

Fill up with a burning desire as you would with anything else that you want. Allow yourself to want what you want. Systematically take your power back from everything that you've given it to. Not only will you get what you want, but your entire life will dramatically improve.

THOUGHTS, FEELINGS, BELIEFS, PATTERNS

When we are changing our reality, we must change all of the thoughts and feelings in the way, without believing them or investing in them. Change your thoughts in a systematic way. Introduce new beliefs to supplant the old ones. Do not believe or trust the old feelings, as they are the product of those beliefs. Feelings are readily transferable and open to change.

The following is an example of the transference of feelings: I was watching my six-year old playing his video game. He was hot on the trail of the bad guys in "Haunted Mansion" when he was caught by one of them, and his character "died." Because I happened to be there, he immediately turned to me and said, "Look what you made me do!"

Cute, isn't it? More than that, it is a fascinating example of the "liar mind" in action. Losing the game caused a feeling in him, and rather than blame himself, his mind turned to whatever happened to be handy, (in this case, me.) His mind assigned his feeling about losing the game to whatever it happened to see.

The mind will scan whatever the circumstances are, and arbitrarily assign blame, so that the feeling equation is satisfied. Though it had nothing to do with reality, the feeling "fit" the circumstances. He could then move on because his "feeling math" was satisfied. It didn't matter to the feeling, or to his mind that none of this was true, it only mattered that the emotional accounting balanced out.

This is how we live. We are ruled by a mind that assigns our feelings to arbitrary events that happen to fit, for now. Our feelings are changeable and assignable. We cannot trust our feelings to give us an accurate account of reality. We can't rely on the mind to reveal the truth through our feelings. Perceptions and interpretations are created through feelings that have nothing to do with the truth. Reality is the first casualty of our emotions.

Because this is the way the mind works it is incredibly pliable and suggestible. Our feelings are readily assignable to whatever circumstances may fit at the time. Just as it would be disaster if we "buy into" that reality, we can use this fertile ground as a means to create.

The first order of business is the effective point of view and management of our feelings. Move through your feelings without believing them. Manage them in any way necessary: cry them out, write them out, talk them out, process them out, but don't believe them. Discipline your mind to enforce only the reality that you choose. Don't let your mind routinely choose a reality that happens to fit in the moment, just to solve your "feeling math." When we understand the nature of mind we are no longer fooled by it. We can direct it toward our purposes.

When you systematically change these manifestors, your reality will change. It isn't that reality might shift; it must shift. As we change our thoughts and feelings, as we alter our perceptions, our choices will change, and our actions will be different. When we get our hands on the wheels and dials that create our reality, we get the results that we choose. This does not only apply to relationship, but to our entire reality. It's a whole new world, one of promise and possibility.

Thoughts: Refuse the negative thoughts and install the positive ones.

Feelings: Don't believe the negative feelings; fill your mind with the pictures that create positive emotions.

Beliefs: Examine and challenge the old beliefs, and deliberately install new, empowering beliefs.

Patterns: Instill new, positive habits and patterns to supplant the old; create patterns that will manifest what you want.

We have been given this incredible instrument called the mind. When we learn how to master it instead of being at its mercy, we create miracle after miracle.

EXERCISE 1

Make a list of thoughts, feelings, actions, perceptions, choices and interpretations. Fill this list in with your manifestors concerning relationships as they exist now.

Next to Thoughts, list a new Empowering Thought about your relationship.

Go down the list and add the Feeling that the new Thought would create about relationship.

List an action you could take after the feeling.

List the positive perception that new feeling would create.

Write down the new choice you would make based on this perception.

Write the positive Interpretation that your new choices create.

Fill your list with all of the positive manifestors that you can think of.

EXERCISE 2

Write out your "programming" about relationship, include everything you've experienced about love since you were a child, and everything you've been led to expect.

Write out the new "programming" that you intend to operate from, as already accomplished fact.

Read this new programming every day for twenty-one days.

Whenever any of the old programming recurs, say "delete."

EXERCISE 3

Create an intention about relationship; state it in the positive as already accomplished fact.

Visualize the achievement of this intention until you feel the emotions that this reality creates.

Turn every negative thought about this intention to a positive. Do this until it becomes habit.

Continue to do this every day until it is your new practice and habit.

TWENTY-THREE

CREATING THE LOVE OF YOUR LIFE

(OR ANYTHING ELSE...)

We have explored many of the real dynamics that operate in relationship. We have explored the mechanisms that make it tick. We've seen the games that we deliberately play, and the bigger game that runs us. When we understand these dynamics we are no longer subject to the game. We are the creators of our reality.

None of this new information will mean anything unless we can translate it into real action and real results in our lives. At some point we must go beyond the theoretical and deal in the practical discipline of change. This means challenging the old identity and determining to do whatever it takes to get the lives that we want. The identity will resist change. We have to be determined in order to break through to a new reality.

We don't need the luxury of belief to change; our minds and our lives will respond to the information they are given. What we require is the courage to stop acting like bit players in our own movie and become the stars that we really are.

MAKE NEW CHOICES

This is not a "practice" life, it is the real deal, and it needs to be treated that way. Beyond a certain point, excuses, or reasons why this or that won't happen, are just that: excuses. We can either have our excuses, or we can have results, but we can't have it both ways. Each occupies the same space, and it is up to us how we will choose to fill our lives.

Don't choose to be "positive" because it's the right thing to do or because it makes you a better person. Create a positive reality because it is what works to create the experience that you want. This is the nature of the pursuit of dreams. At some point we become "practical dreamers" and apply the lessons we have learned.

HIGH RISK, HIGH REWARD

In the pursuit of our dreams we have to abandon the idea of safety. "Safe" is right next to "non-existent" on the life experience meter. As my father used to say, "You can be safe when you're dead!" The pursuit of anything worth having involves risk, and that is part of the thrill when we accomplish what we want. Nothing is more gratifying in life than to face our fears, and beat the odds in spite of everything and to achieve what we set out to achieve.

In fact, the experience that we have along the way is more important than the accomplishment. Who we are and how we feel as we create our lives means much more than the trophies that we may manage to win.

If you are asked, "Who is the most accomplished person in the last two hundred years?" You may come up with answers such as "Thomas Edison" or "Madame Curie." With all of their accomplishments, how often do you think about them in your life? Remember, these are the most accomplished people in a couple of centuries, and you probably don't think about them more than once a month, or even once a year. Our experience along the way determines our happiness; accomplishment should never be our only goal.

The real rewards come from how we shape our experience. Accomplishments, in some way, may be a matter of our destiny, but our experience is under our influence and control. Rise to the challenge of life and really get in the game. Don't sit on the sidelines and let it pass you by. Play big, because that is a better experience.

We should take "intelligent" risks rather than foolish ones, and we can manage the odds in our favor with a little planning and forethought. Don't leave your life in the "planning" stage. Make a plan, get the tools, find your supplies and keep yourself in resourceful states as you execute your plan.

Take the risk of showing up as a different person than who you have been. Let the old him or her go, and deliberately reinvent yourself. Risk your old sense of self. Risk the disapproval of all those that want to keep you where you are. Risk your fear of the unknown and the untried. These are the stakes that we need to put up when we ask for change in life.

RESOURCEFUL STATES
What is a resourceful state of mind and how do we achieve it? The quality of that state of mind is that we see more clearly and we think better. We begin living in possibility. Emotionally, we feel safe and confident, as though we can achieve anything we set our mind to. Intellectually, we see the best possible outcome of the situation and the way to achieve it. Spiritually, we become aligned with our destiny and trusting that we are on our path. Physically, we are in a state of relaxed readiness, energized and ready for life.

We achieve these states all the time, and often go in and out of them without noticing. A pleasant passing thought can bring us into a resourceful state; however, we can deliberately create it by making big plans and believing in them.

Close your eyes and think of the last time you were truly content. Allow yourself to recreate that time in your mind's eye. See it, feel it, smell it, taste it. Watch how your mind goes into a state of ease and delight as you reminisce. Your body relaxes and you "unclench" as you imagine yourself in this contented place. You can feel yourself lift emotionally, as your shoulders drop and the tension fades. This is a resourceful state.

What is the value of this state? Imagine that you can apply that energy anywhere and in any direction at will. Now picture an area of challenge in your present life. Put the image of this challenge side by side with the image of the contented place that you have created. Allow all of the feelings of contentment and peace to pour in to that place of challenge. "See" your contented self entering that challenging place. "See" this version of you handling the challenge with all the ease and clarity of the contented self. Watch as this contented you effortlessly solves every problem and handles the situation masterfully. This is a way of using our resourceful states in our lives; this version of ourselves certainly rises to the challenge.

Accept that you can summon up this wonderfully resourceful version of you at will, and apply it where you want and need it. It is your mind and these are your resourceful states. Don't settle for the state of mind that your challenges and feelings put you in. Deliberately choose your most resourceful states to face your biggest challenges.

As we continue to learn how to manage this incredible instrument known as the mind, we make new and exciting discoveries. We are no longer restricted to an old set of adjustments and the sky becomes the limit. As we routinely make different choices than our old programming dictates, we change something essential in ourselves. We create new patterns and add new success to our lives.

COURAGE

It takes a great deal of courage to buck conventional wisdom. We declare for the entire world to hear that we will live our dreams and get what we want. There is a never-ending supply of nay-sayers who will ridicule and belittle us for daring to believe that we can live our dreams, whatever those dreams may be.

Trying to convince the people that I work with that they can find love, or create that new business, or succeed at a new enterprise is the most difficult challenge of my work. We are willing, and even eager to believe that we can't have and can't achieve what we want. After a lifetime of being diminished, we are reluctant to reach for more. We need no outside force to put us down; we do it ourselves.

It is daunting to dare to believe that we can achieve or have anything. And yet, there is hope. We see people around us getting what they want. Somebody is always finding love, getting rich or hitting a home run. It is all out there for the taking, at least for someone. We must reassemble our spirits and find the courage to declare ourselves and to dare to want more.

Without that first step of creating an intention, nothing more can happen. When we do declare ourselves we call forth a magic and even a surprising assistance from the universe. Unless we believe, we will not perceive. We simply won't see the possibility and won't create any. We are the greatest manifesting mechanism in the universe, infinitely creative and resourceful, but if we never dare to believe, we will never accomplish.

Courage is not fearlessness in the face of danger; that is something else. Perhaps that is denial or even psychosis. Courage is the willingness to take action in spite of our fears. With full knowledge and eyes wide open we choose to take action and we don't let our worries and anxieties stop us. We dare to go forward into life and say "I will do this!" even though we are afraid. This kind of action builds self-esteem and personal power. We also reaps the benefit of living in the possibility of getting what we want.

DARE TO DREAM

Five percent of the people in the world create ninety-five percent of the changes and innovations in the world. These people are visionaries, and they see something that does not exist yet. We could call them delusional, or inspired. Everything that has ever been invented or created started out as a vision that most people did not agree with or even believe. Thomas Edison was a laughing stock for his idea for the electric light. Louis Pasteur was barred from many of the professional associations of his time for his battle with microbes, the unseen danger of infection and death. These people had only their vision and their conviction to sustain them in their quest, and yet they transformed the world.

The human spirit is indomitable. When our vision is clear, we are unstoppable. But life will test us and our resolve. Chances are, what you are trying to create is not so "unbelievable" as flying through the air, or landing on the moon, yet, you are still reluctant to commit.

What is your dream? Who do you want to be? Which percentile do you fall into? Will you dare to find the love of your life? Dare to believe you can? We can hide behind conventional wisdom and statistics and take no action. We can yearn for our dreams but never rise to the challenge. Or we can commit to taking the next step and see what happens. We can borrow a bit of courage from every pioneer of human existence and resolve to explore our dreams.

If it hasn't been made clear so far, let me say this. The reason you don't have the love you want is because you haven't created it. The beginning of creating that love you yearn for is daring to believe that you can create it. It's all up to us. Whether we want to declare that it's our fault or our responsibility, we are the reason we don't have what we want. And we are the solution.

Whether we are up to the challenge of creating new relationship or transforming the one that we are in, we ourselves are our biggest obstacle and our biggest resource. Creating and transforming life starts with having the courage to believe that you can have what you want, despite other's beliefs and opinions, or even your own.

HIGH STAKES

We are playing for high stakes here, so let's roll up our sleeves and get dirty. If someone offered you ten million dollars to walk around in eighteenth century clothes for a week, would you do it? You bet you would. I can think of ten million reasons to do it and so can you. What would your considerations be? "I will look foolish!" "I'll be uncomfortable." "People will laugh at me!" You would risk how you look to yourself and the world. It would challenge your identity, and you would be uncomfortable, but the payoff is so big that it is worth all the discomfort.

You might be uncomfortable all the way to the bank. Perhaps if you actually did walk around this way, people would start dressing like you and you might even start a trend.

The point is that we have to make drastic changes and take risks, including risking feeling foolish, to get what we want. Those are the table stakes in our gamble. What we desire is worth the risk. At the end of the day it won't be other people's opinions that matter to us. We make hundreds of choices every day. When our choices are guided by our intentions, these choices are informed. When we are fueled with the desire to get what we want in life, we are properly motivated.

Freedom is available right now. We can break out of the mind-numbing pattern of caring what other people think; we can begin to play for stakes that mean something in our lives. If we are not going after some dream or goal that drives us, we are just killing time. If this is the case, we are not fully alive. Then there is no mystery; not being fully alive means that we haven't got the power to bring love into our lives.

Stop waiting for something to wake you up; stop relying on life to interest you; stop holding your breath for someone to bring you back to life. We have been given free will in life. This means that we are in charge of our choices, for better or worse. There is no ultimate authority but us. We can choose to turn toward life or turn away. We must break our patterns, find our passion and dare to dream. Nobody will do it for us. We've got to enliven ourselves and in that aliveness we will attract the love that we want.

THE ANSWERS

We walk through life saying, "If only I had the answers to getting what I want, I would do whatever it takes." Now you have real answers, real ways to manifest what you want in life. Let's review. What follows are some of the answers we've arrived at.

1. Know what you want in love. Know that it is possible. Make a distinction between what you have been programmed to believe and what you actually can have. Dispel the fantasy of relationship. Don't be driven by your programming. Examine your own programming and deliberately change that programming.

2. Create an intention. Call forth the relationship that you want. Cultivate a burning desire for that intention. Reclaim your personal power from everything that you have given it away to. With these three actions you will create what you want.

3. Change your thoughts, words and actions, beliefs, perceptions and choices in order to create your reality. Use the tools of manifesting. Control your manifestors. Become aware of your thoughts, and be deliberate in your thinking. Refuse all negative thoughts. Cultivate your new vision, and fill your mind with it. Visualize the outcome you want and invest in that picture. As you change your manifestors to the positive, you will change your reality.

4. Believe you can create what you want. See your history and past as something you created in order to learn from. See your relationship history as a series of spiritual agreements to grow. When we learn what we have chosen to learn, we get to have what we want. Choose to believe in creating what you want, not because it is true, but because belief works to create what we want.

5. Change your life. Create a support system that feeds you and your aspirations. Build your life in a way that supports your dreams. Have a network of positive people that believe in you and what you are creating. Participate in the world in order to get what you want. Get what you need from the world and from yourself. Don't assign your needs to a relationship. Relationship is not meant to fix or fulfill you. It is something that you must be able to afford. Fill your life first so that relationship is something that you can support.

6. Learn to communicate. Master the dynamics of relationship. Understand the law of cause and effect in every relationship, and how that law affects what you can have and what you cannot have. Learn effective communication; by

learning how to identify and ask for what you need, you transform every situation. Learn how to manage conflict. See love as a business partnership and act accordingly.

7. Know that what you want is out there. Know that the universe is infinitely abundant and happy to give you whatever you ask. In fact, the universe is always giving you what you ask. Find ways to continue to ask for what you want, and find ways to continue to affirm that you are getting what you want. Create a discipline or practice in your life to continue to gain power and learn and find inner contentment.

8. Find a purpose for love in your life. Let it be an aspect of your greatness. Find out what fulfills you and work with that purpose. Apply that energy to all other areas of your life. When you are in relationship for the right reasons, your confidence, creativity, inspiration and passion will be never-ending. Love should align with your purpose and your greatness.

9. See the role you are playing. Identify the roles that you and your partner are playing in relationship, now and in the past. Choose to become authentic rather than continuing to play these roles. Identify the games you have played in relationship and may be playing now. Play authentically within that game you are playing. Identify the persona that your relationship is showing up with in the world. Change that persona to one that is more empowering and user-friendly.

10. Identify the stage you are in. See that relationships unfold in stages and note the stage that your relationship is in. Note the characteristics of each stage and how that may be affecting the relationship you are in now. Look around at the relationships surrounding you and see the different stages each is in. Stop taking the dynamics of the stage of relationship, or the game that you are in personally.

APPLY THE RULES

These are some basic rules to understand and create love in our lives. Each point reveals an empowering truth and gives you a tool to work with. Master not only the skill contained in each point but the point of view. Together these points reveal a working philosophy. It is not necessary that we believe this philosophy, only that we use what works in it.

We now know how to structure reality in order to manifest our dreams. We've learned the elements of manifesting: intention, burning desire, and personal power. We know that, in order to achieve the "real" in a relationship we must to dispel the fantasy. Whether we are in a relationship now or in the process of creating one, we must arrive at the truth of what love can offer and what it cannot.

Being realistic doesn't mean lowering our expectations, it means adjusting them. We dispel illusions and roll up our sleeves. We have a mandate to become the person we can be in relationship; when we take up this challenge life meets us halfway.

Deliberately reprogram that incredible instrument, the mind. We can aim ourselves on a fine trajectory toward getting what we want. Create a "stand" in life: determine who you will be and what you will do. Make your life an invitation to the person you want to be with. Show up full of life and engaged in it, not waiting to be rescued or sitting on the sidelines.

We take a practical approach that deliberately changes the mental, physical, emotional and spiritual aspects of our relationship lives in order to get the results that we want. It is as complete a makeover as we can hope to achieve. We embrace the real work of our lives, and as a by-product of doing our work we create what we want in love and in life. We are always manifesting, for better or worse.

You will make a practical plan once the emotions and intellect are on the same page. Make a plan to meet that person that you want to meet. As the old fisherman said of his success, "I go where the fish are!" Adopt a winning attitude: go after your dream as though you can't fail. Remember, if you were offered ten million dollars, you would burn every bridge and passionately pursue your goal.

Intuitively we feel and sense truth. Truth resonates. Take the truth in this book that resonates for you and work with this truth, and it will work for you. When you have truth to work with there are no more excuses for not taking action. Are you the kind of person that truly wants to change, or the kind that is looking for reasons why you can't? People find the love they want every day. As I have helped people find love, the first obstacle I face is their willingness to accept that it can be done. Believe it. "What man can conceive, he can achieve!"

GET ORGANIZED

Get your house in order: Decide that you are going to create love in your life. Let the past be a "cancelled check." The past is over and you have paid for it in full. Start new, and fill your mind with new possibility. We've used the example :when babies attempt to walk, they fail hundreds of times. Each attempt lands them on their backside, again. If that were you or me, we might be tempted to give up, but babies have no particular expectation of succeeding or fear of failing. They have a wonderful single-mindedness of purpose, and they never stop trying. At one point, you and I were that baby. That determination is still alive in us. We are the architects of our life and we make the blueprint of what we want and we have an indomitable spirit.

Choose boldness. Be more daring than you have ever been. Take a stand, make a declaration, map out your plan.

Recapture that spirit. When you begin to execute this plan, notice the obstacles. Learn from them. Be like the baby who is first learning how to walk; have curiosity and determination and the certainty that you will succeed. Use the tools that you've newly learned and create what you want in your life.

If you were a sailboat about to make a great journey you would outfit yourself for the trip. Surround yourself with a positive network of people that support your goals and believe in your ability to get what you want and where you want to go. Cut the naysayers loose; they are only dead-weight anyway. Align yourself emotionally with getting what you want. Fill up with the feelings of winning and having love and contentment. Create the atmosphere necessary to supporting your project. Fill your mind with pictures and ideas of succeeding. Refuse to accept or believe anything else.

PEOPLE, PLACES AND THINGS

What do we need to change in order to change our lives? We need to change our environment. In short, change everything, including people, places and things, and all of the above. Change the furniture, change the color of the walls, change your local haunts. Change everything that you can and embrace and welcome change, change, change.

When we have our mind, our feelings, and our plan in the right place, when we have changed those elements internally, then we must look at our external environment. Let us be excited about introducing newness into our lives as it is the beginning of a great event.

Imagine that you are planning man's first attempt to land on the moon. Who are the people that you will be looking for to participate in your quest? Will they be the ones who say that it is impossible? How about the ones who ridicule you for your plan? Not likely. Wouldn't you pick those that believe in you and believe in the project?

We want people who are assets; that offer constructive ideas and real support. These folks are excited and enthusiastic. They support our determination and believe in our goal.

Our response to the other applicants would be "thanks, but no thanks," We need a "dream team" that is ready, willing and able to support us and believe in us. Do not settle for less, because one negative, one bad "apple" is enough to undermine our confidence.

When we look around in our lives, we may be surprised at who is negative and who is not. We may have to make some hard choices when we realize that even some of the closest people to us do not necessarily wish us well. Close or not, we need to cut them loose. The people in our lives are either part of the problem or part of the solution, and there is no middle ground. When we see with clear eyes, we see accurately. If we want to create love in our lives or success of any kind we must back away from the detractors and embrace the supporters.

"Insanity," said Rudyard Kipling, "is doing the same thing over and over and expecting different results." If we expect to find love, we have to look in different places than we have been looking. For the sake of new energy and new possibility, we must make different choices, even if they are uncomfortable. We cannot go to the same old places, and expect anything new. Take a chance and try some new venue, whether it is a book club or a new salsa dance club. Break the old patterns and release new energy.

It is a relief and a release to break old patterns and routines and let some fresh air into life. Try that new gym that you've wanted to check out, but didn't dare. Go out to coffee with a colleague, if only to sit across from someone new. Join a speaking club, or an acting class. Take Latin dance classes or a course in night school. Change the places that you show up in and you will change you. New locations call forth new personas in us.

The beginning of change for one woman I am working with was a "Tango" class. She is now living in Paris living her dream life. Change begets energy; energy begets possibility.

Try new activities, and especially a program that makes you say "that's not me!" Remember, getting what you want in life is the process of re-inventing yourself. Even if it feels "hokey" try it. Change your wardrobe: deliberately pick colors that you don't wear. Find out whether you are a "winter" or a "summer" in clothing and go with it. Each color is a different frequency and will bring out a different mood or trait in you.

Start a hobby, and get engaged in the world. Get interested in life and you will be interesting. Make a list of ten things you've always wanted to do in your life, and start working on one of them immediately. If you've dreamt of visiting Berlin, get the brochures, even if you can't afford to go right this minute.

We need to enliven every dimension of ourselves and fully engage in life, if we are going to have the energy required for love. We want people to come up to us and say "Wow! What have you been up to?" Get in the game and start to take your rightful share of what life has to offer.

BELIEVE IN YOURSELF

It is time to shatter the old mindset and determine to become the person that you set out to be. Ask a child who they want to be when they grow up. None of them will tell you that they want to be "average" with a "mediocre" job and a "ho-hum" love-life. This is not the nature of the human spirit. When we settle for less than who we are, we are pretending to be something we're not. We are allowing ourselves to be defeated and discouraged by the events of our lives. The spirit within us (it doesn't go away, or die, it just hides,) knows differently. Our spirit knows our greatness. We live in the realm of possibility.

Give yourself permission: Be the wonderfully confident child that you still are; dare to be a star. Be entitled to your birthright of excitement and possibility. Don't settle for this vague hypnosis that you've fallen into.

THE CHILD WITHIN

As you read this chapter, let yourself get excited. Now run with the ball and feed that fire! We have within ourselves right now everything that we need to create our dreams. We've simply lost our way. When we were little children, we could feel the greatness in us, every day. We've simply misplaced our magic, but it is alive and well in us. It is an energy that wants to come out and assert itself in our lives. We are not mundane and earthbound, we are anything but.

Remember the child in you. That child knew she had greatness, and she was right. That part of you had a certainty that you could get anything you wanted, and you possessed a drive and determination that was unstoppable. We've wandered from that path. The way back is lit with our desires and our excitement. By daring to believe in ourselves and our dreams, we find our way back and we recapture that energy.

With this inner light everything is possible, and without this energy, life is just a grind. We are given desires in order to be inspired through life. We are given our fears as the quickening energy that motivates us. We are meant to go toward our fears and our desires, not away from them. Go where you are most energized.

The choice is always up to us. We have been given free will so that we can choose learning and growth or choose to walk away from our lessons. Follow that quickening of your energy and do everything that makes that energy even quicker, and you are back on the path of your magic and your aliveness. When we have recaptured our aliveness we can dare to tackle our dreams. We are not damaged. We are intact.

THE CHALLENGING PATH

We all have the burden of our history and failures that can weigh us down. In the Sanskrit tradition we view that history as merely "maya" or illusion. This is the dream within the dream. None of it is happening now; none of it can hold us back, unless we choose to believe the illusion.

Why would anyone choose to "let" themselves be held back? Because we are afraid of ourselves. We are afraid of our power. We are afraid of the responsibility of maintaining the success that we achieve. We are afraid of getting hurt, of failing, of getting rejected. We are even afraid to find out that we could have accomplished a long time ago and we have wasted our time. We are filled with many illusory fears. When we refuse our greatness, we are not saying "I can't"; we are actually saying "I won't."

We can ignore that spirit within us, but we can't kill it altogether, and there is a "silent witness" inside all of us that sees the choices we make. We may be able to justify to world why it is too hard for us to try, but inside we know the truth. It may be less effort to avoid our dreams, but ultimately, it is not less work. The silent witness holds us accountable, and we pay dearly for letting ourselves down. We are most accountable to ourselves.

RALLY

No matter how irretrievable our dreams may seem, there is still a part of us that is willing to fight and rally. We can feed the part of ourselves that is game or we can feed the part of us that longs to give up. Whatever part of ourselves that we choose to feed will get stronger.

At the end of the day we can't affect change because we should, or for the sake of others. We can only truly fight if we choose. If that is where we come alive and the challenge makes life worth living, then we fight for what we want. It doesn't matter in the end if we succeed or fail, what we accomplish are only the trophies on the wall. What matters is that we do what we can and we don't let ourselves down. When we are in the game and putting out our best effort, life is sweeter, the rewards are better. Even our sleep is well earned.

The most inspiring part of us is our infinite ability to dream and to build from those dreams. Whether that dream is about creating the love of our lives, or curing cancer, we become our best selves by engaging in our dreams.

FANTASTIC RELATIONSHIP

When I first came up with the concept of creating a fantastic relationship, I enjoyed a certain amount of irony. The definition in Merriam-Webster for fantastic is both: unbelievable and excellent. My work is about dispelling fantasies in order to create true love. It amused me that we must dispel what we have been taught, the fantasies (unbelievable) of love, in order to create authentic relationship, which is much truer to the conventional meaning of fantastic (excellence).

By approaching love, feelings and the dynamics of relationship in a very practical way, we create the excellent. The more I see of the real potential of relationship, the more I find myself idealistic and hopeful about the state of love. I know that anyone that puts their mind to it and uses the principles in this book can create and maintain a love relationship in his or her life. I know that we are capable of transforming a relationship that we are in no matter what shape it is in now.

I will never say to someone in a relationship that "this is going to be easy!" but I know that with willing partners, any relationship is can be brought to a place of sanity and peace. Some of the obstacles in the way are from our history and experience and some obstacles are self-induced. The old fantasies are addictive; they are the heroin that we must wean ourselves off of. These fantasies have been so programmed that they seem like reality. We must embrace the idea that relationship is not what we thought it was. It is much more complex and in some ways, so much more. It also has more potential and can be so much better than we ever knew. The reality of what relationship can be is far better and more satisfying than the fantasy could ever be.

The fantasy, by definition, requires that we be "fantastic" whereas the reality requires only that we be real. The difference is night and day. Trying to live up to the fantasy is painful and unworkable. We are never enough. Trying to live the fantasy, we are literally eating the menu instead of the meal. Living the reality of relationship, with genuine relating and by being authentic, is far more satisfying.

We have toxic love games and we have constructive love games. When we identify the games that are manipulative and destructive we can choose not to play them. When we understand the playing field as it truly is, we get to play the game of love the way it is meant to be played: with joy and authenticity.

EXERCISE 1

Close your eyes and go back to the moment of your biggest "win." Let yourself experience that state fully. See it, taste it, feel it, and let it sink into your pores.

Now see yourself in the area of your greatest challenge. Experience it fully. See it, feel it.

Now, split your mental screen, and put the challenging situation on one side and the resourceful one on the other.

Now allow the feelings from the resourceful state to enter the challenging picture. Hold this image as you feel a shift.

Continue to do this until you feel resourceful in the troubled state.

EXERCISE 2

Take the next week and deliberately change the people, places and activities that you engage with in your life.

Interact with different people than you normally would; talk and engage with them.

Go to places around you that you haven't gone but may have wanted to, and allow yourself to engage with the new environment.

Choose an activity (or two) that you've been putting off or meaning to try.

Notice what is different in you, as you change your surroundings.

EXERCISE 3

1. Create an intention.
2. Visualize it and picture it; build a burning desire for it.
3. Practice all of the ways of building personal power around this intention. Take your power back from negative thoughts; practice attention to detail; practice giving. Practice this for twenty-one days.

A FINAL WORD

My intention in writing this book has been to put your hands on the wheels and dials of what makes a relationship work. I hope I've succeeded. If I have given you an objective view of relationships and shown you from the inside out what dynamics are in play, then it is my hope that you will now see with different eyes. When we separate ourselves from the mechanisms that we are subject to, we gain power and perspective. It is my hope that this new perspective will change how you see and respond to relationships and even how you see yourself.

When we understand that so much of what happens in a relationship is not personal, we stop reacting and we start observing. If I could transfer all of my knowledge and experience by some sort of "mind-meld," then how you relate in love would change instantly. There is an experience of relief and release when we realize that we are reacting and interacting in automatic ways to old patterns that have little to do with who we really are and our true intentions.

We all want to love but there are real obstacles in the way. These obstacles are not our fault, but they are our responsibility. Knowledge is power. I hope that the experience and knowledge I've shared with you has given you that power.

I have had two teachers: my experience in love, and you, the clients I've collaborated with. Though hidden, there is a set of rules and inevitable truths that run relationship. A cause and effect collaboration exists, that works seamlessly. There is logic to why and how love works, rules and laws that describe the physics of partnership. When we understand the nature of water, it becomes a blessed and life-giving source. When we don't, we drown. Always, there is an underlying set of agreements and understandings that holds partnerships together.

I hope you have seen in this book that looking at relationships can be simple: there are specific properties that rule what will happen and what will not. When we become aware of these properties we won't get mangled in the machinery. Rather than getting hurt and disappointed, we create an easy, rewarding experience. I am privileged to teach the method of conscious relating and hope that it has served to show you what love is not, what it is, and what it can be. My intention has been to change the context of relationship in a way that dramatically changes the content.

ABOUT THE AUTHOR

THOMAS MICHAEL JONES is a psychotherapist who has been in private practice for more than twenty years. In his work with private clients and couples, his areas of expertise are behavior modification, addiction and relationship reconstruction.

He says, "I often think that the reason that I know so much about relationship is that I have made every mistake that exists in love. I've always contended that we have to be willing to be fools for love, and I know that I am living proof of that contention. My salvation has been my need to understand, to know how and why and in what way it all went so horribly wrong. In the end, that has caused me to learn. It is my desire to share my knowledge with my clients and readers."

An alumnus of CUNY and The University of Hawaii, Thomas Jones gives lectures, workshops and seminars in the fields of addiction, conflict resolution and achievement. He lives in New York City, where is at work on his next book, about The Paradox Process, a concept he co-founded. As he writes, "The Paradox Process is a hands-on transformational tool that allows you to access your negative emotions and change them in the moment, in a way that gives you instant insight and instant emotional relief." For more information visit: www.paradoxprocess.org/

CPSIA information can be obtained at www.ICGtesting.com
Printed in the USA
LVOW08s0837050214

372434LV00001B/104/P